Gender and Ventriloquism in Victorian and
Neo-Victorian Fiction

Gender and Ventriloquism in Victorian and Neo-Victorian Fiction

Passionate Puppets

Helen Davies
Associate Lecturer in English Literature, Leeds Metropolitan University, UK

First published 2012 by
PALGRAVE MACMILLAN

Palgrave Macmillan in the UK is an imprint of Macmillan Publishers Limited, registered in England, company number 785998, of Houndmills, Basingstoke, Hampshire RG21 6XS.

Palgrave Macmillan in the US is a division of St Martin's Press LLC, 175 Fifth Avenue, New York, NY 10010.

Palgrave Macmillan is the global academic imprint of the above companies and has companies and representatives throughout the world.

Palgrave® and Macmillan® are registered trademarks in the United States, the United Kingdom, Europe and other countries.

ISBN 978–0–230–34366–5

This book is printed on paper suitable for recycling and made from fully managed and sustained forest sources. Logging, pulping and manufacturing processes are expected to conform to the environmental regulations of the country of origin.

A catalogue record for this book is available from the British Library.

A catalog record for this book is available from the Library of Congress.

10   9   8   7   6   5   4   3   2   1
21 20 19 18 17 16 15 14 13 12

Printed and bound in Great Britain by
CPI Antony Rowe, Chippenham and Eastbourne

For Madge and Peter Davies, and Robert Francis

Contents

Acknowledgements

In a suitably ventriloquial fashion, many different voices and influences have shaped this book. I am extremely grateful for the intellectual guidance I received from Mary Eagleton, Ruth Robbins and Susan Watkins in the earlier stages of my research, and the continuing advice and support that I receive from Susan. I am indebted to Mark Llewellyn in his role as the reader of this project, who has offered invaluable advice on structuring my work and focusing my ideas. I would like to thank Claire Chambers and Joanne Watkiss for sharing with me their experiences of publishing, and for answering all of my questions. Thanks are also due to Paula Kennedy and Ben Doyle at Palgrave Macmillan for their encouragement and their patience.

Sections of Chapters 1 and 5 originally appeared in my article 'Passive Puppets and Unruly Dummies: Gender and Ventriloquism in Sarah Waters' *Affinity*', in *Autopsia* 1:1 (November 2010), pp. 41–64. Thank you to the editors, Anthony Metivier and Kane X. Faucher, for allowing me to reproduce this work in my book. A short paragraph from Chapter 1 featured in my chapter, 'The Trouble with Gender in *Salome*', in an edited collection by Michael Y. Bennett, *Refiguring Oscar Wilde's Salome* (Amsterdam and New York: Rodopi, 2011). Thank you to Michael and to Esther Roth at Rodopi for giving me permission to re-use this material. A section of Chapter 3 has been adapted from my article '"They whisper into my ears the tale of their perilous joy": The Powers of the Feminine Voice in Oscar Wilde's "The Fisherman and his Soul"', *The Oscholars* e-journal, *A Giant's Garden: Special 'Fairy Tale' Issue*, ed. Naomi Wood, (Spring 2009). Thank you to Naomi and to the general editor of *The Oscholars*, David Rose, for their support with this publication. I also want to thank James Mundie for allowing me to reproduce his picture 'Nightmare in the Works' on the front cover of this book.

There are three people in my life that I could never thank enough. My mother Madge has engaged in endless conversations with me about my work, and everything beyond. She is the dearest of friends. My father Peter has always supported me in every possible way, and has demonstrated remarkable patience in listening to the endless conversations. Both of my parents have always encouraged my research, and respected and accepted my decisions. In some ways, this is a book about double acts; I would like to thank Robert for sharing my life, and for offering me intellectual, practical and emotional support.

Introduction: The Victorians for Dummies? Talking Back to the Nineteenth Century

What might it mean to 'talk back'? In childhood we are warned against 'back-chat', hence the phrase 'talking back' implies a sense of rebellion or challenge to figures of authority. However, children might also be cautioned to 'not speak until you're spoken to', underscoring an alternative interpretation. For 'talking back' suggests a response; one can only engage in a process of 'talking back' after being addressed in some manner, after being brought into being as a subject by a prior discursive agency.[1] Finally, 'talking back also has connotations of historicity; there has been a preceding utterance or voicing that is being answered. I propose that the proliferation of contemporary fiction set in the Victorian era is preoccupied with these multiple implications of 'talking back'. Neo-Victorian fiction suggests that there is a palpable desire to respond to the Victorians in some way, to answer back to the society and culture of this era.

There have been various terms and definitions proposed for contemporary fiction which is set in the nineteenth century. Dana Shiller introduces 'neo-Victorian' in her article, 'The Redemptive Past in the Neo-Victorian Novel', referring to fiction that is 'at once characteristic of postmodernism and imbued with a historicity reminiscent of the nineteenth-century novel' (Shiller, 1997, p. 538). Sally Shuttleworth offers the phrase 'retro-Victorian novel', which she associates with historical novels that manifest nostalgia for the Victorian era (Shuttleworth, 1998, p. 253). In their introduction to the collection of essays *Victorian Afterlife: Postmodern Culture Rewrites the Nineteenth Century*, John Kucich and Dianne F. Sadoff propose the term 'post-Victorian', which 'conveys paradoxes of historical continuity and disruption' in late postmodernism's returns to the nineteenth century (Kucich and Sadoff, 2000, p. xiii). The various merits of and problems with these appellations have been debated in Andrea Kirchknopf's article '(Re-)Workings of Nineteenth Century Fiction: Definitions, Terminology, Contexts' (2008, pp. 59–66) but 'neo-Victorian' is emerging as the most frequently used phrase for delineating contemporary engagements with the nineteenth century. The most pertinent definition of 'neo-Victorian' has come from Ann Heilmann and Mark Llewellyn: 'the "neo-Victorian" is *more than* historical fiction set in the nineteenth century. To be part of neo-Victorianism [...] texts [...] must in some respect be *self-consciously engaged with the act of (re)interpretation, (re)discovery and (re)vision concerning the Victorians'* (Heilmann and Llewellyn, 2010, p. 4, emphasis in original).

Following Heilmann and Llewellyn, I prefer the term 'neo-Victorian' as it implies a genre of writing that is *doing something with* the Victorian era; critically engaging with nineteenth-century fiction, culture and society as opposed to *just* repeating or nostalgically harking back to a past era (as the phrase 'retro-Victorian' might imply). Attempts to define the genre of contemporary literature set in the nineteenth century thus bring multiple critical 'voices' into play and, as these various definitions indicate, the diversity of texts that constitute 'neo-Victorianism' cannot be reduced to a unified body of work. This book's deployment of the terms 'neo-Victorian' and 'neo-Victorianism' is conscious of the plurality of textual voices – literary and critical – that are at work within this rapidly expanding field of writing, and does not seek to fix these voices to a finite location or address.[2]

It is thus significant that in recent academic commentaries on neo-Victorianism there is a recurring emphasis placed upon the metaphor of 'voice'. For example, Mark Llewellyn has written of neo-Victorianism as 'the desire to rewrite the historical narrative of that period by representing marginalised voices, new histories of sexuality, post-colonial viewpoints and other generally "different" versions of the Victorians' (Llewellyn, 2008, p. 165). Similarly, Marie-Lusie Kohlke comments on 'the neo-Victorian's preoccupation with liberating lost voices and repressed histories left out of the public record' (Kohlke, 2008, p. 9). Peter Widdowson's remarks on 'contemporary re-visionary fiction' also emphasize the 'process of restoring a voice [...] to those hitherto exploited, marginalised and silenced by dominant interests and ideologies' (Widdowson, 2006, pp. 505–6) and the 'voice' metaphor is invoked – either explicitly or implicitly – by numerous other critics.[3]

An association between 'voice' and social agency is clearly at work within such accounts of neo-Victorianism, and it is in this context that the notion of 'having a voice' has become one of the more compelling motifs of identity politics.[4] The above examples repeatedly relate neo-Victorian 're-voicings' to the representation of subjects who have been largely absent from the traditional master discourse of history, a narrative which privileges patriarchy, heteronormativity, euro-centricity and the 'able-bodied'. Furthermore, such accounts invoke a power dichotomy between 'voicing' and 'silencing'. We see that the 'silenced' Victorians are granted a 'voice' by contemporary authors and this is largely perceived as a noble, politically-aware enterprise, an attempt to challenge and redress the broader social and cultural ine-qualities that lead to this 'silencing' in the first instance. In this sense, then, neo-Victorian fiction might be interpreted as subversively 'talking back' to the Victorians.

Nevertheless, we must not forget that other connotation of 'talking back' which suggests that we cannot speak until being spoken to. To what extent does our sense of historical dialogue with the Victorian era actually depend upon 'us' being interpellated into discourse by 'them'? To pursue the implications of the parent/child relationship offered in my opening paragraph, surely neo-Victorian authors are challenging an authority which has necessarily formed them; if we are the rebel-lious (grand)children of the Victorians, then doesn't our 'talking back' belie an anxiety about influence – 'We're not like you! (Are we...?)'.[5] Hence another 'voice'-related concern emerges, for even as certain neo-Victorian texts are apparently rebelliously 'talking back' the Victorian era and literary production, they also – in varying degrees – emulate and are indebted to the cultural artefacts of this historical period. As Andrea Kirchknopf notes, such texts have a tendency to:

> keep the average length and structure of Victorian novels [...] they imitate prevalent genres of the nineteenth century, such as the Bildungsroman, or the social, industrial and sensation novels [...] The narrative design of these novels tends to be like that of their Victorian predecessors' and they typically employ narrative voices of the types dominant in nineteenth-century texts, i.e. the first person character narrator or the third person omniscient one. (Kirchknopf, 2008, p. 54)

Kirchknopf's observations are certainly relevant to the novels of Sarah Waters, for instance, with her use of the bildungsroman and first-person 'character' narrator in *Tipping the Velvet* (1998) or her indebtedness to the sensation fiction genre in *Fingersmith* (2002). This sense of indebt-edness to Victorian tropes becomes more pronounced when we con-sider novels such as Jean Rhys' *Wide Sargasso Sea* (1966) which offers a specific engagement with Charlotte Brontë's *Jane Eyre* (1847), or even Will Self's *Dorian: An Imitation* (2002). Although Self's rewriting of Oscar Wilde's *The Picture of Dorian Gray* takes place in the 1980s–1990s and hence does not have a Victorian setting as such, the novel's dependence on the characters, plot and themes of Wilde's original, as well as its self-conscious announcement of its 'imitative' status, offers justification for positioning Self's *Dorian* within the remit of neo-Victorianism. Whether via direct rewritings of Victorian texts, stylistic and generic similarities, broader thematic or cultural echoes, neo-Victorian novels evidently manifest some degree of dependence upon their Victorian precursors. In this sense, the issue of 'voice' becomes a matter of *repetition*; as well as neo-Victorianism 'speaking for' the silenced subjects of the Victorian era, Victorian authors and texts are also 'speaking through' neo-Victorian literature.

It is at this complex juncture between the 'speaking through' and 'speaking for' where I position the metaphor of ventriloquism as central to neo-Victorianism. It is a truism to suggest that ventriloquism is intrinsically bound up with ideas about 'voice' and, considering the preoccupation with 'voices' in academic commentaries on neo-Victorianism, it is unsurprising that the term 'ventriloquism' is also regularly mentioned. Eckart Voights-Virchow refers to the 'unabashed Victorian ventriloquism' of Sarah Waters' neo-Victorian novels and claims that the narrative voice of Michel Faber's *The Crimson Petal and the White* (2002) 'counters the charge of historicist ventriloquism' (Voights-Virchow, 2009, pp. 119; 116). In her study of the 'women's historical novel', Diana Wallace discusses the trope of the female medium in the neo-Victorian writings of A. S. Byatt, Sarah Waters and Michèle Roberts, suggesting that 'the female medium becomes a suggestive figure of the historical novelist herself, ventriloquizing the voices of the past' (Wallace, 2005, p. 208). The connection between ventriloquism and spiritualism is also made by Tatiana Kontou in her monograph *Spiritualism and Women's Writing from the fin de siècle to the Neo-Victorian*, which repeatedly uses the term 'ventriloquism' to describe nineteenth-century mediums' channelling of spirit voices and to explore the quasi-mediumistic role of contemporary female authors rewriting the Victorian era (Kontou, 2009, pp. 5; 99; 101).

The word 'ventriloquism' is often mentioned in critical writings on A. S. Byatt's *Possession: A Romance* (1990). John O'Neill associates the novel's 'reviving [of] voices' with ventriloquism and, like Wallace and Kontou, links this 'ventriloquism' to spiritualism (O'Neill, 2006, p. 336). Catherine Burgass' 'Reader's Guide' to *Possession* discusses ventriloquism as a key theme in the text, highlighting the 'multiplicity of voices and other texts' at play in the novel (Burgass, 2002, pp. 50–4). In an article titled 'Forgery, Dis/Possession, Ventriloquism in the Works of A. S. Byatt and Peter Ackroyd', Catherine Bernard delineates contemporary authors as being 'ventriloquists [...] condemned to be spoken by the past without necessarily transcending it' (Bernard, 2003, p. 16). After noting the recurrence of the term 'ventriloquism' in Byatt's novel, Christian Gutleben argues:

> this notion of ventriloquy may serve as a metaphor not only for the past-obsessed characters [of *Possession*] but also for the writers of much contemporary fiction. Indeed, far from looking for a new idiom of the present, British novelists of the 80s and 90s have been bringing back to life voices of the past and particularly of the Victorian era. (Gutleben, 2001, pp. 15–16)

Gutleben's analysis implies that ventriloquism is at the heart of neo-Victorian rewritings of the nineteenth century. But what is meant by 'ventriloquism'? In various ways, the above critics all indicate that neo-Victorian ventriloquisms are something to do with authorial 'voice' yet they also demonstrate a notable lack of consensus as to what the implications of this might be. For Voights-Virchow, 'historicist ventriloquism' is a 'charge' that must be countered, insinuating that there might be something dubious about the practice of 'voicing' the past. Whether this is artistically or ethically suspect remains unsaid. Ventriloquism is apparently an artistic failing in the accounts of Bernard and Gutleben, a symptom of the postmodernist realization that everything has always already been said and thus the contemporary author might only speak in the 'voices' of her or his forebears. In this sense, it is significant that both Bernard and Gutleben express sympathy with Fredric Jameson's indictment of postmodernism as typified by pastiche: 'speech in a dead language' (Jameson, 1991, p. 17), in itself a ventriloquial image.[6] In contrast to these largely negative remarks on the ethical and aesthetic implications of ventriloquism, Diana Wallace's account proposes that cross-gendered ventriloquism (the female author speaking in the voice of a male character) is a subversive strategy which exposes the constructed status of all gender roles, hinting that there might be more to neo-Victorian ventriloquisms than just 'repetition' of Victorian precursors (Wallace, 2005, p. 23).

 I am aware that I have indulged in an act of ventriloquism myself in attempting to reconstruct these critics' stance on the ventriloquial metaphor, yet I make no apology for this presumptuous 're-voicing'. For what is surprising in the repeated recourse to 'ventriloquism' as a way of articulating neo-Victorian preoccupations is the *lack of engagement* with what 'ventriloquism' might actually mean. Ironically enough, ventriloquism is left to speak for itself. I contend that it is not enough to make a vague equation between 'ventriloquism' and 'voice'. The fundamental aims of this study are to position the ventriloquial metaphor as a focal point for negotiating the politics of neo-Victorian literature, to establish the possibilities that the ventriloquial metaphor offers for neo-Victorian re-voicings of the Victorian era and to consider the problems that might be encountered in neo-Victorian ventriloquisms. I offer the insight that in attempting to define ventriloquism we will also encounter neo-Victorianism's tension between 'transformation' and 'repetition' in a variety of ways. Indeed, as the deployments of the ventriloquial metaphor in existing academic commentaries on neo-Victorian fiction have implied, ventriloquism might be either a 'subversive' or 'conservative' enterprise. It might challenge the patriarchal, heteronormative, euro-centric discourse of history, but it might also repeat it. In fact, like neo-Victorianism, it might be simultaneously 'subversive' and 'conservative' and throughout this study I will repeatedly underscore the centrality of this paradox to the metaphor of ventriloquism.

Who's the dummy?

As Chapter 1 will explore in further detail, the word 'ventriloquism' conjures up the image of a person making a dummy appear to speak. The origin and agency of the voice in such a scenario is not seriously called into dispute; the dummy might well 'talk back' to the ventriloquist yet we know that the dialogue between ventriloquist and dummy is entirely orchestrated by the performer. This dichotomy of agency/passivity haunts prior usages of the ventriloquial metaphor in relation to neo-Victorian literature, even if it is rarely acknowledged.[7] For who is the 'dummy' in this ventriloquial exchange? Does neo-Victorian fiction 'speak for' the Victorians, or do Victorian precursors ultimately dictate the script of neo-Victorian fiction, figuring contemporary authors as 'puppets' without voices of their own? The limitations of such a metaphor should be obvious; this use of the concept of ventriloquism must locate the agency of voice somewhere and thus oscillates around a fundamental imbalance of power. There are both aesthetic and ethical implications in thinking of ventriloquism in this way. As the commentaries of Bernard and Gutleben imply, neo-Victorian ventriloquism can be perceived as an aesthetic failure in the sense that there is no significant alteration of Victorian 'voices' and thus neo-Victorian fiction might just be for dummies after all. However, if we want to emphasize the revisionary component of neo-Victorian literature – contemporary rewritings of the Victorian era as 'giving voice' to the oppressed or forgotten subjects of the nineteenth century – then we must also be attuned to the differences between recovering suppressed voices and imagining lost voices. Can such a distinction even be made? For if, as many commentaries on neo-Victorianism suggest, certain Victorians have no voice, then what are the ethical stakes at play in contemporary authors providing such voices?[8] Such a conceptualization figures neo-Victorian authors as the all-powerful ventriloquists of the show. Albeit with benevolent intentions, the initial 'silencing' of Victorian subjects is surely compounded by this ventriloquial process.[9] There can be no dialogue, no exchange, only neo-Victorianism talking to itself.

This study offers an alternative vision of the ventriloquial metaphor. In Chapter 1, I explain how the dummy/ventriloquist performance genre is only a relatively recent development in the history of displaced voice. We shall see that the late nineteenth century was a turning point in ventriloquism; prior to the dummy/ventriloquist stage act, the topic of ventriloquism encompassed the prophecies at the Delphic oracle, accounts of demon possession, the strange mimicries of distant voice ventriloquism and the mysterious utterances of nineteenth-century spiritualism. What will become apparent is a crucial *uncertainty as to the origin of voice*. I want to propose that 'ventriloquism' can actually be a 'talking back' and 'speaking through' of *subjects* as opposed to objects, offering multiple possibilities for voice, agency and intention that cannot be simply reduced to a finite dichotomy of power.

A further aim of this book is to demonstrate the significance of ventriloquism not just as a metaphor for articulating the textual echoes and 're-voicings' that occur between selected Victorian and neo-Victorian novels, but also as a *thematic* preoccupation in the literature of both periods. I argue that the late nineteenth century is a significant era in the history of ventriloquism, a time when the ambiguous fluctuations of voice/agency were increasingly moving towards the dummy/ventriloquist stage performance. This tension between ventriloquism as a supernatural, mysterious process and ventriloquism as a form of popular entertainment focusing on the manipulation of a puppet is manifest in a collection of texts dating from this period: Henry James' *The Bostonians* (1886); George Du Maurier's *Trilby* (1894); Oscar Wilde's *The Picture of Dorian Gray* (1891) and *De Profundis* (1897–8).[10] My analysis of these texts highlights a selection of key ventriloquial themes: anxiety over the 'origin' of voice; the figure of the 'sinister' ventriloquist; currencies of influence and possession; the motif of the double; the use of puppet/dummy imagery. A vital aspect of the history of ventriloquism becomes discernable in these texts for we see repeatedly that to be 'ventriloquized' manifests as a feminized condition, whereas the agency of 'voice' and ventriloquial prowess is linked to masculinity. My readings of the nineteenth-century texts highlight the gendered power imbalance between the masculine 'ventriloquist' and the feminized dummy/puppet. Despite moments of rebellion, the subject fulfilling the 'dummy' or 'puppet' role is largely condemned to repeat a patriarchal heteronormative script of passivity and objectification.

It has become *de rigueur* to acknowledge that neo-Victorian fiction is preoccupied with issues of gender and sexuality, but my reading of neo-Victorian novels emphasizes specifically the relationship between gender and ventriloquism in contemporary fiction set in the Victorian era. For if gender and sexuality have emerged as particularly fertile areas in terms of 'talking back' to the nineteenth century, then I identify that the gendered inflection of ventriloquial issues in late Victorian writing has also received sustained attention in neo-Victorian fiction. The figures of Verena Tarrant, Trilby, Olive Chancellor, Basil Ransom, Svengali and Lord Henry Wotton (amongst others) and their attendant ventriloquial concerns return in neo-Victorian novels such as Angela Carter's *Nights at the Circus* (1984), Margaret Atwood's *Alias Grace* (1996), Janice Galloway's *Clara* (2003) and Sarah Waters' *Tipping the Velvet* (1998) and *Affinity* (1999). My analysis suggests that these 'repetitions' of ventriloquial texts can be read, in Judith Butler's terms, as 're-citations' of the script of gender and ventriloquism that subversively 'talk back' to visions of Victorian ventriloquism. Such re-citations generate a forum to re-evaluate the hierarchical relationship between 'ventriloquist' and 'dummy' or 'original' and 'copied' voice, both in terms of literary production (the relationship between the Victorian and neo-Victorian) and in terms of gendered models of ventriloquism.

Talking back to Butler: neo-Victorian ventriloquism and historical performativity

It is in the context of the tension between 'repetition' and 'transformation' that I want to discuss the link between gender, ventriloquism and Judith Butler's theories of gender as performance, and my use of these ideas in this book. Butler's well-known argument is that gender is performative; 'a set of repeated acts within a highly rigid regulatory frame that congeal over time to produce the appearance of substance, of a natural source of being' (Butler, 1999, pp. 43–4). Butler conceptualizes gender as 'script' – a discourse produced by social and cultural imperatives – and it is the repetition of this 'script' of gender that constructs the gendered subject. A central aspect of Butler's theory of a repeated gendered script is an emphasis on *temporality*; performative gender is not a single, isolated 'act' but a continuous, compulsory repetition. The construction of gender is an incessant process of becoming and it is within this framework of perpetual repetition that Butler perceives the potential for the subversion of conventional gender roles: 'As an ongoing discursive practice, it is open to intervention and resignification' (Butler, 1999, pp. 43–4). The implications of the potential for 'resignification' are important. Gender subversion stems from the prospect that the 'acts' constructing gendered identity might be performed differently. Deviations from the script of heteronormative gender could serve to expose the utterly constructed 'nature' of coherent gender identity and thus alter the script that the subject is compelled to enact or recite.

The famous example which Butler provides to demonstrate the subversive potential of re-citing an alternative version of the gendered script is of drag performance. For Butler, the critical promise in drag performance is in its *parody* of the notion of an original gender/sex: 'gender parody reveals that the original identity after which gender fashions itself is an imitation without an origin [...] It is a production [...] which postures as an imitation' (Butler, 1999, pp. 175–6). The resignification of gender enacted in drag performance offers a parodic microcosm – an allegory – of the acts that must be repeated to produce all gender roles. Drag performance's purported ability to deconstruct the relationship between 'original' and 'copy' thus echoes Butler's broader dismantling of the hierarchical relationship between 'originary' sex and the ostensible 'copy' of gender (Butler, 1999, pp. 10–11).

Butler's theories have had an enormous cross-disciplinary impact upon gender studies and her work has already received considerable attention in the field of neo-Victorianism, particularly in relation to theme of cross-dressing/drag performance. In this respect the novels of Sarah Waters, specifically *Tipping the Velvet*'s world of male impersonation, have emerged as particularly ripe for Butlerian readings, foreshadowed by the quotation on the cover of the 1999 paperback edition of *Tipping the Velvet* which reads 'Imagine Jeanette Winterson on a good day, collaborating with Judith Butler to pen a sapphic Moll Flanders.'[11] Chapter 1 will consider some of the extant applications of Butler's work to neo-Victorian literature, and suggests that there is a tendency to perceive 'gender as performance' as having unequivocally subversive and/or liberatory implications for neo-Victorian texts which engage with the construction of gender roles. This assumption largely stems from an elision of the differences between the terms 'performance' and 'performativity'. Butler's use of the term 'performative' is borrowed from linguistic terminology and refers to the *conventions* of language use that pre-exist the utterance/agency of any individual subject. Her deployment of this concept in the context of gender construction is to underscore the conventional 'acts' and utterances that must be recited to produce a gendered identity. Performativity is the repetition of a script and the subject has no 'choice' as to whether to engage in these conventions. This script dictates the terms under which the individual comes into being as a gendered subject in the first place. Butler emphasizes the restrictive and conventional force of performativity in her introduction to *Bodies That Matter* (1993):

> For if I were to argue that genders are performative, that could mean that I thought that one woke in the morning, perused the closet or some more open space for the gender of choice, donned that gender for the day, and then restored the garment to its place at night. Such a wilful and instrumental subject, one who decides *on* its gender, is clearly not its gender from the start and fails to realize that its existence is already decided *by* gender. (Butler, 1993, p. x)

There is thus a distinction to be made between the 'performative' as the compulsory, restrictive script of gender that all subjects must recite and 'performance' as the expression of the subject's agency to alter these repetitions, to produce a subversive transformation in the very process of repetition. I argue that it is this tension between repetition and transformation that is so relevant the neo-Victorian texts discussed in this book. *Performativity is the process of historical repetition.* Even the most 'subversive' of performances – whether in the forum of gender or neo-Victorianism – is necessarily dependent on the prior 'script' on which it attempts to alter. This raises a crucial question: how can we tell if a re-citation is enacting a subversion of the prior script, or if it is mere repetition? Butler repeatedly returns to this quandary in her work since *Gender Trouble*, yet never posits a strategy for negotiating this fluctuation between subversion and reconsolidation. In the various commentaries on neo-Victorian novels that use a Butlerian framework, it is rare that such a tension is contemplated. Rather than simply celebrating neo-Victorian literature's subversive 'performances' of Victorian scripts, then, this book seeks to position the problematic aspects of performativity as being particularly informative in understanding the complexity of neo-Victorianism's 'talking back' to the Victorian era. To what extent do neo-Victorian ventriloquisms transform the script of Victorian gender? To what extent do they repeat it? These questions will be consistently addressed in my discussion of the neo-Victorian novels in this study. Furthermore, how might Butler's vision of the performative constraints of the script of gender versus the subversive agency in the performance of gender be relevant to the gendering of the history of ventriloquism? In my reading of the history of ventriloquism in Chapter 1, I shall highlight the ways in which Butler's theories can help us to rethink the passive/active dichotomy suggested by some uses of the ventriloquial metaphor. In addition, I will also elaborate on how my understanding of the ventriloquial metaphor can offer a new way to chart and negotiate the fluctuations between agency and constraint in Butler's theories, specifically in relation to neo-Victorian fiction.

However, there is a further ventriloquial issue that needs to be addressed here, which links back to my earlier discussion of the ethical considerations of 'voicing' the Victorians. As the chapter outline below will demonstrate, this book studies ventriloquism in both Victorian and neo-Victorian fiction and seeks to emphasize a sense of ventriloquial dialogue between these eras. This is not to suggest that my use of Butler's theories can somehow be mapped onto the Victorian era; put another way, that the late Victorian texts should be analysed through the lens of late twentieth-century queer theory and be denounced as lacking and the neo-Victorian as 'better'. Such an approach would reveal a desire to make the Victorians speak for 'us', to position Victorian precursors in the role of dummies to be manipulated and voiced to suit contemporary concerns. Although this is certainly a way of perceiving the neo-Victorian impulse to 're-voice' the past, it is not productive and returns to that image of neo-Victorianism *endlessly* talking to itself. Rather, what I aim to demonstrate in this study is the ways my ventriloquial metaphor – initially conceptualized via Butlerian performativity – can aid us in exploring neo-Victorian fiction, but that current understandings of 'performativity' also potentially act as a barrier to re-articulating Victorian texts. Indeed, the dominance of Butlerian understandings of gender performativity in neo-Victorian fiction runs the risk of muting Victorian voices all together. My purpose in including chapters discussing the theme of ventriloquism in Victorian texts is to provide a context for the ventriloquial themes which emerge in the work of Carter, Atwood, Galloway and Waters. I suggest that texts such as *The Bostonians, Trilby, Dorian Gray* and *De Profundis* provide the outlines of a 'script' of gendered ventriloquism that is re-voiced in the neo-Victorian novels but do not simply produce an illusory 'origin' for neo-Victorianism to return to and redress. Instead, my analysis is attuned to what is re-voiced by neo-Victorian fiction but also to what might be silenced, the ways in which neo-Victorian fiction does 'talk to itself' – to 'our' contemporary preoccupations – as opposed to 'talking back' to the nineteenth century. This will be part of Chapter 6's focus, where I examine A. S. Byatt's *Possession* (1990) and writings on historical fiction and ventriloquism, Sarah Waters' *Fingersmith* (2002) and Kathe Koja's *Under the Poppy* (2010). Although these texts do not enter into a specific dialogue with Du Maurier's, James' and Wilde's work they are invoking broader issues surrounding neo-Victorianism and ventriloquism and engaging with some of the more problematic issues of ventriloquism as a aesthetic and ethical strategy. An additional concern in this chapter is the 'voices' of critics and readers of neo-Victorian literature, which is necessarily a self-conscious reflection on my own role as a critical reader of neo-Victorian texts. In what ways does a critical reader 'talk back' to the complex ventriloquism of neo-Victorianism? Are critical readers encouraged to engage in this dialogue, or do certain texts actually seek to silence such critical reflection? What is at stake when additional voices enter into the Victorian/neo-Victorian dialogue?

The late Victorian 'script' of ventriloquism is not self-originating, it is in itself a re-voicing of concerns about agency, voice and gender that were being expressed at the turn of the eighteenth century. The earliest text I study in this book is Charles Brockden Brown's *Wieland, Or the Transformation* (1798). Again, this is not to install this text as an 'origin' for Victorian attitudes towards ventriloquism (though it is worth noting that this is one of the first novels about the dangers of ventriloquial utterances). My commentary on Brown's novel serves to highlight the ventriloquial aspect of discussions about ventriloquism, the sense that the late Victorian authors studied were also re-voicing a 'script' of ventriloquism and gender and, like neo-Victorianism, re-articulating some 'voices' at the expense of others.

Gender and ventriloquism in Victorian and neo-Victorian fiction: chapter outline

As suggested above, Chapter 1 will consider the ways in which the history of displaced voice can offer an alternative interpretation of the concept of ventriloquism. Instead of fixing the source of agency to an all-powerful ventriloquist or delineating the dummy as an object to be manipulated and voiced, my reading of pre-twentieth-century ventriloquism offers the possibility of the 'passionate puppet'; an ostensible dummy that can 'talk back' to the master discourses by which she is manipulated. Emphasizing the gendering of the 'dummy' role, this chapter explores the connections between ventriloquism and Judith Butler's work on gender as performance. The problematic aspects of Butler's uncertainty about the agency of the subject caught between restrictive performativity and the subversive potential of performance are also discussed, demonstrating how my ventriloquial metaphor provides a strategy for articulating and negotiating the ambiguity of Butler's work. Furthermore, this chapter highlights the anxiety about transformation through repetition manifest in critical accounts of neo-Victorianism, providing a context for the book's investment in ventriloquism as a key trope in dialogues between Victorian and neo-Victorian texts.

Chapter 2 provides the foundation of the Victorian 'script' of ventriloquism that will be re-voiced in the neo-Victorian texts of this study. Positioning the nineteenth century as a transitional period in cultural understandings of ventriloquism, I argue that the practice of ventriloquism encompassed a range of fears about the concept of influence, specifically in relation to gender and sexuality. This chapter's reading of Brown's *Wieland, or the Transformation* and Henry Cockton's *The Life and Adventures of Valentine Vox the Ventriloquist* alongside contemporary attitudes towards ventriloquial performance outlines the trope of the masculine, penetrative ventriloquist and the feminized, penetrated 'dummy' that will reappear in late Victorian literature. James' *The Bostonians* and Du Maurier's *Trilby* are located as the central texts of Victorian narratives of ventriloquism, and my analysis of the novels emphasizes contemporary anxieties surrounding 'vocal' women. Though both Verena and Trilby appear to possess influential voices, it is ultimately revealed that their vocal abilities are always under the influence of another; they are 'possessed' by the masculine potency of male ventriloquists. The chapter also introduces the theme of the queer ventriloquist; although the manipulative agendas of Olive Chancellor and Little Billee are ultimately thwarted, we shall subsequently see that the queer ventriloquist has a significant cultural afterlife in neo-Victorian fiction.

Chapter 3 considers how Carter's *Nights at the Circus* and Atwood's *Alias Grace* 'talk back' to the Victorian script of ventriloquism outlined in Chapter 2. Although these novels depict women with influential voices from ambiguous sources, they challenge the 'dummy' status of women in the late Victorian texts by offering specific engagements with the connections between gender, voice, agency and influence. The respective roles of ventriloquist and dummy shift and blur as the desire of Jack Walser and Simon Jordan to 'script' their female subjects is thwarted by Fevvers' and Grace Mark's ventriloquial strategies to produce voice. The potential queerness of ventriloquial exchanges is also discussed. Although the work of Carter and Atwood provides a reappraisal of ventriloquial agency, the novels also dramatize the perilously fine line between repetition and transformation in ventriloquism as a thematic and metatextual preoccupation in neo-Victorian fiction. This chapter considers the aspects of Victorian ventriloquism that are silenced in neo-Victorian ventriloquism narratives, namely the vulnerability of the masculine ventriloquist. I argue that this omission is redressed in Galloway's *Clara*, a novel that interrogates the instability of would-be ventriloquist figures rather than attempting to provide its female protagonist with a subversive 'voice'.

Chapter 4 offers the opportunity to hear alternative 'voices' in the script of late Victorian ventriloquism: Wilde's *The Picture of Dorian Gray* and *De Profundis*. My reading of *Dorian Gray* emphasizes the potential for influence to be a multi-voiced process, not confined to a static dichotomy of power between ventriloquist and dummy. Exploring the concept of the double in ventriloquism, this chapter considers the multiple possibilities for agency suggested by the novel's depiction of ventriloquial influence. However, such freedom is not granted to the women of Wilde's novel. In the analysis of *De Profundis* I explain Wilde's prison letter as a ventriloquial text on several levels; the process of Wilde 'talking back' to his silencing by his conviction, and articulating a perspective on his relationship with Lord Alfred Douglas. Discussing the ventriloquial imagery deployed in the text, I suggest that Wilde creates a vision of a 'passionate puppet' who must find alternative strategies to produce 'voice' when it has apparently been denied, and the queerness of ventriloquial negotiations of power and desire are highlighted.

Chapter 5 studies two of Sarah Waters' neo-Victorian novels: *Tipping the Velvet* and *Affinity*. Waters' first novel is an act of metatextual ventriloquism, providing a voice for the silenced history of desire between women through re-citing the Wildean underworld of renters and same-sex coteries. Although the text redresses the marginalization of women in Wilde's work to an extent, my analysis considers the ways in which Wilde's misogyny is replicated by Waters' characters. The issue of gender as performance is central to *Tipping the Velvet* and this chapter emphasizes the ventriloquial inflection of the tension between repetition and transformation in Nancy's attempts to develop a sexual subjectivity. *Affinity* contains echoes of *De Profundis* and *The Bostonians*. My gloss of the novel discusses the connections between mediumship and ventriloquism, and reads *Affinity* as a development of the concept of queer ventriloquism in late Victorian literature. I argue that Waters' work provides a self-conscious reflection on the promise of and problems with neo-Victorian ventriloquism, engaging with the repetition of past voices and the quandaries of agency and subversion in relation to gender and ventriloquism.

Chapter 6 is concerned with the *critical* voices of neo-Victorian ventriloquism, self-consciously asking the question: how does the voice of the critical reader figure in neo-Victorian ventriloquial dialogues? As mentioned above, Byatt's *Possession: A Romance* is often read as a text about ventriloquism, but I am interested the power dynamics of authorial/critical voices as a theme in the novel and as a metatextual enactment of the dummy/ventriloquist relationship. Byatt's own commentary on the novel attempts to distance herself from the 'moral' implications of repeating prior historical scripts by utilizing the concept of ventriloquism. Throughout this book I argue that ventriloquism is intimately related to the politics of voice, gender and agency, and my analysis of *Possession* explores the ways in which Byatt, perhaps inadvertently, imposes the script of Victorian ventriloquism upon her characters and, crucially, upon the critical readers of the novel. Sarah Waters' *Fingersmith* depicts a queer dummy, Maud Lilly, who appears to find a 'voice' for her desire in the pornographic scripts that have ensured her oppression in the first instance. My study of the ventriloquial themes within the novel leads on to a reflection on the afterlife of Waters' work in television adaptation. To what extent does Waters, like Maud, have her attempts to 'talk back' to patriarchal, heteronormative scripts of women's sexuality silenced by the voices of her audience? Kathe Koja's *Under the Poppy* is a novel about a queer ventriloquist, but demonstrates a lack of critical reflection upon the gendered politics of ventriloquism and the process of neo-Victorian 're-voicing'. Although the critical reader is in a position to trace the novel's Victorian and neo-Victorian references, bringing a critical voice to the novel exposes the limits of its subversive potential, and the depiction of 'Victorian' sexuality is both disturbing and stereotyped.

The Afterword to this book offers a space to listen to textual voices from beyond the Victorian/neo-Victorian dialogue in Wesley Stace's *Misfortune* (2005) and *By George* (2007). Although both novels are concerned with issues surrounding gender and ventriloquism – *By George* tells the story of a family of ventriloquists – neither find a 'voice' that is securely located in the Victorian era. What might this suggest to us about the limitations of the nineteenth century as a locus for thinking about ventriloquism? What parables do Stace's novels provide for thinking about the position of the author as always already ventriloquial? Although *Gender and Ventriloquism in Victorian and Neo-Victorian Fiction* clearly has an investment in thinking about Victorian and neo-Victorian voices, to ignore the peripheral voices in this debate would be the antithesis of my understanding of ventriloquism in this book: poly-vocal, fluid, and engaging in perpetual negotiations of gendered subjectivity.

1
Voices from the Past: Rethinking the Ventriloquial Metaphor

In his book entitled *The Culture of the Copy*, Hillel Schwartz discusses the distribution of power in the relationship between ventriloquist and dummy: 'The dummy's destiny is finally determined from above, but in the meantime it makes one articulate gesture after another in the direction of free will. Together, ventriloquist and dummy allude to power and powerlessness through stand-up comedies of insolence' (Schwartz, 1996, p. 136). Why, in a study focusing on 'the culture of the copy', does Hillel Schwartz offer ventriloquism as an example? What is the connection between ventriloquism and 'copying', or repetition? My Introduction's discussion of extant uses of the ventriloquial metaphor in neo-Victorian scholarship highlighted a dearth of engagement with what 'ventriloquism' might actually signify. Despite this inclination to let ventriloquism speak for itself, there is still a recurring association between ventriloquism and 'copying' in the context of neo-Victorianism. For instance, Catherine Bernard argues that the 'pervading presence' of ventriloquism in contemporary fiction suggests: 'The very concept of creativeness seems to have become depleted and replaced with a weaker version of invention that equates writing with the mere reactivation of past idioms, with a form of clever if exhausted mimicry' (Bernard, 2003, p. 11). Put another way, 'ventriloquism' represents the lack of an independent authorial voice; neo-Victorian fiction can only produce inferior 'copies' of the Victorian 'original'. In a similar vein, Christian Gutleben proposes the mythical figure of Echo as a fitting allegory for neo-Victorian authorship: 'Is contemporary fiction [...] like Echo, doomed to have no voice of its own and to repeat the words of others?' (Gutleben, 2001, p. 16) Ventriloquial authorship is again deemed derivative, imitative, condemned to repetition as opposed to originality.

In the above quotation Schwartz makes explicit the image that is only hinted at in Bernard's and Gutleben's commentaries. The 'dummy' is symbolic of repetition in several ways. The ventriloquist's puppet is often a simulacrum (or 'copy') of a human being but, more importantly, the dummy is compelled to recite a script authored by another. As Schwartz's gloss suggests, the dummy might appear to 'talk back' to its master – therein lies the comedy of the dummy/ventriloquist performance – yet its fate is sealed; 'the dummy's destiny is finally determined from above'. For in the specific context of the dummy/vent performance, ventriloquism is an *illusion* of abnegated autonomy on the part of the ventriloquist as s/he orchestrates her/his own lack of control. The audience also engages in a willing self-deception as, although the personality of the dummy is often captivating, we still know that it is just a puppet animated by the hand and voice of the ventriloquist.[1] The 'origin' of voice is never seriously in doubt. As a metaphor for articulating the relationship between Victorian 'originals' and neo-Victorian 'copies', this understanding of ventriloquism is disappointing and limited. A fixed hierarchy is constructed between 'original'/'copied' voice and no matter how dazzling the ostensible 'dialogue' between texts we are ultimately left with neo-Victorian dummy-authors, belatedly speaking in voices which can be sourced to the nineteenth century.

There is another way in which the ventriloquial metaphor is deployed in relation to neo-Victorianism and this is also relevant to the dummy/vent exchange outlined by Schwartz: the stark division between 'power and powerlessness'. As C. B. Davis has remarked in his commentary on uses of the ventriloquial metaphor in critical theory, ventriloquism operates as 'a general term for any variety of speaking for and through a represented Other [...] By analogy the represented Other is the implicitly mute puppet or "dummy" of an authorial voice or Western "master discourses"' (Davis, 1998, p. 133). As I discussed in the Introduction, 'voice' and social subjectivity have important conceptual links and in the above quotation, Davis highlights the metaphorical link between 'voice' and agency. His assessment of the generally negative connotations of the ventriloquial metaphor in relation to identity politics and lack of agency is exemplified in neo-Victorian criticism by Christine Ferguson's article on the after-life of the Jack the Ripper story in the film version of Alan Moore's graphic novel *From Hell* (2001). She condemns the Hughes Brothers, the directors of the film, for 'ventriloquizing the suffering of a victim of brutal sexual homicide' (Ferguson, 2009, p. 45). Ferguson's distaste for this re-voicing is palpable. The most vicious silencing of the female murder victims is further perpetrated by patriarchal, misogynist accounts of their stories; the women are figured as puppets to be manipulated and ventriloquized by neo-Victorian discourses.

This gendered inflection of the ventriloquial metaphor is not confined to commentaries on the power inequalities within neo-Victorian re-voicings. For instance, in her book *Ventriloquized Bodies: Narratives of Hysteria in Nineteenth-Century France* (1994), Janet Beizer uses the notion of ventriloquism to encapsulate the process of the repression of women's speech, manifesting itself as inarticulate hysteria which must then be provided with a narrative explanation by male doctors (Beizer, 1994, p. 9). The silenced woman is implicitly forced into a 'dummy' role and her social subjectivity is articulated by the male ventriloquist-doctors. Naomi B. Sokoloff also invokes the concept of ventriloquism to discuss the power politics of men speaking for women in textual narratives (Sokoloff, 1989, pp. 113–37) and in a comparable usage Elizabeth Harvey's study of texts from the early modern era states: 'I [...] argue that ventriloquism is an appropriation of the feminine voice, and that it reflects and contributes to a larger cultural silencing of women' (Harvey, 1992, p. 12).

From a different perspective, Lori Hope Lefkovitz imagines the impulse to tell her antecedents' Holocaust survival narratives as a form of ventriloquism on the part of the younger Jewish generation (Lefkovitz, 1991, p. 41). These examples refer to different scenarios charged with a variety of intentions. We can see an exposé of the mechanisms of patriarchal ideology at work in Beizer's usage but Lefkovitz's deployment of the ventriloquial metaphor is motivated by noble impulses in terms of the desire to re-tell and remember Jewish history. 'Speaking for' a particular group does not necessarily mean that the speaker/ventriloquist has personally imposed the 'dummy's' silence. Although the word 'ventriloquism' is not mentioned, M. L. Kohlke's introduction to the inaugural issue of *Neo-Victorian Studies* also seems to allude to the ethical quandaries of ventriloquizing the Victorians:

> To properly 'address' the manifold spectres of the nineteenth century [...] also means addressing our own complex investments with resurrecting the past, acknowledging how desire makes the spectres dance to our tune, delimiting what we choose to hear when we make the ghosts speak – or speak for them. (Kohlke, 2008, p. 14)

Kohlke's statement draws upon mediumistic imagery – and as we shall see, spiritualism and ventriloquism are closely linked – but her concept of making the Victorians 'dance to our tune' also figures neo-Victorian authors as manipulative puppet-masters. She identifies a tension between allowing 'the Victorians' to speak and speaking for them but her comment on what 'we choose to hear' implies that the ventriloquial agency ultimately resides with neo-Victorian authors and critics.

Each of these examples retain the passive/active dichotomy of manipulated 'dummy' and manipulative 'ventriloquist'. As in a ventriloquist stage show, the self is figured as having utter control over the other, despite the illusion of a dialogue, and the 'dummy' is compelled to repeat a script authored by the ventriloquist. Within such a model of ventriloquism multiple voices are not permitted to exist in unison but can only oscillate between the 'dummy' and it's 'master'. In a commentary on the ethics of the voice in literary and cultural criticism, Steven Connor notes that such usages suggest:

> For my voice to issue from an other means that my voice can be no longer in my possession. If, by contrast, another forces his voice upon me then it is again impossible for me to speak with my own voice, because the voice of the other must wholly supplant my own. (Connor, 1999a, p. 221)

An intractable dualism defines these uses of the ventriloquial metaphor, resonating with concerns about passive possession and active possessing of 'voice'. How might our understanding of ventriloquism alter if the ventriloquist/dummy power dichotomy is challenged? What if the so-called 'dummy' actually could talk back to the ostensibly all-controlling ventriloquist? As a context for this book's exploration of the generative potential – and perils – of ventriloquism, this chapter will give a brief overview of the history of ventriloquism to demonstrate how the ventriloquial metaphor can be released from the constraints of active/passive dualism. Prior to dummy/ventriloquist performances of the twentieth century, the state of being 'ventriloquized' is gendered; it is women who have generally fulfilled the role of 'dummy' in ventriloquial exchanges. I will then examine how Judith Butler's theories on gender as performance can assist in rethinking two issues that are central to the concepts of ventriloquism, gender and neo-Victorianism: the relationship between 'original' and 'copy' and the notion of transformation through repetition. Indeed, I argue that Butler's theory of performativity/performance can actually be elucidated by thinking ventriloquially about the tension between repetition and subversion, constraint and agency. The final section of this chapter will bring the focus back to neo-Victorian fiction, underscoring the ways in which my ventriloquial rethinking of Butler's theories is relevant to the 're-voicing' and 're-scripting' of Victorian discourses on ventriloquism in neo-Victorian texts.

The gendering of ventriloquism: Butler, performance and performativity

Despite the ubiquity of puppet-based understandings of ventriloquial exchanges, the ventriloquist/dummy performance is a relatively recent development in the history of ventriloquism; it was only to become the standard demonstration of ventriloquial prowess from the late nineteenth century onwards. The history of ventriloquism can be traced back to the ambiguous speech of the priestesses of the Delphic oracle, through medieval accounts of demonic possession to the séances of spirit mediums in the nineteenth century.[2] Significantly, the displacements of voice encompassed by this genealogy of ventriloquism are not limited to objects (in other words, a literal dummy) but can also be enacted upon people. In each of these scenarios, it is a *subject* fulfilling the role of the 'dummy'.

We can begin to understand the challenges this poses to the dichotomy of agency/passivity in the ventriloquial metaphor by thinking through the dynamics of these exchanges. For example, at the site of the Delphic oracle a priestess would be possessed by the voices of the gods, who supposedly used her voice to transmit their messages to the mortals. The priests present at the scene had the responsibility of interpreting the prophecy, and so their voices are added to the ambiguous voices of the gods and priestess. These already multiple voices are further complicated by the written accounts of this scene throughout history, the narrative perspectives of the authors whose information we rely upon for imagining these strange events. Steven Connor's gloss of the ventriloquial currencies of the Delphic oracle also recognizes this multiplicity of voice: 'The voice of the oracle is plural; and its plurality also involves temporal multiplicity. It does not speak of one time alone, or at one time. Any number of people may be speaking through this act of forced speech' (Connor, 2000, p. 65). The question raised by this act of ventriloquism is *who* is speaking? Where is the origin and agency of voice located? This quandary repeatedly surfaces in the history of displaced voice. In the case of possession, a similar ambiguity with regards to the agency behind the ventriloquial voice occurs. The subject under possession (most often female) has her own voice appropriated by the demon who has entered her body. This demon is then enticed into conversation with the exorcists and the account is subsequently recorded in written documents.

A comparable pattern is apparent in the situation of the nineteenth-century spirit medium. She is seemingly spoken through by numerous spirit voices yet these voices manifest themselves alongside the medium's own voice. The other participants in the séance must interpret the messages imparted by the medium and so effectively impose their own voices upon her. Again, we often have the later narrative voice of the writer who might transcribe these events.

A crucial issue to emphasize in these instances of ventriloquial speech is the *gender* of the ventriloquized body. The state of being 'ventriloquized', of having the voice suppressed or appropriated by external forces repeatedly manifests as a feminized condition. Following the usages of the ventriloquial metaphor by Beizer, Sokoloff and Harvey, one could speculate that the apparent susceptibility of women to possession or mediumship merely reiterates the deeply entrenched patriarchal association between femininity and penetrability. Is the female body therefore condemned to be silenced, spoken for and manipulated by this historical genealogy of ventriloquism? Is femininity for dummies? However, such an analysis rests on the assumption that the voices of these gods/demons/spirits were authentic. What if (a reasonable contention) they were not? We are then faced with the prospect that it is the subject of possession who is the ventriloquist, producing – consciously or otherwise – numerous voices alongside her own whilst posing as a mere 'dummy'. In contrast to the dummy/ventriloquist stage performance the origin and intention of these ventriloquial voices cannot be easily quantified. There are many voices, many ventriloquists, many 'dummies' and these roles are in a constant state of negotiation. In each of these ventriloquial scenarios, we are presented with women whose occupation of the feminine subject position should ostensibly condemn them to silence, manipulation and otherness. Indeed, it is these very traits that necessitate their fulfilment of the 'dummy' role. Nevertheless, ventriloquial strategies provide the opportunity to produce 'voice', to exercise agency where it has socially and culturally been denied. What we are presented with is strategy of *performance*; a performance of the 'dummy' role which simultaneously invokes patriarchal norms of femininity – passivity and penetrability – even as they are subverted by the production of voice/agency. The 'dummy's' performance allows space to 'talk back' to the machinations of patriarchal ventriloquisms. The concept of subversive 'performance' in relation to gender clearly echoes the work of Judith Butler, and the ways in which the ventriloquial metaphor and Butler's work on gender as performance might be connected bear further consideration.

There are two strands of Butler's work that prove relevant to my broadening of the ventriloquial metaphor and which also have ramifications for neo-Victorianism: her challenge to the hierarchical relationship between 'original' and 'copy' and the recognition that repetition can enact subversive transformations. It is an established feminist contention that gender is constructed, but in *Gender Trouble* (1990) Butler argues that we might also perceive 'biological' sex as being constructed. Sex is produced by a regulatory system of discourses that serve the agenda of heteronormative society: 'Gender is not to culture as sex is to nature; gender is also the discursive/cultural means by which "sexed nature" or "natural sex" is produced and established as "prediscursive", prior to culture, a politically neutral surface *on which* culture acts' (Butler, 1999, p. 11, emphasis in original). Biological sex is not the 'original' to gender's 'copy', there is not a 'mimetic relation of gender to sex whereby gender mirrors sex or is otherwise restricted by it' (Butler, 1999, p. 10). As a consequence, the homophobic argument that 'unintelligible' gender roles – where there is a dissonance between sex and gender, or sexual behaviour and either sex and/or gender – are inferior 'copies' of heteronormative 'originals' is also challenged: 'The replication of heterosexual constructs in non-heterosexual frames brings into relief the utterly constructed status of the so-called heterosexual original. Thus, gay is to straight *not* as copy is to original, but, rather, as copy is to copy' (Butler, 1999, p. 41, emphasis in original).

This concept of 'copying' or replication is the key issue in understanding Butler's theorization of the way in which gender/sex is socially constructed. Butler states that the illusion of a coherent gender identity – heterosexual or otherwise – is formed through a set of acts that must be repeated. Gender is constructed via the recitation of a discursive script and it is in the very process of this performative repetition that gender has the potential to be constructed in alternative ways to subvert patriarchal, heteronormative expectations. As outlined in the Introduction, Butler argues that drag performance offers an allegory for the construction of all gender roles. Drag provides an overt parody of the script which must be recited to produce the illusion of a coherent, stable gender. It reveals that there is no 'original' gender/sex, only ever 'copies': '*In imitating gender, drag implicitly reveals the imitative structure of gender itself – as well as its contingency*' (Butler, 1999, p. 175, emphasis in original).

Most aptly, Butler's work has spawned many transformations through critical repetition, not all of which have met with her approval. The theory of gender as performance risks being interpreted as suggesting that the individual subject has the agency to 'choose' a gender to perform and that 'subversion' will be automatically within the gender-bending subject's grasp. Such a reading stems from a conflation of 'performativity' with 'performance' and the potential for confusing these terms is exemplified by Seyla Benhabib's critique of Butler's *theatrical* metaphor for gender identity. Benhabib ponders whether there is 'ever any chance to stop the performance for awhile, to pull the curtain down, and to let it rise only if one can have a say in the production of the play itself?' (Benhabib, 1995, p. 21). In her subsequent response Butler condemns Benhabib's failure to 'read carefully' and explains that her use of 'performativity' is rooted in linguistic theory, namely J. L. Austin's coining of the term in *How to Do Things With Words* (1962). An Austinian performative is a speech act which 'brings into being that which it names' and thus emphasizes the generative power of discourse (Butler, 1995, p. 134). The distinction between a theatrically-inflected metaphor of 'performance' and a linguistically-grounded notion of a performative utterance has significant consequences for thinking about the concept of agency:

> To the extent that a performative appears to 'express' a prior intention, a doer *behind* the deed, that prior agency is only legible *as the effect* of that utterance. For a performative to work, it must draw upon and recite a set of linguistic conventions which have traditionally worked to bind or engage certain kinds of effects. The force or effectivity of a performative will be derived from its capacity to draw on and reencode the historicity of those conventions in a present act. This power of recitation is not a function of an individual's *intention*, but is an effect of historically sedimented linguistic conventions [...] In other words, when words engage actions or constitute themselves a kind of action, they do this not because they reflect the power of an individual's will or intention, but because they draw upon and reengage conventions which have gained their power precisely through a *sedimented iterability*. (Butler, 1995, p. 134, emphasis in original)

This quotation bears careful consideration. It emphasizes not only Butler's indebtedness to poststructuralist interpretations of language but also the strict limitation exercised upon the subject's agency by a performative theory of gender. There is no subject that can position itself prior to language or, specifically in relation to Butler's argument, gender. Our access to a gendered subject position is dependent upon discursive laws and conventions that predate the individual subject and that will always already dictate how gendered subjectivity can be expressed. There is a sense that we can never 'own' the language that we speak. The subject is always 'spoken through' (or ventriloquized) by existing discourses, evacuating the privileged position of illusory originality. Butler's invocation of the performativity of gender in her work stems from a similar position. The gendered subject inherits a discourse (or 'script') or gender that defines the terms under which the individual will appear as a subject at all. We do not have the option of 'stepping outside' of a gendered script to subvert its dominant meanings.

However, *Gender Trouble* does have a tendency to slide between the linguistic connotations of 'performative' and the theatrical metaphor of 'performance' without accounting sufficiently for the tension between the terms. In an earlier essay, Butler offers a clearer rejection of the theatrical model of *agency* that might imply that there is a gendered subject who pre-exists the performative construction of gender and who has the option of performing a gendered self. She does – rather confusingly – suggest that there are similarities to be drawn between gender constituted through discursive 'acts' and a theatrical context, and this underscores her emphasis on the *restrictions* of performativity:

> The body is not passively scripted with cultural codes, as if it were a lifeless recipient of wholly pre-given cultural relations. But neither do embodied selves pre-exist the cultural conventions which essentially signify bodies. Actors are always already on stage, within the terms of the performance. Just as a script might be enacted in various ways, and just as the play requires both text and interpretation, so the gendered body acts its part in a culturally restricted corporeal space and enacts interpretations within the confines of already existing directives. (Butler, 1988, p. 526)

In other words, there is a theatrically-inflected 'performance' aspect to Butler's theory of gender performativity but only in the sense of there being an irrevocably blurred boundary between 'real' life and the 'copy' of theatrical performance. The 'gender-as-performance' thesis only functions alongside performativity if we image the social realm as a perpetual, compulsory theatre with a ubiquitous imperative not only to perform an 'act' but to keep on performing it.

The development of Butler's work on gendered subjectivity since the publication of *Gender Trouble* has been a sustained attempt to distance her self from the 'voluntarist' model of gender as performance. In *Bodies*

That Matter (1993) and *The Psychic Life of Power* (1997) there is a growing incompatibility between the concepts of performance and the performative. An essential issue to understand in Butler's refining of her theory of performative gender is that her emphasis on construction does not suggest that gender has an element of 'choice' and can thus be easily cast aside. On the contrary, the 'constructedness' of gender emerges as a deeply rooted social, cultural and psychic phenomena (Butler, 1993, p. xi). She increasingly acknowledges the *paradoxical* aspect of the subject's social agency. How will a subject – whose very existence as a subject is dependent on regulatory power regimes – appropriate a strategy of agency from *within* those power regimes to attempt to *subvert* those power regimes?

To reiterate the constraints of gender performativity, Butler returns to her interpretation of drag and its relationship to subversive parody. At the conclusion of *Gender Trouble*, Butler admits that there is nothing inherently subversive about parody and ponders the difficulty in determining: 'what makes certain kinds of parodic repetitions effectively disruptive, truly troubling, and which repetitions become domesticated and recirculated as instruments of cultural hegemony' (Butler, 1999, p. 177). This quandary is not resolved but is returned to in *Bodies that Matter*, where Butler provides several examples of gender performances that fail to fulfil the expectations of drag's subversive potential.[3] At best, drag serves to expose the way in which all gender identities are formed by rendering this process of cross-gendered identification transparent and hyperbolic (Butler, 1993, p. 131). Is exposing the mechanisms of gender formation sufficient to enact a critique of these norms? How might we judge when a gender performance is subversive of the heteronormative construction of gender or when it is just a recapitulation of these discourses?

This is another dilemma that has drawn much criticism of Butler's interest in parody as a political strategy, considering the emphasis it appears to place on both the performer's intentions and the audience's interpretation. Carole-Anne Tyler has commented on the difficulty in distinguishing between a gendered performance which is a subversive repetition and a representation of gender which merely repeats the script: 'The answer, it seems, are the author's intentions: parody is legible in the drama of gender performance if someone meant to script it, intending it to be there' (Tyler, 1991, p. 54). As Tyler's remarks indicate, 'authorial' intention might demarcate a performance that is supposed to challenge heteronormative, patriarchal expectations but the success of such a performance is still dependent upon an 'audience's' interpretation. The subversive intentions of a performance are always liable to be recuperated or construed in ways that are beyond the control of the 'author' of a performance. This highlights a broader issue about parody as a strategy for subversion. There has been copious academic speculation on the definitions, intentions and meanings of parody, with little consensus or agreement. The only consistent factor of parody is its dependence on a prior work or practice, as Simon Dentith suggests: 'Parody includes any cultural practice which provides a relatively polemical allusive imitation of another cultural production or practice' (Dentith, 2000, p. 9). One of the difficulties in recuperating parody as a potentially subversive practice is this symbiotic, or pejoratively speaking, parasitic, relationship to the 'original'; it is paradoxical, both incorporating and challenging the object of the parody (Hutcheon, 1988, p. 11).

A further, more fundamental, quandary can be raised with the notions of 'subversion' or 'transgression' as there is, of course, nothing inherently 'good' from a political perspective about either of these concepts. Nancy Fraser makes a comparable criticism of Butler's apparent privileging of 'resignification' as implicitly having positive implications. Fraser comments: 'Why is resignification good? Can't there be bad (oppressive, reactionary) resignifications? [...] Butler seems to valorise change for its own sake' (Fraser, 1995, p. 68). Butler does acknowledge the ambiguity of 'subversion' as a concept. She notes that the emergence of fascism in Hitler's Germany certainly functioned as a significant 'subversion' or 'resignification' of human rights. The difference between a 'radically democratic' subversion and a subversion founded on violent exclusion resides in the notoriously thorny issues of intention, perception and effects (Butler, 2004, pp. 223–4). She also recognizes that sometimes an act will ultimately exceed its author's intentions (Butler, 1993, p. 241).

Performativity and ventriloquism: neo-Victorian genders, neo-Victorian voices

It is this stress on both the restrictive aspect of performativity and the unpredictability of performer intention/audience interpretation that is largely absent from the application of Butler's work to neo-Victorian literature. For instance, Cheryl A. Wilson's article on Sarah Waters' *Tipping the Velvet* applies a Butlerian framework to Nancy's time as a cross-dressing renter and approvingly terms this part of the novel as 'a literal embodiment of sexuality and performance' (Wilson, 2006, p. 299). Cross-dressing is celebrated as a liberating, subversive act and yet such a gloss fails to mention the performative imperatives of gender which dictate the terms under which Nancy will 'pass' as a young man and which thus offer no challenge to the broader script of masculinity. In a commentary on the motif of cross-dressing in the historical novel more generally, Diana Wallace writes of 'the transgressive possibility of flexible gender identity acted out through clothes [...] what Judith Butler [...] theorises as gender as performativity' (Wallace, 2005, p. 21). We see here that Wallace elides the distinction between performance and performativity; subversion can seemingly be accessed via a costume change. Sarah Gamble's article discussing *Tipping the Velvet* alongside Angela Carter's *Nights at the Circus* and Wesley Stace's *Misfortune* has argued that such neo-Victorian novels are 'intimately related' to Butler's theories of queerness and performativity: 'In placing the theme of gender performativity at the centre of their texts, they attempt to expose the provisional nature of all enactments of gender, past and present, and in doing so reveal the performative nature of the neo-Victorian literary mode itself' (Gamble, 2009, pp. 128–9). She also posits that arguments surrounding the 'authenticity' of the neo-Victorian novel, which position it as a mere 'copy' to the Victorian 'original', also find resonance in cultural anxiety over the 'authenticity' of the transsexual subject (Gamble, 2009, p. 131).

I want to pause here to interrogate Sarah Gamble's vocabulary, for it strikes me that a slippage is at work in her terminology which cuts to the heart of the problems with prior usages of Butler's work in neo-Victorian scholarship. Gamble's application of Butler's deconstruction of the 'original'/'copy' dichotomy to Victorian 'originals' and neo-Victorian 'copies' is extremely pertinent. As I seek to demonstrate throughout this book, the blurring of the boundaries between 'original' and 'copy' is also at the centre of my ventriloquial metaphor, both in relation to Victorian/neo-Victorian exchanges and in relation to the repetition/ transformation of the normative script of gender. However, Gamble continually conflates the terms 'performative' and 'performance' and thus appears to replicate this most common misreading of Butler's work.

Butler's vision is of agency with prescribed boundaries – subversion within limitation – but she does not proffer a workable model for theorizing this ambiguity. Subversion may happen spontaneously but then merely submerge itself back into the realm of the restrictive performative. It is this tension that Butler consistently returns to throughout her work from *Bodies that Matter* onwards and it is never resolved. It seems that Butler spends much of *Bodies* and *Psychic Life* explaining just how paradoxical and difficult such subversion actually is, emphasizing the pervasiveness of performative imperatives. She argues that the achievement of subversion will be tortuous, unpredictable and open to debate:

> One is, as it were, in power even as one opposes it, formed by it as one reworks it [...]The incalculable effects of action are as much a part of their subversive promise as those that we plan in advance [...] The reach of the signifiability cannot be controlled by the one who utters or writes, since such productions are not owned by the one who utters them. They continue to signify in spite of their authors, and sometimes against their authors' most precious intentions [...] This not owning of one's words is there from the start, however, since speaking is always in some way the speaking of a stranger through and as oneself, the [...] reiteration of a language that one never chose, that one does not find as an instrument to be used, but that one is, as it were, used by. (Butler, 1993, pp. 241–2)

Butler acknowledges that the subversive potential of either gender performance or performative gender is never wholly predictable, both in terms of the volatility of audience perception and in relation to the pressures of gender formation that the individual subject can never fully acknowledge or control. Subversive repetition will happen from within the system which is being challenged and its effects will be 'incalculable'. For Moya Lloyd, it is this paradox that represents the limitations of Butler's theories. Without the possibility of calculable effects: 'political intervention may be construed as either totally meaningless (why bother?) or entirely spontaneous (it just happens)' (Lloyd, 1999, p. 207). Neither Butler nor Lloyd posit a strategy, however, for conceptualizing or negotiating this fluctuation between the performance of gender (as an expression of agency) and the performative script of gender (the repressive, subjugating imperatives of compulsory gender performance).

How can my ventriloquial metaphor offer a strategy for negotiating the tension between performance and performativity? The first section of this chapter demonstrated that the ventriloquial metaphor is generally used as an expression of absolute power (the ventriloquist) exercised over complete passivity (the dummy). This active/passive dichotomy is played out, for instance, in Janet Beizer's study of the repression of women's speech, manifesting itself as inarticulate hysteria, which must then be provided with a narrative explanation by male doctors. Autonomy is denied to these women, their identity and 'voice' is ultimately constructed through the agency of the men who treat their 'illness' and the women fulfil a 'dummy' role to the doctors' role of 'ventriloquist' or puppet-master. We can understand this metaphor as having broader applications to the construction of gender in society. Following Butler's theory, from birth a subject is inaugurated into a gendered subject position ('girl' or 'boy') or, put another way, the individual inherits a 'script' of gender that they must continually recite or perform to maintain a coherent subjectivity within society. The use of the word 'script', however, does not suggest that the subject can be considered to be an actor with a sense of autonomous agency. The 'script' of gender is enforced and necessary – to refuse to cohere with performative imperatives is to be relegated to a position of non-being. In spite of this emphasis on the restrictions of the gendered script, Butler explicitly rejects the implication that the subject is merely a puppet or dummy: 'The body is not *passively* scripted with cultural codes, as if it were a *lifeless recipient* of wholly pre-given cultural relations' (Butler, 1988, p. 526, my emphasis).

If we return to the examples of ventriloquism where the subject fulfilling the dummy/puppet role is actually a subject (the medium, the possessed subject, the prophetic priestess) the division between activity and passivity begins to unravel and agency becomes an increasingly debateable issue. The image of a subject's body being 'spoken through' by voices from an indeterminate source (that may well be produced by the subject herself), represents *agency under constraint*; an unruly performance of a pre-scripted role that exceeds the expectations of the puppet-master/ventriloquist. The script of gender might well be prescribed and the recitation compulsory, seemingly casting us in the role of 'dummies', but a sense of agency can become manifest within the possibility of altering a recitation, of 'talking back' (in terms of performative acts) to the cultural discourses that ventriloquize us and hence enacting an alteration of our compelled performance of gender. If ventriloquism is about repetition of scripts, my broadened view of the ventriloquial metaphor is about the *potential* for repetition with a difference.

This is not a utopian vision of subversive potential. The women who perform the 'dummy' role in the history of ventriloquism might be 'talking back' yet this can only occur within their recitations of a script which has dictated the terms of their cultural 'silencing' in the first place. Although my ventriloquial metaphor dismantles the dichotomization of 'original'/'copy' in relation to 'voice', the agency provided by exposing this construction does not exist beyond the discursive laws that have generated and consolidated these binaries initially. The subject fulfilling the 'dummy' or 'puppet' role is implicitly animated as a subject by the discourses that seek to repress it. This understanding of ventriloquism provides a strategy for representing and articulating Butler's ambiguous excursions between performance and performativity, intention and interpretation, subversion and reconsolidation, agency and subjection. Thinking ventriloquially about the flux or oscillation of this subversion of/adherence to dominant power structures provides a model for channelling and exploring these fluctuations that are not satisfactorily accounted for in Butler's theory. There is space for multiple 'voices' and various intentions; a continuum between agency and constraint, original and copy, that does not have to be just one or the other but can articulate both at the same time. To return to Schwartz's comment at the beginning of this chapter: the 'dummy's destiny' is not *finally* determined from above, yet it is still uncertain.

Butler's vision of language – 'not owning of one's words is there from the start [...] since speaking is always in some way the speaking of a stranger through and as oneself' (Butler, 1993, p. 242) – is charged with ventriloquial connotations: the displacement of voice, the uncertainty of agency in language use, the ambivalent condition of possession. Although Butler's work is indebted to a linguistic model for understanding gender construction, it is her study of 'hate speech' in *Excitable Speech: A Politics of the Performative* (1997) which makes the connection between language and transformation through repetition most transparent. Her main topic of enquiry in this book is 'injurious speech' and the potential for combating 'hate speech' without legal intervention. Despite having borrowed J. L. Austin's concept of 'performative utterances' – words or phrases that perform a certain action in the very process of articulation – as a theoretical underpinning for her previous work, it is not until *Excitable Speech* that Butler offers a sustained engagement with his notion of the performative. In *How to Do Things With Word*'s attempts to define the various components of language which might constitute the 'total speech act', Austin introduces the term 'illocutionary' to delineate the 'performance of an act *in* saying something as opposed to performance of an act *of* saying something' (Austin, 1962, p. 99), explaining that the illocutionary has a 'conventional force' that has much in common with the performative (Austin, 1962, p. 108). Butler recapitulates Austin's idea of 'illocutionary' (or performative) words conveying a 'force' upon the listener but adds emphasis to the *temporal* or *ritual* quality of the performative utterance. An act might be performed at the moment of utterance but it also invokes a historicity of usage, a 'sphere of operation that is not restricted to the moment of utterance itself' (Butler, 1997, p. 3). In an exposition overtly influenced by Derrida,[4] Butler suggests that it is the *excessive* aspect of the speech act that is the key to its instability and unpredictability. The speech act (the name-calling, the insult) is perpetually vulnerable to failure because we cannot determine every possible context or interpretation of the utterance. It is this vulnerability of the performative utterance to re-citation that has the potential to be exploited to counter the threat implied by injurious language (Butler, 1997, p. 12).

In the next passage Butler is arguing against recourse to legislation prohibiting the use of certain words due to the unpredictability of intention, context and effect. Her remarks also underscore my interest in interpreting performative re-citation via a ventriloquial metaphor:

> That no speech act *has* to perform injury as its effect means that no simple elaboration of speech acts will provide a standard by which the injuries of speech might be effectively adjudicated. Such a loosening of the link between act and injury, however, opens up the possibility for a *counter-speech, a kind of talking back* that would be foreclosed by the tightening of that link [...] The interval between instances of utterances not only makes the repetition and resignification of the utterance possible, but shows how words might, through time, become disjointed from their power to injure and recontextualized in more affirmative modes. I hope to make clear that by affirmative, I mean 'opening up the possibility of agency', where agency is not the restoration of sovereign autonomy in speech, a replication of conventional notions of mastery.[5] (1997, p. 15; my emphasis)

The image of language – and the construction of subjectivity through language – as a chain of signifiers that must be repeated to create meaning reminds us that the possibility for the subversion of a master discourse becomes apparent in the fissures between these repetitions; the potential to re-cite a 'script' of language to transform its implication. 'Talking back' is figured as a strategy of redressing prior scripts, of offering agency to the 'dummy' who is either compelled to repeat the words dictated from a prior source or who runs the risk of being silenced by oppressive language. The term 'excitable speech' is taken from legal discourse and refers to utterances that cannot be used in court as they do not reflect the balanced mental state of the speaker. Butler contends that all speech might have an 'excitable' quality as it is 'always in some ways out of our control' (Butler, 1997, p. 15). We do not 'possess' the language that we use, it predates all and any speaking subjects as 'an inherited set of voices, an echo of others' (Butler, 1997,

p. 25). In this sense, it is not only the script of gender that dictates the terms of subjectivity; the performative aspect of all language use could conceptualize the speaking subject as a 'dummy' of discursive convention that is condemned never to speak in her 'own' language. However, by deploying an understanding of ventriloquism which resists positioning the ventriloquist/dummy relationship as a fixed imbalance of power we can imagine a ventriloquial dialogue in which 'dummies' might 'talk back' to the master discourses which possess them.

It is important to acknowledge that despite Butler's recourse to imagery which may be interpreted as ventriloquial, her explicit use of the term 'ventriloquism' is very limited. In *Antigone's Claim: Kinship Between Life and Death* (2000), Butler uses the concept of subversive re-citation to explore Antigone's relationship to the master discourse of the state in Sophocles' play. In a paragraph discussing the curse of Oedipus, Butler makes her sole specific reference to ventriloquism in her body of work to date: 'The one who within the present recites the curse or finds oneself in the midst of the word's historical effectivity does not precisely ventriloquize words that are received from a prior source. The words are reiterated, and their force is reinforced' (Butler, 2000, pp. 65–6). For Butler it appears that ventriloquism is shackled to exact repetition, an assumption that is incongruous considering her own theoretical and political investment in the transformative potential of repetition and which leads me to speculate that she is reiterating the passive/active model of ventriloquism that this study seeks to challenge. In this sense, then, *Gender and Ventriloquism in Victorian and Neo-Victorian Fiction* is also 'talking back' to Butler: demonstrating that her ambiguity about agency and intention in her understanding of performativity can be more clearly articulated by thinking ventriloquially about gender, and also responding to the notion that ventriloquism is irrevocably shackled to the power imbalances between 'original' and 'copied' voice. In the following chapters, I will rarely be making specific reference to Butler's theories. This is not an attempt to 'silence' Butler from discussions of neo-Victorian fiction's representations of gender – as if such an aim could be realized. This chapter has, of course, served to underscore the ways in which Butler's ideas have influenced my understanding of ventriloquism. Instead, my ventriloquial interpretation of gender within neo-Victorian fiction and my positioning of ventriloquism as a way of thinking about neo-Victorian authorship are aiming to address some of the silences within Butler's work, to amplify the fissures between repetition and transformation, reiteration and subversion, which she certainly acknowledges but has stopped short of articulating.

It is the ventriloquial condition of language use – the sense of not 'owning' our words, of always already speaking in echoes – that can help us to contemplate neo-Victorian 're-voicings' of the nineteenth century. It is a truism to suggest that neo-Victorian fiction is not 'original' in the sense that it necessarily depends upon a prior script of Victorian texts and discourses. However, the extent to which neo-Victorian writing transforms and even subverts this script is contentious. Cora Kaplan is attuned to the danger of contemporary culture's returns to the Victorian era being a form of nostalgia. However, she also stresses the subversive or challenging aspects of neo-Victorianism (or 'Victoriana'), particularly in relation to nineteenth-century master narratives of sexuality or race (Kaplan, 2007, p. 3). In a comparable vein, Ann Heilmann's and Mark Llewellyn's recent work argues that neo-Victorianism is engaged in the process of *doing something* with the Victorian era but they are also cautious about the ways in which some neo-Victorian texts are 'also inherently conservative because they [...] recycle and deliver a stereotypical and unnuanced reading of the Victorians and their literature and culture' (Heilmann and Llewellyn, 2010, p. 6). This is a significant observation as it indicates the ways in which neo-Victorianism can be perceived as 'talking to itself' as opposed to entering into any sense of dialogue with the past. Indeed, at times the 'script' that neo-Victorianism repeats is one of its own invention. Christian Gutleben has also queried the 'subversive' aspects of neo-Victorian fiction in relation to what he terms 'the tyranny of the politically correct'. For Gutleben, the inclusion of the 'silenced' voices of the Victorian period (non-heterosexual, non-patriarchal, non-white) has now become something of a cliché in neo-Victorianism: 'Repeated from one novel to another, these politically correct perspectives, far from being subversive or innovative, become predictable [...] from an aesthetic point of view, it can hardly pretend to any originality' (Gutleben, 2001, p. 169). Ironically enough, attempts at 'transformation' have become a form of repetition.

What emerges, then, is a debate as to whether neo-Victorian fiction can be considered as 'subversive' or 'conservative', 'repetitive' or 'transformative', and the majority of commentators appear to concede that it is both. We can again see that the tensions between 'original'/'copy' or transformation/repetition come into play with regards to the relationship between Victorian and neo-Victorian 'voices'. Considering the gendering of the history of ventriloquism, it is surely significant that the 'script' about Victorian ventriloquism was articulated by men writing in the nineteenth century and is being ventriloquized by women writing in the neo-Victorian genre. This is not to suggest that either group of authors are articulating a univocal position on ventriloquism due to their gender/sex, or that they 'share' a voice because of being male or female. I am making no broad claims about the differences between the writing of 'women' and 'men'. Such an attitude would erase the multiple and sometimes conflicting social identities which any individual subject will necessarily occupy, and over-simplify the position which such identities will hold in relation to access to 'voice' at any given historical moment. For instance, Oscar Wilde can be understood as possessing the privileges of being male and middle class in late nineteenth-century British society, but simultaneously marginalized due to his non-normative sexuality. However, it will become apparent in the chapters on neo-Victorian texts that the relationship between 'voice' and gender is a preoccupation and will provide opportunities to reflect upon the way in which voices might be authored within the world of the novels and also metatextually. At times neo-Victorian authors repeat aspects of the Victorian script of ventriloquism, at times they are 'passionate puppets' who 'talk back' to this script. There are instances where they become ventriloquists, either giving voice to silenced subjects, or even silencing aspects of the Victorian voices discussed in this book. This is a multi-voiced exchange, taking into account Victorian texts, neo-Victorian texts and also neo-Victorian criticism. This is why the duality of prior usages of the ventriloquial metaphor have proved inadequate for conceptualizing neo-Victorian 're-voicings' and also why my ventriloquial metaphor offers an important intervention in this forum. Encompassing both the repetitions and the subversive transformations of Victorian scripts, thinking ventriloquially about neo-Victorianism allows space for ambiguity of authorial intention and reader interpretation and can articulate subversion within limitations.

Conclusion

This chapter has reflected upon the history of ventriloquism to provide an alternative way of considering the relationship between 'ventriloquist' and 'dummy' in existing uses of the ventriloquial metaphor. Instead of associating the 'dummy' with being an inferior copy, passively manipulated by the voice of another, I have offered the possibility that dummies might be subjects with voices of their own, 'talking back' to master discourses and acting with agency under the guise of silence and/or repetition. Crucially, this performance of the dummy role has been related to gender; it is women who have typically been cast in the position of being penetrated, manipulated and possessed but who simultaneously might have re-cited this script to generate 'voice'. By thinking about the intersection between Butler's theories of gender performance and performativity and the tension between 'original' and 'copy' and 'repetition' and 'subversion' in debates surrounding neo-Victorian literature, we can also see the ways in which ventriloquism becomes a key strategy for considering the re-citation of gendered and Victorian scripts. Performativity is concerned with historical repetition and Butler's use of this concept in her work on gender and language has ventriloquial connotations, despite her lack of engagement with the word 'ventriloquism'. The critical reception of Butler's work has indicated a weakness in her initial distinction between 'performance' as expressing a subject's agency and 'performativity' as representing the pre-existing scripts which dictate and constrain subjectivity. Although her later work has offered a clearer definition of the differences between these terms, Butler has never offered a method for negotiating the ways in which these concepts interact. This is where my ventriloquial metaphor can address her silence on this issue. Ventriloquism can encompass multiple voices, intentions and degrees of agency and one of the chief aims of the subsequent chapters of this book is to use Victorian and neo-Victorian representations of ventriloquism to offer examples of these fluctuations.

Criticism on neo-Victorian literature which utilizes the concept of ventriloquism often relies on 'ventriloquism' as exemplifying a passive/active dichotomy of agency; neo-Victorian authors are either dummies who 'copy' Victorian voices, or ventriloquists who impose their own voices upon silenced subjects, manipulating 'the Victorians' for contemporary concerns. Acknowledging the uncertainty of voice, agency and intention in the history of ventriloquial utterances allows for broadening existing understandings of neo-Victorian ventriloquisms, critically engaging with the notions of 'repetition' and 'subversion' and redressing the denigration of 'copying'. Indeed, repetition is a condition of all language use but to engage in the dummy-esque practice of 'copying' is the only way in which we might be able to 'talk back' to the historical script which has shaped contemporary literature. The neo-Victorian texts of this study engage in a ventriloquial dialogue with their Victorian forebears in a metatextual sense, but also represent ventriloquism as being a significant theme in Victorian literature. If ventriloquial repetition is dependent on the *historical* sedimentation of social scripts, then what 'script' of ventriloquism can the late nineteenth century offer us? The next chapter will explain why the nineteenth century was a transitional period in the history of ventriloquism. This was an era when ventriloquial skill became increasing associated with the exercise of dangerous influence over others and the sense that the individual was vulnerable to manipulation, could be made a 'dummy' of by the sinister ventriloquist. We shall also see that the gendering of this script becomes significant; the ventriloquist comes to represent masculine potency and penetrative ability and the 'dummy' – silenced, influenced, objectified – is aligned with femininity.

2
Victorian Ventriloquists: Henry James and George Du Maurier

In Chapter 1 I addressed several examples of ventriloquial voices, ranging from the Delphic oracle in Ancient Greece to nineteenth-century spirit mediums. The 'origin' of the voice(s) in each of these circumstances is certainly debateable but there is a common theme in which the source of the voice was traced to a supernatural agency, whether demonic or divine. However, Leigh Eric Schmidt identifies a shift in popular ideas about ventriloquial voices from the eighteenth century onwards: 'In performative practice, the ventriloquist's art shifted the focus [...] from the divine struggle over the soul to the protean malleability of personal identity, the fears and attractions of imposture, and the sheer pleasures of amusement' (Schmidt, 1998, p. 274). It was during the eighteenth century that ventriloquism began to be billed as an overt performance art, becoming a form of popular entertainment as opposed to the manifestation of supernatural forces (Vox, 1981, p. 47) and we can see that this correlates with the eighteenth century's increased questioning of and scepticism towards superstition. Ventriloquism became a mainstay of travelling fairs and outdoor markets. At these demonstrations the performer would produce the illusion of voices issuing from a variety of sources, imitating sounds, 'throwing' voices at a distance or into people or objects. Such performances, then, did not always feature the 'dummy' component that comes to dominate ventriloquism-as-entertainment from the twentieth century onwards. Some ventriloquists, such the Irish-born James Burns who frequented the fairs and markets of Nottinghamshire, would use a small doll as part of their act, but the use of puppets only became popular during the nineteenth century when ventriloquial performances moved into theatres and playhouses. George Sutton, an English ventriloquist performing during the 1830s, was one of the earlier practitioners to make use of automata in his stage show and the American ventriloquist John Wyman Jr also employed a dummy in his act which became popular during the 1850s. By the mid- to late nineteenth century ventriloquists on both sides of the Atlantic were using some sort of dummy or puppet but would also still feature 'distant voice' illusions as part of the show. Fred Russell is credited as being the 'father of modern ventriloquism', first using a single knee-figure named Coster Joe in the final decades of the Victorian era; Russell inaugurated the convention of a performance solely focusing on the exchange between dummy and ventriloquist.[1]

The nineteenth century was clearly the era when the voicing and manipulation of puppets became an increasingly popular aspect of ventriloquial performance but it is also important to recognize that the dummy was not yet the sole focus of the act. The nineteenth century can thus be understood as a transitional era in the history of ventriloquism. The literal puppet has always been lurking around in the history of displaced voice but we shall also see that prior to the twentieth century the 'dummy' role could also be imposed upon human subjects. Of course, this is the basis of my rethinking of the ventriloquial metaphor in Chapter 1. However, this chapter serves to underscore a crucial difference between ventriloquism as 'supernatural' and ventriloquism as secular. For from the early nineteenth century onwards the origin of ventriloquial voice was not in dispute. It is increasingly located in the skill and talent of an individual performer, a performer whose prowess has the potential to make a 'dummy' – with all those connotations of being a 'copy', manipulated, influenced, possessed, silenced, voiced – out of any unfortunate subject he might encounter. My gendering of the ventriloquist is intentional here, as the historical shift in explanations of ventriloquial voice correlates with a change in the gendering of the source of voice. As Steven Connor has noted: 'From the late eighteenth century onwards, ventriloquial performers, as opposed to the possessed victims of ventriloquial speech, are nearly always male' (Connor, 2000, p. 328). The ventriloquized women may have been perceived as 'victims' yet at the same time they can also be interpreted as being ventriloquists as well, performing the role of both ventriloquist and dummy. However, as we shall see below, male ventriloquists in narratives dating from the period where ventriloquism was recognized as a trick or skill rarely find themselves in the role of dummy; indeed, they are accomplished in making 'dummies' of others. To be a 'dummy' – passive, penetrable, malleable, the 'copy' – recites the traditional script of femininity, but to be a ventriloquist – powerful, penetrating, the 'origin' – invokes typically masculine characteristics.

Ventriloquism thus increasingly becomes associated with masculine potency and prowess.

As I aim to demonstrate in the first section of this chapter, we can understand ventriloquism as encompassing a variety of fantasies and fears which cluster around the dangerous potential of influence and anxiety over the concept of voice and agency. By examining several narratives about ventriloquism – Charles Brockden Brown's *Wieland, Or the Transformation* (1798) and Henry Cockton's *The Life and Adventures of Valentine Vox* (1840) – I will underscore the connection between influence and ventriloquism and highlight the gendered inflection of literary representations of ventriloquism. The subsequent sections of this chapter will discuss how such themes are developed in two late nineteenth-century novels, Henry James' *The Bostonians* (1886)[2] and George Du Maurier's *Trilby* (1894). Although both of these texts represent women with influential voices they are still concerned with the gendered power dynamics of ventriloquism. Both novels feature women – in the shape of Verena Tarrant and Trilby O'Farrell – who apparently possess the ability to captivate their respective audiences via the compelling powers of their vocal performances. Verena gives electrifying speeches on the rights of women and Trilby develops a singing voice of such quality that her audiences are manipulated into a frenzy of adoration and hysteria by her dulcet tones. However, we shall see that the origin and agency of these influential voices is repeatedly located in manipulative, masculine ventriloquist figures. I suggest that each novel ultimately cannot figure the performing woman as anything other than a feminized dummy, the 'copy' of an originating masculine voice. Both women are finally silenced at the end of the texts by either marriage or death. Verena and Trilby are returned to the patriarchally prescribed role of the passive puppet that can only be animated by the manipulations of a masculine force.

Both novels also imply an association between ventriloquial manipulation and queer genders/sexualities: Verena is 'rescued' from her father by Olive Chancellor, an intense, wealthy young woman whose desire to 'possess' Verena has strong connotations of same-sex desire. Olive's appropriation of the role of ventriloquist is thwarted by the heteronormative powers of her cousin, Basil Ransom, who also yearns to 'possess' Verena and who succeeds in taking her away from the world of women's rights and public speaking. *Trilby* depicts a coterie of homosocial bonding in Bohemian Paris and I will discuss the figure of Little Billee, a character whose slight build, feminine features and susceptibility to oral/aural influences align him with the feminized realm of the 'dummy'. Despite his apparent cross-gendering, Billee's desire to mould Trilby into a 'respectable' woman displays traces of the desire to provide her with a socially-prescribed 'script' to recite. I argue that characters who display sexual/gendered ambiguity are portrayed as pivotal figures in the currencies of ventriloquial manipulations in the texts. In both novels we see that such figures cannot triumph and are ultimately punished for their attempts to appropriate the 'ventriloquist' role that remains the privilege of heteronormative masculinity.

Considering the centrality of 'voice' to the plot of both texts, it is unsurprising that some of the existing criticism on the novels has touched upon ventriloquial issues. Lynn Wardley's article on *The Bostonians* considers Verena's voice as emanating from 'a ventriloquial body', suggesting that the source of her speeches on women's rights is divided between the 'voice' of democracy and the potentially disruptive implications of women's bodies upon democratic speech (Wardley, 1989, p. 647). In a comparable vein, Claire Kahane identifies James' novel as engaging with contemporary anxieties about the figure of the speaking woman, particularly in relation to the challenge posed by the female speaker to the typically male tradition of oratory (Kahane, 1995, p. 64). According to Kahane, Verena is depicted as the 'object rather than a sub-ject of speech', represented as a 'vessel, a medium' rather than an active agent (Kahane, 1995, p. 66). Critical commentaries on *Trilby* are divided with regards to how much agency the eponymous heroine can be perceived as exercising over her voice. Contesting the amount of atten-tion that the theme of mesmerism has received in Du Maurier's novel, Fiona Coll explores how the representation of Trilby coheres with the nineteenth-century fascination with automata (Coll, 2010, pp. 742–63). Similarly, Christine Ferguson remarks that Trilby becomes a 'mere pup-pet' of the sinister musician Svengali (Ferguson, 2006, p. 135). In con-trast, Phyllis Weliver argues that the novel refuses the objectification of Trilby, emphasizing the contribution the singer makes to the brilliance of her performances (Weliver, 2004, p. 69). Interestingly, this body of work employs ventriloquial imagery but generally silences the word 'ventriloquism' from their arguments. Even Wardley's passing reference to ventriloquism in the context of *The Bostonians*' preoccupation with gendered voice fails to acknowledge the ways in which the history of ventriloquism is already embroiled in gendered politics. The unspoken connotation of the power dynamics of ventriloquism in neo-Victorian criticism's interest in 'voice' therefore finds resonance in scholarship on late-Victorian texts which feature ventriloquial themes. A further aim of this chapter is to redress this silence and to locate *The Bostonians* and *Trilby* as narratives that are centrally concerned with nineteenth-century anxieties about gender, sexuality and ventriloquism.

Under the influence: conceptualizing the fantastic fear of ventriloquism

According to the *Oxford English Dictionary* the noun 'influence' originated as an astrological term. The development of the definitions of 'influence' is worth quoting at length:

> 1. The action or fact of flowing in; inflowing, influx: said of the action of water and other fluids, and of immaterial things conceived of as flowing in [...]
> 2. a. *spec.* in *Astrol.* The supposed flowing or streaming from the stars or heavens of an ethereal fluid acting upon the character and destiny of men, and affecting sublunary things generally. In later times gradually viewed less literally, as an exercise of power or 'virtue', or of an occult force [...]
> b. *transf.* The exercise of personal power by human beings, figured as something of the same nature as astral influence [...]
> 4. a. The exertion of action of which the operation is unseen or insensible (or perceptible only in its effects), by one person or thing upon another; the action thus exercised [...]
> c. Under the influence: affected by alcoholic liquor; intoxicated, drunk.
> 5. The capacity or faculty of producing effects by insensible or invisible means, without the employment of material force, or by the exercise of formal authority; ascendancy of a person or social group; moral power *over* or *with* a person; ascendancy, sway, control, or authority, not formally or overtly expressed.

This list of definitions charts a series of subtle changes from the sublime to the ridiculous, from the influence of the Spirits to being under the influence of alcoholic spirits. There are several recurring themes in the explanation of the word. We should note the consistent reference to power relationships or, more accurately, an *imbalance* of power involving the exercise of the agency of one individual over another. The concept of being 'under' the influence connotes suppression, domination or inferiority.

Several of the definitions make reference to influence being associated with 'flowing in' and according to John Ayto: '[the word influence] was coined in medieval Latin as *influential* from the present participle of Latin *influere* "flow in"' (Ayto, 2006, p. 286). The ramifications of the etymological basis of 'influence' in fluidity take a queasy turn when we recognize that the word 'influenza' comes from the same root (Ayto, 2006, p. 223). So, to 'influence' also has implications of infection and unhealthiness. Considering this connection between influence and infection literally, it can be understood as the body being infiltrated and taken over by an invisible force. The body is revealed to be penetrable under the process of influence, and the introduction of 'morality' into the above definition implies that there is the potential for sinister intentions to be fulfilled in the practice of influence. The influenced subject must enact the will of another, for better or for worse. Influence reveals that we might not be wholly in control of our selves. Indeed, I go so far as to suggest that to be under the influence is to be controlled, puppet-like, by another.

The relationship between ventriloquism and *spiritual* influence are clear in the cases of displaced voice discussed in Chapter 1, and yet from the late eighteenth century onwards the *moral* influence of a ventriloquist who could not only displace his own voice but appropriate the voices of others became a cause for concern. The production of the voice is on one level a physical process yet it is also intrinsically tied to an individual's sense of self. Mladen Dolar, commenting on the individuality of the voice, emphasizes its identifying properties: 'We can almost unfailingly identify a person by the voice, the particular timbre, resonance, pitch, cadence and melody, the peculiar way of pronouncing certain sounds. The voice is like a fingerprint, instantly recognisable and identifiable' (Dolar, 2006, p. 22). The voice is personal and can function as an expression of personal self or subjecthood, hence the connection between 'voice' and social agency discussed in the Introduction and Chapter 1. Voice is always somewhere between the boundaries of the physical body and mental subjectivity; an outward expression of an inward state. Steven Connor observes that in the nineteenth century ventriloquism 'comes to be associated with the fearful sense that there may be no place in which the private self is safe from *influence* or assault' (Connor, 2000, p. 243, my emphasis). The use of the word 'influence' at this juncture is important. The shifting of the source of ventriloquial voice from supernatural to human agency brought with it a profound suspicion with regards to the morality of the ventriloquist. If the voice is the physical, external manifestation of psychic, internal self, the notion of a subject who can dissociate their own voice from their self and impose it upon other subjects and objects reveals the body/self to be permeable and manipulable. Connor's term 'assault' is suggestive, implying the forceful intrusion of the ventriloquist on his vulnerable victim and such language holds overtly gendered and sexualized connotations. Bearing this assortment of negative connotations in mind, then, I want to turn now to several examples of late eighteenth-/early nineteenth-century ventriloquist narratives to demonstrate the ways in which ventriloquism comes to be associated with dangerous influence and to explore the increasingly gendered implications of either possessing the potency of ventriloquial voice or being subjected to the penetration of ventriloquial influence.

The North American author Charles Brockden Brown wrote one of the earliest novels to engage with the dangers of ventriloquial influence. *Wieland, Or the Transformation* tells the story of a small community living on the outskirts of Philadelphia. Theodore Wieland, his wife Catharine and their children, Catharine's brother Henry Pleyel and Wieland's sister Clara are joined by an enigmatic stranger named Carwin. The family begin to hear mysterious voices which disclose warnings and ominous information about their peers. This atmosphere of confusion and suspicion culminates in Wieland murdering his wife and children under the instruction of a seemingly disembodied voice. In his madness, Wieland also attempts to murder Clara but is ultimately prevented by a ventriloquial utterance from Carwin. The ethical issues surrounding the practice of ventriloquism evidently play an important role in the novel, but the majority of critical commentaries on *Wieland* mention the theme of ventriloquism only in passing.[3] *Wieland* is significant for the purposes of this study due to it's invocation of a series of ideas about ventriloquism, specifically the figure of the ventriloquist, which will be repeatedly revisited throughout nineteenth-century ventriloquist narratives and that subsequently return in neo-Victorian texts concerned with ventriloquism. The novel was published at a pivotal moment in the evolution of understandings of ventriloquism, when the notion of voices issuing from supernatural sources was giving way to locating the ventriloquial voice in a human origin. The figure of Carwin represents this ambivalence; is he a demonic presence, a pernicious manipulator, or merely a misguided trickster?

The novel's representation of Carwin's ventriloquial abilities demonstrates a range of talents. He is able to perform distant voice ventriloquism, 'throwing' the voice to make it appear to issue from locked rooms and the ceiling, but he also revels in imitating the voice of others – effectively 'stealing' the voices of his victims. Most importantly, both of these manifestations of ventriloquism underscore his ability to manipulate and influence the behaviour of the other characters. Put another way, Carwin's ventriloquial influence actually reduces his peers to the state of puppets forced to perform his will, emphasized when Clara hears the voices of two men, produced by Carwin, debating her murder: 'My terrors urged me forward with almost a mechanical impulse' (Brown, 1998, p. 54). She is forced into an automaton-like state by Carwin's whisperings. Clara flees her room and collapses at Wieland's door, where he is roused by a further voice issuing from Carwin summoning him to find his unconscious sister (Brown, 1998, p. 55). This scene thus depicts Carwin's ability to orchestrate the actions of various people; his ventriloquial influence will make puppets of the family group. There is a repeated emphasis on the invasive properties of his ventriloquial utterances. The voice Wieland hears is of 'almost piercing shrillness' (Brown, 1998, p. 55) and Clara is later prevented from entering a room by a cry of 'Hold! hold!' She explains the effect this utterance has upon her:

O! May my ears lose their sensibility, ere they be again assailed by a shriek so terrible! Not merely my understanding was subdued by the sound: it acted on my nerves like an edge of steel. It appeared to cut asunder the fibres of my brain, and rack every joint with agony. (Brown, 1998, p. 78)

She experiences this ventriloquial manipulation as a form of visceral penetration and this is related explicitly to the vulnerability of aural influence; Clara would rather be deaf to these utterances than compelled to experience them and perform under their effect yet she is passive in the experience of such aural domination.

Carwin's ventriloquial prowess is most frequently employed in imitating female voices. The first example of ventriloquial mimicry in the novel comes when Wieland hears the voice of his wife summoning him home. Catharine is understandably disturbed by this appropriation of her speech and despite being 'endowed with an uncommon portion of good sense' her 'mind was accessible, on this quarter, to wonder and panic' (Brown, 1998, p. 32). The stealing of her voice underscores the 'accessibility' of her mind and her internal sense of self – represented by her voice – is under assault. The ventriloquist's talent for imitation has the potential to be interpreted as a feminized characteristic. Steven Connor, for example, comments upon the 'potentially emasculating play of dissimulation and mimesis' involved in this form of ventriloquism (Connor, 2000, p. 328). An alternative reading of Carwin's propensity for imitating women, however, would emphasize the particular susceptibility of women to being 'copied' and influenced in this way. Carwin's 'copying' of the female voice suggests that the 'original' lacks substance or is not especially secure or 'authentic' in the first place. There are dire consequences for Clara when her voice is adopted by Carwin. Her burgeoning relationship with Pleyel is destroyed when he overhears a 'conversation' between Clara and Carwin which leads Pleyel to believe she is 'the most profligate of women' (Brown, 1998, p. 124). We never learn the details of Carwin's use of Clara's voice but the implication is that she is exposed in a lover's tryst with the visitor. Clara's vulnerability to ventriloquial imitation accentuates her liability to sexual inconstancy or attack. Clara's response to Pleyel's accusations is striking: 'Wrapped up in the consciousness of innocence [...] it was my province to be passive and silent' (Brown, 1998, p. 98). Carwin's occupation of her voice enacts her silencing; she is unable to talk back to his ventriloquial machinations.

Although she never acts upon her desire, Clara is attracted to Carwin and it is worth noting that it is his voice which initially excites her interest:

> I cannot pretend to communicate the impression that was made upon me by these accents [...] The voice was not only mellifluent and clear, but the emphasis was so just, and the modulation so impassioned, that it seemed as if an heart of stone could not fail of being moved by it. It imparted to me an emotion altogether involuntary and uncontrollable. (Brown, 1998, p. 48)

The ventriloquist's voice is represented as inspiring 'involuntary and uncontrollable' sensations. Clara cannot be held accountable for her response, she implies that anyone else would have been influenced in such a way, yet she is suitably enthralled by Carwin's mellifluous tones that she spends the following evening sketching his face (Brown, 1998, p. 49). Not only can Carwin invoke such passion in the otherwise very serious and reserved Clara, his voice also has the effect of rendering her inarticulate: 'I cannot pretend to communicate the impression that was made upon me by these accents'. The dangerous voice of the ventriloquist is not only seductive but also silencing.

Carwin explains his ventriloquial abilities by revelling in the sense of power they bring him, speaking of 'the possession of so potent and stupendous an endowment' (p. 182). He represents ventriloquism as an ultra-masculine force, able to control and manipulate all he encounters but also expounds on the sinister potential of his 'gift': 'the dangerousness of that instrument I employed' (Brown, 1998, p. 184). Ventriloquism is couched in terms of 'potency' and Carwin's use of the terms 'instrument' and 'endowment' have phallic connotations, made even more apparent by his penchant for exercising penetrative influences over the women that he encounters. However, we must remember that the most dramatic – and ambiguous – manifestation of the malign potential of ventriloquial influence is in the manipulation of Wieland. In Wieland's confession of his brutal murder of his wife and children he blames a divine voice for inciting him to commit the act. After the revelation of Carwin's dubious talents, Clara jumps to the logical conclusion that he produced this voice in order to manipulate Wieland yet Carwin denies such an accusation. He admits, somewhat incriminatingly, that he was in the house when the killings took place and that he was the first to discover Catharine's body. His explanation for Wieland's actions is decidedly confusing: 'Surely my malignant stars had not made me the cause of her death; yet had I not rashly set in motion a machine, over whose progress I had no control, and which experience had shown me was infinite in power?' (Brown, 1998, p. 197). Carwin implies that the voices he has previously produced have reduced Wieland to such a state of madness that he imagines the instructions which prove so fatal to the family. We are thus introduced to a theme that will undermine the figure of the all-controlling ventriloquist; the limits of ventriloquial control. For despite Carwin's boasts of his 'stupendous' powers, he seemingly cannot predict the consequences of his ventriloquial influence. Although he uses an automaton image to describe Wieland's behaviour Carwin claims to lose control of this 'puppet'. When the origin of ventriloquial voice comes to be located in a human source it is fallible; the ventriloquist is revealed to be powerless over the events which he sets in motion. However, it is essential to realize that at this moment in the history of ventriloquial narratives it is only the influenced *man* who is granted the agency to exceed the ventriloquist's expectations. Clara and Catharine do not experience such (albeit questionable) autonomy; the female 'dummy' is still in thrall to the sinister ventriloquist's machinations. It is Carwin who saves Clara's life at the novel's climax. Wieland escapes from jail and comes to murder his sister but Carwin manages to intervene by issuing a final ventriloquial command and Wieland takes his own life.

So what does this heady mix of sex, suicide, murder and mayhem teach us about ventriloquism? Ironically it seems that during the era when ventriloquism was coming to be understood as a human accomplishment a series of new dangers emerged: the fear of malign ventriloquial influence, the masculinized ventriloquist as a potential sexual predator, the sense that human voice and agency might be appropriated by another, and also that women might be particularly disposed to such manipulations. *Wieland* offers the components of the script of ventriloquism that would be repeated in various guises throughout the nineteenth century. Although never quite so sinister, the ventriloquist narratives of the late eighteenth and first half of the nineteenth century (both in the form of texts focusing on ventriloquial abilities and in the guise of ventriloquists' publicity materials) represent a similar vein of dangerous tendencies which associate the figure of the ventriloquist with the fear/fantasies of influence.

Valentine Vox's history of ventriloquism, for example, recounts the story of James Burns, an Irish-born ventriloquist who frequented the markets and fairs of Nottinghamshire:

> Burns was a great practical joker, and in 1789, at a market in Nottingham, he began calling a young village girl in the assumed voice of a tiny child who appeared to be in distress. The girl became so distraught at not being able to locate the infant that she fainted. At the time the mayor was not amused by this hoax and ordered Burns to spend three days in the local gaol. (Vox, 1981, pp. 47–8)

Vox's anecdote couches Burns as a 'trickster' figure and yet his 'prank' is deemed pernicious enough to warrant punishment. Alexandre Vattemare was a French ventriloquist who was famous throughout Western Europe during the 1820s. Vattemare's memoirs describe a trick played whilst a medical student in Paris, producing the sound of a voice crying for help from the cellars of the hospital mortuary (Connor, 2000, p. 258). The ventriloquist's prowess is associated with an illusory transgression of the boundaries between subject and object, life and death but also with the ability to humiliate and control others, to reduce them to the condition of objects to be manipulated at the ventriloquist's whim.

Connor notes that the memoirs of various notable ventriloquists of this era contain comparable anecdotes and that it is difficult to confirm the veracity of such stories as they are generally derived from publicity materials (Connor, 2000, p. 257). I would add to this that the interest in these stories in terms of understanding the fears of ventriloquial influence actually lies in their fictional quality. It is not unreasonable to imagine that these stories were wildly exaggerated and similarly to assume that there is nothing particularly morally dubious about a speech practice that is, after all, just a trick that anyone could accomplish. Despite the mundane reality of ventriloquism as a practice, these narratives contribute towards the *myth* of vocal power, the fantasized *potential* of ventriloquial influence to make a 'dummy' of the other.

This process of myth-making surrounding the figure of the ventriloquist found a further outlet in Henry Cockton's *The Life and Adventures of Valentine Vox*, serialized in 1839 and published as a novel in 1840. It is perhaps difficult for a twenty-first-century audience to appreciate the popularity of this text; Cockton's novel generated enthusiastic reviews which hailed the author as the next Dickens and in 1899 was listed as one of the top 100 novels of the nineteenth century by *The Daily Telegraph*.[4] *Valentine Vox* contains a curious combination of themes, filled with 'amusing' pranks concocted by the ventriloquist-protagonist. The novel is part bildungsroman, part tirade against the evils of private lunatic asylums and critique of avaricious relatives. Vox's escapades involve a gamut of ventriloquial talents, involving throwing his voice to incite riots (Cockton, 1889, pp. 15–22), appropriating the voices of politicians to provoke outrage in the House of Commons (Cockton, 1889, pp. 47–56) and displaying comparable pseudo-necromantic abilities to Vattemare in a scene where he animates the skull of a deceased murderer with ostensibly spiritual utterances (Cockton, 1889, pp. 141–7). The silliness of the ventriloquial scenarios in Cockton's text is evidently far-removed from the blood-thirsty and sensational machinations of Carwin in Brown's *Wieland*. The texts are comparable, however, in the depiction of the ventriloquist's potential for manipulating others and also the ventriloquist's apparent imperviousness to the powers of influence himself. Clara describes Carwin's abilities as creating an 'impenetrable veil' around the ventriloquist (Brown, 1998, p. 86) and Valentine's resistance to influence is expressed in terms which explicitly relate 'voice' to agency: 'His tongue had never learnt to assume the accents of a slave' (Cockton, 1889, p. 15). Like Carwin, Valentine perceives himself to be in possession of a 'power' (Cockton, 1889, p. 15) though it is worth noting that the latter is rather more democratic in the exercise of this power than Carwin; Valentine displays no predilection for imitating the voices of women and is content to make 'dummies' of both men and women alike.

The exception to this is Valentine's relationship with Louise, a young woman he falls in love with and eventually marries. Although Louise is never the direct object of Valentine's ventriloquial manipulations, his relationship with her is couched in ominously ventriloquial terms. When it appears that Louise's affection towards him is dwindling, he rages: 'Could she expect him to submit to every species of indignity? Could she expect that he would ever suffer himself to be her slave? [...] never would he consent to become the puppet of her caprice [...] He would *not* surrender his spirit as a man!' (Cockton, 1889, p. 338). Valentine rarely employs a dummy – although he does make a statue in the British Museum speak (Cockton, 1889, p. 100) – yet his use of a puppet metaphor to articulate his fear of losing his autonomy is suggestive. Even more salient is his conflation of the 'puppet' role with the loss of *masculine* spirit. The role of the puppet, it would seem, is not for 'real' men. Bearing this in mind, what should we make of the exchange between Valentine and Louise when he proposes marriage? She responds:

> 'I really – I don't at all know – I – it is such a question [...] I don't know how to give an answer really – '
> 'Let me teach you – say "yes". It will save a lot of trouble. Say "yes" and have done with it. Take my advice and say "yes" [...]
> 'Have you forgotten that I have a father?' (Cockton, 1889, p. 371)

We can interpret this as a further incarnation of Valentine's desire to 'voice' others, as he attempts to dictate Louise's speech. He compels her to speak under his instruction, to recite his words. Louise's refusal to answer could be perceived as a failure of Valentine's powers and yet she is merely demurring to speak without having her father's consent. One way or another, Louise must have a patriarchal puppet-master to provide her with voice. This hint of a dummy/ventriloquist relationship is developed on the announcement of the couple's engagement, for Louise retreats to a non-speaking role: 'She scarcely said a word. She looked, and blushed, and occasionally smiled' (Cockton, 1889, p. 374). The reason for Louise's silence is never made clear and we are left to speculate on the unsavoury implications of a master ventriloquist with a dumbstruck wife. *Valentine Vox* demonstrates that even in ostensibly comic ventriloquist narratives the ramifications of being made a 'dummy' are no laughing matter; to be silenced, manipulated and penetrated by ventriloquial influence are feminized traits. I want to turn now to two texts written towards the end of the nineteenth century which develop these themes in a slightly different way. *The Bostonians* (1886) and *Trilby* (1894) are novels centring on *women* who have influential voices but which still reveal that the origin and agency of voice is always more securely located in a masculine ventriloquist. The figure of the silenced woman will return, but the role of ventriloquist will also be appropriated by characters with queer genders and/or sexualities and the relationship between ventriloquist and 'dummy' will become increasingly symbiotic.

The preposterous puppet, the queer ventriloquist and the silencing Southerner: ventriloquial power struggles in Henry James' *The Bostonians*

Set against the backdrop of the east coast of America in the late nine-teenth century, Henry James' *The Bostonians* depicts a world where the practice of giving voice is important. On the first meeting with her cousin, Basil Ransom, an aspiring journalist from the Deep South, Adeline Luna describes the city as being populated by 'witches and wizards, mediums and spirit-rappers and roaring radicals' (James, 1998, p. 3). Boston's milieu is thus couched in ambiguous terms, representing a melting pot of superstition, spiritualist high jinx and political activism. The most prominent contingent of these 'roaring radicals' in *The Bostonians* is the women's rights movement, passionately supported by Adeline's sister, Olive Chancellor: 'The unhappiness of women! The voice of their silent suffering was always in her ears [...]They were her sisters, they were her own, and the day of their delivery had dawned' (James, 1998, p. 33). Olive's rhetoric aligns silencing with oppression and voic-ing with agency, a use of terminology which pre-empts the prevalence of 'voice' metaphors in second-wave feminist politics.[5] However, this statement is paradoxical, for how can women who suffer silently have a voice? We are introduced to a key theme of the novel; a tension between gendered voicing and silencing and the ventriloquizing of women.

If in Olive's terms speech is the key to women's liberation it is no wonder that she is so captivated by Verena Tarrant, a young woman on the Boston lecture-circuit whose verbal prowess is becoming famous. Basil is also fascinated by Verena but his antipathy towards the women's movement ensures his disapproval of her public speaking and moti-vates his desire to prevent his prospective wife from further involve-ment in this world. This dichotomy between speech/silence in relation to gender is fraught with ventriloquial concerns which positions *The Bostonians* within the genealogy of discourses on ventriloquism in the nineteenth century. For what James' novel demonstrates is an anxiety about the origin and authenticity of the female voice which repeatedly positions women as susceptible to ventriloquial influence.

Both Olive and Basil first encounter Verena at a meeting on women's rights. She is introduced as 'a fresh young voice [...] a voice which, on

Basil turning, like everyone else, for an explanation, appeared to have proceeded from the pretty girl with red hair' (James, 1998, p. 46). An initial incongruity between the voice and its origin is established, as this turn of phrase hints at a sense of doubt about as to where this utterance might have come from. Do the assembled group expect 'pretty' redheads to be seen and not heard? Why is there this uncertainty? We learn subsequently that it is due to the 'nature' of Verena's speeches: 'They call her inspirational [...] She has to have her father start her up. It seems to pass into her' (James, 1998, p. 49). Verena's influential voicings must apparently be inaugurated by her father. The expression 'start her up' is repeated throughout the novel and represents a mechanization or objectification of the speaking woman. Such a reading is underscored by Verena's denial of possession of her own voice. She claims '"It is not *me*, mother"' and the refusal of Verena's agency as a speaking subject is reiterated by Selah Tarrant: 'he and Mrs Tarrant and the girl herself were all equally aware it was not she [...] The voice that spoke from her lips seemed to want to take that form [...] She let it come out just as it would – she didn't pretend to have any control' (James, 1998, p. 51).

Verena's voice is positioned beyond her own agency – 'the voice that spoke from her lips' – and it is Selah that takes on the role of the ventriloquist in stimulating her speech. However, the description of her actual 'performance' is more ambiguous:

> She proceeded slowly, cautiously, as if she were listening for the prompter, catching, one by one, certain phrases that were whispered to her a great distance off, behind the scenes of the world. Then memory, or inspiration, returned to her, and presently she was in possession of her part [...] at the end of ten minutes Ransom became aware that the whole audience – Mrs Farrinder, Miss Chancellor, and the tough subject from Mississippi were under the charm. I speak of ten minutes, but to tell the truth the young man lost all sense of time. He wondered afterwards how long she had spoken. (James, 1998, pp. 55–6)

This complex passage deserves careful consideration. Verena is initially positioned as being 'prompted'; put another way, she is possibly reciting a script she has been given and therefore is not in possession of her own utterances. On the other hand, we witness the process of the possessed object talking under the influence becoming a subject in 'possession of her part'. The double meaning of the term 'possession' is at work; is she an object to be possessed, or owning her own performance? The phrase 'her part' might imply that she is in control of her own performance. The effect upon her audience is also significant. Verena 'charms' all who listen to her, her influenced speech comes to influence the assembled group in turn; even the sceptical Basil loses track of a rational time scale and is similarly enthralled by her voice. Nevertheless, it is important to note that Basil is not moved in the same way as the women in the party: 'It was not what she said; he didn't care for that, he scarcely understood it [...] The effect was not in what she said, though she said some pretty things, but in the picture and figure of the half-bedizened damsel' (James, 1998, p. 56). He is impermeable to her ventriloquial influence, therefore, but admires her from the privileged position of the male gaze – an assertion of his masculine power and superiority.

Olive is impressed by Verena's talent and recognizes the young woman's potential for influential speaking in the feminist movement: 'the girl had moved her as she had never been moved, and the power to do that, from whatever source it came, was a force that one must admire' (James, 1998, p. 74). Yet this statement also reveals Olive's uncertainty as to the 'source' of Verena's eloquence, an ambiguity that will prove crucial in their subsequent relationship. There is a dual desire motivating Olive's interest in Verena, the noble work of the women's movement and a rather more personal agenda:

> she found here what she had been looking for so long – a friend of her own sex with whom she might have a union of soul. It took a double consent to make a friendship, but it was not possible that this intensely sympathetic girl would refuse. Olive had the penetration to discover in a moment that she was a creature of unlimited generosity. (James, 1998, pp. 74–5)

There has been much critical discussion as to whether Olive's desire for Verena should be interpreted as representing a recognisably 'lesbian' identity and, perhaps more revealingly, the extent to which same-sex desire is sympathetically depicted in the novel.[6] Anthony Scott has argued that Olive's designs on Verena are not problematic due to 'the sexuality of the tie as such but its structural resemblance to conventional (married) heterosexuality – that is, its asymmetry of power, its possessiveness, its use of coercion disguised as consent – that subjects it to critique' (Scott, 1993, p. 60). Scott's observation is pertinent to Olive's thoughts as quoted above for there is a disconcerting attitude towards the issue of 'consent'. In Olive's view, Verena is so malleable it is as if she has no choice in the development of their 'friendship'. We should also be attuned to the masculinist metaphor for Olive's insight into Verena's character; she has the power of 'penetration'. Although Olive has evidently been deeply influenced by Verena's oratory abilities, she is astute enough to use her to fulfil her own needs and mould her as she sees fit. Crucially, then, Olive seeks to prevent Selah's role of ventriloquial manipulator of Verena and claim this position for her self: 'The girl had virtually confessed that she lent herself to it only because it gave him pleasure [...] anything that would make her quiet a little before she began to "give out". Olive took upon herself to believe that *she* could make her quiet [...] and lay her hands upon her head' (James, 1998, p. 110). The connotations of this 'making quiet' of Verena are thought-provoking; this queer ventriloquist desires to be able to control the terms under which Verena will speak and when she will be silent and Olive's plans are inflected by possession of 'voice'/agency and gendered power dynamics.

Verena's autonomy in this relationship is debateable. She is described as being 'completely under her [Olive's] influence' (James, 1998, p. 132) and although Verena has willingly left her parents' home to live with Olive and devote more time to the women's movement, she is depicted as a prop in Olive's feminist aspirations. The description of Verena's participation in Olive's various societies and meetings is revealing:

> Verena's share in these proceedings was not active; she hovered over them, smiling, listening, dropping occasionally a fanciful though never an idle word, like some gently animated image placed there for good omen. It was understood that her part was before the scenes, not behind; that she was not a prompter. (James, 1998, p. 167)

There is a real sense of a ventriloquist/dummy power relationship between Olive and Verena. Verena is 'gently animated' by Olive's polemical thinking but is denied the agency of independently producing speech. The admission that 'she was not a prompter' reminds us of Verena's earlier speech under her father's influence where she is figured as 'listening for the prompter', a performer perpetually in need of a script to repeat. We also learn that Verena has an aptitude for repetition: she 'could repeat, days afterwards, passages that she appeared only to have glanced at' (James, 1998, p. 169). Verena is thus repeatedly positioned in the role of 'copier' to the 'origin' of voices that always reside elsewhere; a dummy that can only speak under ventriloquial influence.

The final, and most potent, ventriloquizer of Verena is Basil Ransom. Despite my emphasis on the ways in which Olive's desire to manipulate

Verena echoes that of Selah Tarrant, we should recognize that Olive also has the wider aims of the feminist movement in mind in her relationship with Verena. She warns her protégé: 'There are gentlemen in plenty who would be glad to stop your mouth by kissing you!' (James, 1998, p. 130) and her statement foreshadows Basil's plan to simultaneously win Verena's affections and to silence her. Although we have seen that Basil is initially 'charmed' by Verena's speeches he is repulsed by the spectacle of the speaking woman and her manipulating father: 'He grew more impatient [...] of Tarrant's grotesque manipulations, which he resented as much as if he himself had felt their touch, and which seemed to dishonour the passive maiden' (James, 1998, p. 55). The use of the word 'manipulations' aligns Selah with the role of puppet-master, particularly as Verena's passivity is emphasized. As Claire Kahane has also identified, this is a strange, even queer moment of Basil's identification with Verena (Kahane, 1995, p. 76). He imagines how he would resent the touch of this man, suggesting that to be in the role of manipulated puppet is a threat to masculinity and therefore implicitly a feminine experience. Basil clearly perceives himself as a chivalrous rescuer of the 'passive maiden' Verena (ironically, Olive also sees herself as a protector of Verena's honour) yet he also has ventriloquial designs upon her: 'he wanted to take possession of her' (James, 1998, p. 307). Basil aspires to 'possess' Verena as one might an object, with patriarchal connotations of sexual ownership and mastery. He articulates this project as a desire to liberate Verena from the machinations of the feminist movement:

> you ought to know that your connexion with all these rantings and ravings is the most unreal, accidental, illusory thing in the world. You think you care about them, but you don't at all [...]It isn't *you*, the least in the world, but an inflated little figure [...] whom you have invented and set on its feet, pulling strings, behind it, to make it move and speak, while you try to conceal and efface yourself there. Ah, Miss Tarrant, if it's a question of pleasing, how much you might please some one else by tipping your preposterous puppet over and standing forth in your freedom as well as in your loveliness!' (James, 1998, pp. 325–6)

In a telling metaphor Basil describes her public speaking, feminist self as a puppet and he claims to imbue her with the autonomy to construct her own performance; the suggestion of her 'pulling the strings' is an important expression of this. Verena's 'freedom' at the hands of Basil will involve silence, for he has already suggested that 'if he should become her husband he should know a way to strike her dumb' (James, 1998, p. 309). This is also the moment when his words exercise an acute influence over her, a 'revelation' that she is not being 'true' to herself and trying to please others (James, 1998, p. 326). It is difficult to resist a depressing conclusion; it is Basil, with his own oratory powers, that reveals Verena's 'authentic' (heterosexual) self and precipitates the first, and only, insight we have into Verena's personal opinions in the novel. However, is it not significant that it must take another man to tell her that she must be free, to dictate a new script that she can follow, enacted through the power of his compelling voice? At the moment when Basil encourages Verena to free her self from her 'puppet' status she falls under the ventriloquial influence of yet another manipulator. His words are described as being 'most effective and penetrating, had sunk into her soul and fermented there' (James, 1998, p. 370); Basil is now the masculine ventriloquist, exercising his penetrative spell upon the feminine dummy who will fall silent under his command.

This silencing is most poignantly demonstrated in the final scene of the novel. Olive has arranged for Verena to lecture in a Boston theatre but Verena's speech is prevented by the appearance of Basil. Verena explains: 'I went out to those steps that go up to the stage and I looked out, with my father – from behind him – and saw you in a minute. Then I felt too nervous to speak! I could never, never, if you were there!' (James, 1998, p. 429). Basil has truly usurped the role of her father-ventriloquist and although both Selah's and Olive's manipulations might have denied Verena's agency, she did actually have a 'voice' under their influence. She is afforded no such option in Basil's possession. Hearing the baying of the assembled crowd, Verena protests: '"I could soothe them with a word!" "Keep your soothing words for me – you will have need of them all, in our coming time" Ransom said, laughing' (James, 1998, p. 432). His final words are both sinister and foreboding and as she is led away by her future husband the narrative voice underscores Verena's uncertain future: 'But though she was glad, he presently discovered that, beneath her hood, she was in tears. It is to be feared that with the union, so far from brilliant, into which she was about to enter, these were not the last she was destined to shed' (James, 1998, p. 435). Basil might triumph as the master ventriloquist in this novel, but we are not encouraged to celebrate in his 'victory'; this ventriloquist is a figure of threat and menace.

Despite this discouraging ending, there are moments of instability and uncertainty the novel's representation of ventriloquial influence. If Selah, Olive and Basil all play the role of ventriloquists to the puppet of

Verena, they are also united by lacking a voice of their own. In a scene where Selah's wife considers her husband's talents she admits: 'the only very definite criticism she made of him today was that he didn't know how to speak [...] He couldn't hold the attention of an audience, he was not acceptable as a lecturer. He had plenty of thoughts, but it seemed as if he couldn't fit them into each other' (James, 1998, p. 69). Olive also confesses that she does not have an aptitude for public speaking: 'Oh, dear, no, I can't speak; I have none of that sort of talent. I have no self-possession, no eloquence; I can't put three words together. But I do want to contribute' (James, 1998, p. 32). Despite Basil's ability to influence Verena with his mellifluous Southern tones, he is lacking a social 'voice'; as Susan Wolstenholme has noted, Basil cannot find a publisher to print his anti-feminist articles (Wolstenholme, 1978, p. 584). Each ventriloquist is thus defined by their personal voice-related inadequacies. Although the ventriloquist might be positioned as having the ability to exercise influence and possess other subjects, s/he is always dependent on another. There are limits to the ventriloquist's power. Steven Connor emphasizes the contradictory aspect of nineteenth-century understandings of the ventriloquist:

> literary and dramatic representations of ventriloquism co-operated in the creation of a powerful and seductive dream of an art of power, a dream that would nevertheless be shadowed by the comic threat of impotence and absurdity [...] The ventriloquist, it seems, could do everything, and yet could do nothing. (2000, p. 327)

Although *The Bostonians* can hardly be considered as a comic reflection of the inadequacies of the ventriloquist, it does still reveal the ventriloquist's abilities to be unstable. This is amply demonstrated by the relative ease with which Selah's and Olive's ventriloquial influence is usurped yet the image of the potent, masculinized ventriloquist is restored through the representation of Basil's ability to silence and manipulate Verena. Although the neo-Victorian texts discussed in Chapters 3 do pose a challenge to the figure of the all-powerful Victorian ventriloquist, we shall see that they do not always recognize that this power could be rendered unstable in Victorian ventriloquist narratives in the first instance. This is part of the script of Victorian ventriloquism that will be silenced.

Another unpredictable consequence of Basil's usurpation of Olive's power of Verena is that Olive must finally find a voice of her own. In the absence of Verena, Olive is compelled to go out and address the crowd herself. Nina Auerbach has interpreted this scene as a triumph of Olive's feminist spirit (Auerbach, 1978, pp. 134–5) although Philip Page has contended that we never actually discover whether Olive does 'find her voice' as the novel stops short of representing this scene (Page, 1974, p. 377). Nevertheless, we are left with the sense that this lonely woman who previously could only voice her aims through Verena might have been stirred to eloquence. As we shall see in later chapters, it is the neo-Victorians who will imagine what Olive Chancellor – the queer ventriloquist bereft of her dummy – might actually have said.

'Svengali, Svengali, Svengali!': Ventriloquial vocality in George Du Maurier's *Trilby*

Although set in nineteenth-century Paris as opposed to the lecture theatres of Boston, George Du Maurier's *Trilby* has some significant thematic parallels with *The Bostonians*. *Trilby* tells the story of a young artist's model, lovely but tone-deaf, who falls under the influence of Svengali, a talented yet sinister musician, who manipulates her voice in such a way that she becomes a singing sensation who entrances the concert audiences of Europe. The extant critical commentaries on *Trilby* have tended to emphasize the novel's preoccupation with the dangers of mesmeric influence; Daniel Pick is the only scholar to have mentioned the concept of ventriloquism in relation to Svengali's use of Trilby's voice (Pick, 2000, p. 20).[7] As Pick has discussed, there is a resonance between fears/fantasies about mesmerism and ventriloquism and the dangerous influence such practices might exercise over a vulnerable subject, particularly as mesmerism/hypnotism is, in part, enacted via verbal suggestion/aural influence (Pick, 2000, p. 20; p. 60). However, I feel it is useful to consider *Trilby* in the light of Victorian ventriloquist narratives as it displays comparable preoccupations to the other texts discussed in this chapter and also Oscar Wilde's *The Picture of Dorian Gray* (Chapter 4). Importantly, the relationship between Svengali and Trilby also forms a key component of the 'script' of Victorian ventriloquism which is in turn ventriloquized and redressed in several of the neo-Victorian texts studied in this book, most notably Angela Carter's *Nights at the Circus*, Margaret Atwood's *Alias Grace* and Janice Galloway's *Clara*.

Trilby's first appearance in the novel is as a voice calling upstairs to the rooms of a group of artists: 'a portentous voice of great volume that might almost have belonged to any sex (even an angel's)' (Du Maurier, 2003, p. 14). Svengali is present at the gathering, captivating the assembled party with his musical talents and Trilby is inspired to demonstrate her own vocal abilities:

> From that capacious mouth and through that high-bridged bony nose there rolled a volume of breathy sound, not loud, but so immense that it seemed to come from all around, to be reverberated from every surface in the studio [...] It was as though she could never once have hit upon a true note, even by a fluke – in fact, as though she were absolutely tone-deaf, and without ear [...] She finished her song amid an embarrassing silence. The audience didn't quite know whether it were meant for fun or seriously. (Du Maurier, 2003, p. 22)

Trilby evidently is not a gifted singer, but this first performance introduces several issues that will resonate throughout the text. Her singing voice is already represented in ventriloquial terms. It appears displaced, it echoes around the room in such a way as to occlude its origin. Trilby's performance raises the quandary of authenticity and intention in relation to voice – does she intend to sing in this way (and is therefore enacting a parody, a 'copy' of an original) or is she actually guileless and unconscious of her inadequacies? Her audience cannot quite believe the voice is truly coming from her and are uncertain of the agency behind the voice, hence Trilby reminds us of Verena Tarrant, who speaks in a voice of dubious origin and intentions. Women, it seems, are not expected to have such powerful voices and the gendering of Trilby's voice is called into question the first time it is encountered. Even in its most raw state, Trilby's voice has the ability to render her audience dumb-struck. This silencing of her auditors foreshadows the influence her voice will have later in the novel when she performs as 'La Svengali'.

Despite her voice's faults, Svengali recognizes some potential in Trilby. She proudly informs her friends: 'He said I breathed as natural and straight as a baby, and all I want is to get my voice a little more under control. That's what *he* said' (Du Maurier, 2003, p. 23, emphasis in original). Trilby's comment ironically comes to fruition as her voice does come under control, though not necessarily her own. Svengali sets himself the task of bringing Trilby under his influence so he can transform her voice. He has a vital trait in common with the assorted ventriloquists of *The Bostonians*, for despite his musical abilities Svengali in fact lacks a voice of his own: 'He had ardently wished to sing [...] But nature had been singularly harsh to him in this one respect – inexorable. He was absolutely without voice, beyond the harsh, hoarse, weak raven's croak he used to speak with' (Du Maurier, 2003, pp. 56–7). Although Svengali is represented as a master musician, he is compelled to use ventriloquial strategies to realize his ambitions. Indeed, we learn that he has already exhausted the voice of one unfortunate singer, Mimi la Salope, who as a result is condemned to silence (Du Maurier, 2003, pp. 58–63). As discussed in relation to *The Bostonians*, the ventriloquist is an ambivalent figure, sinister and powerful in the sense that he can steal and manipulate the voice of others, even silencing them in the process, yet also inadequate, masking his own vocal impotency. The ventriloquist must have a dummy and the relationship is symbiotic, demonstrated by the rapid demise of Trilby after Svengali's death.

Nevertheless, the balance of power between Svengali and Trilby is clearly unequal. He offers to hypnotize her to cure her neuralgia and he issues a series of commands which she is compelled to follow, one of which silences her: 'She strained to open her mouth and speak, but in vain' (Du Maurier, 2003, p. 68). She can only make a sound on his command and is obliged to adhere to his manipulations and the roles of Svengali as puppet-master/ventriloquist and Trilby as dummy are inaugurated. Although Trilby's friends sneer at Svengali they also fear him, contributing towards the myth of the all-powerful ventriloquist. After hearing that Trilby allowed Svengali to mesmerize her, the Laird remarks: '"He mesmerised you; that's what it is – mesmerism! [...] They get you into their power, and just make you do any blessed thing they please – lie, murder, steal – anything! and kill yourself into the bargain when they've done with you!"' (Du Maurier, 2003, p. 72). It is mesmerism, but the Laird's dire warnings also cohere with the dangers of ventriloquial influence. We are reminded of Wieland, inspired to murder by ventriloquial utterances. There is an emphasis on the manipulative and malign aspects of influence as the subject under this spell will become a puppet of the desires of the other, objectified and without agency.

Trilby is particularly susceptible to Svengali's powers and the novel underscores the aural aspect of this process of influence. On leaving her after her first time under hypnosis, Svengali issues a menacing prophecy: '*you shall see nothing, hear nothing, think of nothing but Svengali, Svengali, Svengali!*' (Du Maurier, 2003, p. 72, emphasis in original). This ominous statement comes to fruition:

> She had a singularly impressionable nature, as was shown by her quick and ready susceptibility to Svengali's hypnotic influence. And all that day, [...] 'Svengali, Svengali, Svengali!' went ringing in her head and ears till it became an obsession, a dirge, a knell, an

unendurable burden, almost as hard to bear as the pain in her eyes. *'Svengali Svengali, Svengali!'* (Du Maurier, 2003, p. 73, emphasis in original)

There is a sense that Trilby's body is infiltrated and possessed by the voice of Svengali, highlighted by the repetition of his name 'ringing in her head and ears'. The penetrative and pervasive quality of this aural influence represents Trilby's feminized role as her internal space is shown to be breached by Svengali's voice. Again we see that women are acutely vulnerable to such ventriloquial manipulations.

The chant 'Svengali, Svengali, Svengali!' will echo throughout the rest of the novel. After a failed relationship with Little Billee, Trilby loses contact with her artist friends and disappears from view. Some years later, news of a new singing sensation – 'La Svengali' – reaches the men. The singer Glorioli informs them of the effect of her performance: 'but bah! the voice is a detail. It's what she does with it – it's incredible! [...] Mon ami, when I heard her it made me swear that even *I* would never try to sing any more – it seemed *too* absurd! and I kept my word for a month at least' (Du Maurier, 2003, p. 246). As yet the group do not make the association with the Svengali they knew in Paris and neither they nor the reader has the knowledge of Trilby's new identity. This is important, for at this stage the agency behind the performance is located with the singer; as Glorioli suggests, the actual voice is not important, 'it's what *she* does with it'. Such vocal prowess has the ability to render not only Glorioli silent but also Billee, Taffy and the Laird who attend a performance: 'But our three friends found little to say – for what *they* felt there were as yet no words!' (Du Maurier, 2003, p. 312). Of course, this is an ironic echo of their silence when she first sings 'Ben Bolt' and is so dreadful. Both Billee (pp. 325–6) and the Laird (pp. 331–2) are haunted by Trilby's voice – it is stuck in their heads, repeating itself over and over. In other words, they are possessed by her voice, thus Trilby (at this moment) appears to possess ventriloquial powers of influence, penetration and silencing. Her performance is so impressive that it will make dummies of her audience.

However, we should not forget her stage appellation, 'La Svengali', for Trilby is appearing under her master's name and we have the first hint that she might also be using her master's voice in the description of her effect on the crowd. She appears to be able to exercise a profound influence with the power of her voice in a similar way to Verena Tarrant yet, like Verena, the origin of Trilby's voice is also queried: 'I am *Svengali*; and you shall hear nothing, see nothing, think of nothing, but *Svengali,*

Svengali, Svengali!' (Du Maurier, 2003, p. 310, emphasis in original). At this moment a slippage occurs, as she loses her feminine pronoun and just becomes *'Svengali'*. Unquestionably the crowd fall under the influence of the voice but Trilby's voice is not her own, underscored by the repetition of the very phrase that Svengali uttered to his protégé back in Paris. The echo of his voice through hers, his words being imagined as coming out of her mouth, is an important ventriloquial image. She is merely the copy of his original utterances, a dummy for his ventriloquial prowess and his manipulations are now extended to the audience who come to listen to La Svengali perform.

The mantra 'Svengali, Svengali, Svengali!' will make one more textual appearance. After Svengali dies Trilby loses all ability to sing and her health fails. On her death-bed she is shown a photograph of her former master and she falls into a trance and regains her lost voice. The description of Trilby's last song is important: 'She hardly seemed to breathe as the notes came pouring out, without words – merely vocalising' (Du Maurier, 2003, p. 417). The lack of breath is symbolic of the unnaturalness of her performance and foretells of her impending death. At this moment Trilby is practically an inanimate object, emphasizing her dummy role. After this uncanny vocalization she falls into a deep sleep and Trilby's final words are *'Svengali... Svengali... Svengali...'* (Du Maurier, 2003, p. 420) before she dies. The ventriloquist has pursued his partner to the grave and she is possessed by him to the last.

The secret of Trilby's amazing voice is not fully revealed until after her death. Her friends meet Gecko, a musician who associated with Svengali and Trilby whilst she (or, rather, he) was at the height of his success. Gecko constructs Svengali's powers as ubiquitous; he is described as a quasi-supernatural figure: 'Monsieur Svengali was a demon, a magician! I used to think him a god!' (Du Maurier, 2003, p. 435). He does, however, acknowledge that Trilby had some abilities yet his expression of this is ambivalent: 'she could do anything – utter any sound she liked, when once Svengali had shown her how – and he was the greatest master that ever lived! and once she knew a thing, she knew it' (Du Maurier, 2003, p. 439). It is thus her capacity for repetition that makes Trilby so able at singing; as we have already seen in the representation of Verena in *The Bostonians*, feminized dummies do have a talent for copying their master's voices but the origin and agency behind the utterance must lie in a masculine ventriloquist. Gecko suggests *'There were two Trilbys'* (Du Maurier, 2003, p. 440, emphasis in original) and La Svengali 'was just a singing-machine – an organ to play upon – an instrument of music – [...] a voice, and nothing more – just the unconscious voice that Svengali sang with – for it takes two to sing like La Svengali, monsieur – the one who has got the voice, and the one who knows what to do with it' (Du Maurier, 2003, p. 441). Gecko emphasizes the process of objectification that Trilby has undergone. She is an automaton, a mere 'instrument' or vessel for the projected voice of Svengali but again Gecko exposes the symbiotic relationship between ventriloquist and dummy, as 'it takes two' for the ventriloquial exchange to occur. Some critics have suggested that this might be an expression of Trilby's triumph over Svengali. For instance, Nina Auerbach contends that Trilby's malleability is her power and that this 'metamorphic power enervates her master', citing the scene where Svengali dies whilst trying to manipulate Trilby's voice to further glories (Auerbach, 1981, p. 285). Phyllis Weliver suggests that La Svengali's performances provide a forum for the singer's 'own interpretative voice' to be heard (Weliver, 2004, p. 68). Nevertheless, in her time under Svengali's spell Trilby is ultimately denied any independent agency beyond her submission to her master whereas Svengali, albeit with a croaky voice, is able to leave his dummy for long enough to arrange concerts and collect his earnings.

There is another would-be ventriloquist figure in the novel that provides an interesting counterpart to the queer ventriloquial manipulations of Olive Chancellor in *The Bostonians*. The artist Little Billee is an ambiguous character who is aligned with both Trilby (dummy) and Svengali (ventriloquist) at different textual moments. In contrast to the muscular masculinity of his companions, the Laird and Taffy, Little Billee 'was small and slender [...] and had a straight white forehead veined with blue, large dark eyes, delicate, regular features' (Du Maurier, 2003, p. 6). Little Billee is feminized, underscored by his diminutive name and his 'almost girlish purity of mind' (Du Maurier, 2003, p. 9) and his cross-gendered characteristics are further emphasized in Billee's susceptibility to the influence of Svengali's music (Du Maurier, 2003, p. 30) and beautiful singing voices: 'he had for the singing woman an absolute worship. He was especially thrall to the contralto – the deep low voice that breaks and changes in the middle and soars all at once into a magnified angelic boy treble. It pierced through his ears to his heart, and stirred his very vitals' (Du Maurier, 2003, p. 59). The gendering of the voice is important; although this quotation seems to suggest that women's voices can also have penetrative and influential qualities, Dennis Denisoff has noted Billee's preference for a woman's voice that *sounds like a boy's* (Denisoff, 1999, p. 158). The feminized dummy role can indeed be performed by a man but only a man who looks and behaves much like a girl. There is certainly some gender trouble at work in *Trilby*, both in the representation of Little Billee and the eponymous heroine, who wears men's clothes and whose voice is ambiguously gendered when we first meet her, yet Billee's potential queerness is challenged by his strange similarity with Svengali, the master masculine ventriloquist.[8]

At the beginning of the text it is suggested that Billee has a hint of the Jewishness which so defines the novel's representation of Svengali: in his face 'there was just a suggestion of some possible very remote Jewish ancestor' (Du Maurier, 2003, p. 6).[9] A link is formed between these two characters, but from a ventriloquial perspective it is their shared desire to manipulate Trilby which is noteworthy. Billee is attracted to Trilby but repulsed by her work as a nude model and wishes she could have a more respectable background as to be worthy of his adoration: 'the longing was a longing that Trilby could be turned into a young lady – say the vicar's daughter in a little Devonshire village – his sister's friend and co-teacher at the Sunday school, a simple, pure, and pious maiden of gentle birth' (Du Maurier, 2003, p. 46). Billee's longing is to mould Trilby, to write a script for her to recite based upon the requirements of chaste Victorian femininity. The ventriloquial inflection of this desire to create another version of Trilby becomes more apparent in the description of her altered behaviour. As her friendship with the three men blossoms: 'She knew when to talk and when to laugh and when to hold her tongue' whilst she is fulfilling various domestic tasks for them (Du Maurier, 2003, p. 89). It is when she is at her most feminine and domesticated that she is able to fulfil the requirements for the appropriate feminine balance of speech/silence. On understanding Billee's need for her to change, Trilby's modification of her speech is the most important signifier of his influence upon her: 'She was no longer slangy in French, unless it were now and then by a slip of the tongue, no longer so facetious and droll' (Du Maurier, 2003, p. 126). Albeit in a rather less dramatic way than Svengali, Billee still has the ability to alter Trilby's voice in an attempt to construct a more securely feminine role for his beloved.

Svengali's relationship with Trilby does appear to be threatened by her attachment to Billee, even when she is living under his influence: 'He had for his wife, slave, and pupil a fierce, jealous kind of affection that was a source of endless torment to him; for indelibly graven in her heart, which he wished to occupy alone, was the never-ending image of the little English painter' (Du Maurier, 2003, p. 357). This is another moment where the concept of Svengali's omnipresent ventriloquial power over Trilby is destabilized yet we must understand that this is not because Trilby is retaining some degree of agency. The image of Billee also occupying – possessing – Trilby's internal space retains the sense of her body being easily penetrated by manipulative influences and consolidates the connection between Billee and Svengali. However, the ventriloquial potency of Svengali should not be underestimated; neither should his ability to reduce the already vulnerable Little Billee to a state of feminized incoherence. After Trilby's death, Billee has a hysterical outburst:

> 'She d-d-died with Sv-Sv-Sv... damn it, I can't get it out! that ruffian's name on her lips!... it was just as if he were calling her from the t-t-tomb! She recovered her senses the very minute she saw his photograph – she was so f-fond of him she f-forgot everybody else! She's gone straight to him, after all – in some other life! ... to slave for him, and sing for him, and help him to make better music than ever! Oh, T-T-oh-oh! Taffy – oh! oh! oh! catch hold! c-c-catch...' (Du Maurier, 2003, p. 424)

Billee is recalling the moment of Trilby's last words – 'Svengali, Svengali, Svengali' – and recognizes this as the affirmation of his ultimate influence over her. Billee cannot compete with Svengali's powers of penetration and possession of his dummy, he has not managed to wholly appropriate the role of masculine ventriloquist. As in the defeat of Olive Chancellor at the hands (and voice) of Basil Ransom, queer subjects cannot triumph in the Victorian world of ventriloquial power struggles and this is underscored by Billee's positioning in the role of feminized dummy; his speech disintegrates under the superior powers of Svengali. Perhaps there is some significance in the fact that Billee does not actually repeat that phrase, 'Svengali, Svengali, Svengali'. Unlike Trilby he resists reciting the words of the master ventriloquist, implying that even the most feminized man could not be such a dummy as Trilby. Nevertheless, Billee swoons, cannot recover from this fit and dies; Svengali's silencing of both Trilby and Billee is complete.

Conclusion

James' and Du Maurier's novels have an important position in the history of narratives on ventriloquism as they were written during the period when ventriloquial performances increasingly utilized actual dummies yet also during a time when ventriloquism still held connotations of influencing, possessing and manipulating human subjects. The chapter's opening discussion of the etymology of the word 'influence' revealed its invasive and penetrative properties and also emphasized its representation of an imbalance of power. As my analysis of Brown's novel indicated, one of the first novels about ventriloquism was preoccupied with the dangers of ventriloquial influence that invoke these very qualities. Women were revealed to be particularly vulnerable to Carwin's prowess, highlighting the tendency for men to be figured as the potent origin of ventriloquial voice and women to be compelled to fulfil the role of the 'dummy'; malleable, penetrable and easily silenced. If my commentary on Cockton's text suggested that Valentine Vox does not confine his ventriloquial manipulations to just women, we also saw that Vox's relationship with his wife consolidated the dichotomy between the active, masculine agency of voice and the feminine passivity of silence.

Initially *The Bostonians* and *Trilby* appear to alter this script, presenting two women who are seemingly able to influence others with the respective powers of their voices. However, the texts also expose an anxiety about the figure of the vocal woman; both Verena's and Trilby's voices are revealed to be mere copies of a masculine original. They are denied the agency of voice and are confined to the role of dummy – objectified, manipulated, influenced and, ultimately, silenced. For what unites Verena and Trilby is their ultimate lack of a voice. As Philip Page has noted, the words of Verena's influential speeches are never actually transcribed and so the narrative voice itself colludes with her vocal stifling (Page, 1974, p. 380). We very rarely have access to the internal monologue of either Trilby or Verena. They are only ever represented as projections of other characters' desires, never as autonomous beings in their own right. This is an aspect of the Victorian script of ventriloquism that will be redressed by the neo-Victorian texts of this study, as we shall encounter a variety of quasi-Verena and Trilby-esque figures who do find a voice to 'talk back' to their masters and exceed the expectations of their patriarchal puppet-masters.

The ventriloquists in these Victorian novels are ambivalent. In *The Bostonians*, the patriarchal authority of Selah Tarrant is usurped by Olive Chancellor but she is subsequently defeated by the supreme ventriloquist, Basil Ransom. Would-be ventriloquists often emerge as queer figures; Olive and Little Billee are defined by either queer desires or cross-gendered characteristics and they both trouble the gendered currencies of ventriloquial influence. However, heterosexual masculinity triumphs; Basil succeeds in silencing and speaking for Verena and Billee cannot undo Svengali's objectification and possession of Trilby.

Nevertheless, neither Svengali nor Basil is not wholly secure in their ventriloquial potency. Lacking voices of their own they must steal the voices of women. We will see that elements of this script will return in Angela Carter's *Nights at the Circus* (1984), Margaret Atwood's *Alias Grace* (1996), Janice Galloway's *Clara* (2002) and Sarah Waters' neo-Victorian trio of novels (1998–2002). However, this chapter has also highlighted an aspect of the Victorian script of ventriloquism that is silenced by these neo-Victorian texts. *The Bostonians* and *Trilby* both construct the myth of the masculine potency of the ventriloquist but also, at times, undermine this. The work of Carter and Atwood is so concerned with 'talking back' to the image of the feminized dummy that it misses the often precarious quality of the ventriloquist's power in the Victorian novels. Chapter 3 will consider the process of this 'talking back' in more detail, discussing *Nights at the Circus, Alias Grace* and *Clara* in the light of the script of Victorian ventriloquism that has been identified in this chapter.

3
Sirens and Svengalis: *Nights at the Circus, Alias Grace* and *Clara*

Chapter 2 identified various key themes which are manifest in nineteenth-century narratives of ventriloquism. Although Henry James' *The Bostonians* and George Du Maurier's *Trilby* feature women with compelling voices, the origin of 'voice' and the agency associated with the exercise of oral/aural influence is ultimately located in masculine ventriloquist figures such as Basil Ransom and Svengali. Verena Tarrant and Trilby O'Farrell are represented as feminized 'dummies' to be manipulated and voiced by a succession of ventriloquists and both novels conclude with the silencing of these unfortunate women. The gendered power dynamics of ventriloquism have an additional dimension in *The Bostonians*. The novel is largely written in a third-person, omnipresent style and yet there are moments when the narrative self-consciously acknowledges the process of the textual construction of 'voice'. Verena has been invited to speak on the topic of women's rights at the home of Mrs Burrage and although we are party to a brief example of her rhetoric, her performance is abruptly interrupted by the narrator:

> The historian who has gathered these documents together does not deem it necessary to give a larger specimen of Verena's eloquence, especially as Basil Ransom, through whose ears we are listening to it, arrived, at this point, at a definite conclusion. (James, 1998, p. 257)

Basil's 'definite conclusion' appears to be that Verena's success as an orator is due to her physical attractiveness as opposed to the content of her speeches or the quality of her voice. Of course, this is a pertinent example of Basil's resilience to aural influence but it also offers an important insight to the way in which certain textual voices are privileged over others in the script of Victorian ventriloquism. The narrative voice at this juncture is positioned as belonging to a historian, with implications of authenticity, reliable documentation and authority. Verena's speech has no place in such an account; women's voices are deemed unnecessary and our access to Verena's voice is mediated by Basil, for in the world of the novel it is men such as him who will dictate who is heard and who is silenced. The reader is compelled to collude with Basil's – and James' – judicious editing of Verena's utterances.

The above quotation thus provides us with a microcosm of the broader silencing and marginalization of women's voices from the patriarchal script of history. Women such as Verena – working class, potentially queer, affiliated with subversive social movements – have, traditionally speaking, been muted from male-authored versions of the historical record. As the Introduction outlined, the ways in which this balance might be redressed is a significant strain in neo-Victorian fiction and criticism. In an article on Angela Carter's *Nights at the Circus* and Sarah Waters' *Affinity*, M. L. Kohlke identifies that the use of 'extremely socially marginal characters' as narrators in these neo-Victorian novels:

> Metaphorically give[s] voice to the historically silenced and forgotten who *have no history*. Critiquing the blind spots in 'official' history's methodology, they query the basis of its partisan authority, which legitimates one gender, class, race and sex's speech at the expense of its excluded Others. (Kohlke, 2004, p. 155)

Kohlke's insight is loaded with ventriloquial imagery and the tension between speech and silence is aligned with identity politics and the struggle for self-definition. It is in this sense that neo-Victorian fiction can be understood as 'talking back' to the Victorian era. I want to suggest that such a process is fraught with concerns about power, agency and influence in a comparable way to the fears/fantasies surrounding ventriloquism discussed in Chapter 2. Which 'voices' will be included and which will be disregarded in neo-Victorian ventriloquisms? Is there a risk of replicating the power structures of speech/silence that have ensured the marginalization of certain 'voices' in the first place?

In this chapter I seek to explore the ways in which Angela Carter's *Nights at the Circus*, Margaret Atwood's *Alias Grace* and Janice Galloway's *Clara* are narratives of ventriloquism, both in terms of metatextual engagements with the politics of 'talking back' to the gendered inequalities of the nineteenth century and in relation to specific thematic issues surrounding voice, gender, agency, influence and desire; the 'script' of Victorian ventriloquism dictated by *The Bostonians* and *Trilby*. We shall see that the Verena/Selah, Verena/Olive, Verena/Basil and Trilby/ Svengali relationships are echoed in various ways in these three neo-Victorian novels, but also reappropriated and, to an extent, challenged. Ventriloquism emerges as a multi-voiced process in neo-Victorian novels and the roles of 'ventriloquist' and 'dummy' become blurred in a way that consistently refuses to reduce the location of 'voice' to a finite origin. I also identify a further tension in each text between repetition and transformation. I will explore the ways in which some aspects of Victorian ventriloquism are replicated and even how some features of the Victorian novels are marginalized and silenced in the dialogue between Victorian and neo-Victorian versions of ventriloquism. My analysis of each novel is attuned to the ways in which these texts deal with the power dynamics of 'giving voice' to the silenced and positions the concept of ventriloquism as being central to negotiating the tension between speech and silence in neo-Victorianism.

'A prisoner of her voice': questioning the 'authenticity' of voice in *Nights at the Circus*

In the opening section of *Nights at the Circus*, the journalist Jack Walser interviews the enigmatic, seemingly winged trapeze artist Fevvers. Walser's purpose in meeting Fevvers is to compose an exposé, the proposed title being 'Great Humbugs of the World' (Carter, 1985, p. 11). Walser thus positions himself as a confirmed sceptic, immune to the influence of such a woman's charms and determined to manipulate Fevvers' story of her life to serve his own agenda. We should remember that Basil Ransom of *The Bostonians* is also a journalist, although he is not as successful as Walser and struggles to get his own work published and so in Carter's novel the initial 'voice' of the would-be ventriloquist is more secure than his Victorian counterpart. Jennifer Gustar has argued that Walser's assumption that his transcription of Fevvers' voice will be more valid that her oral narrative can be connected to Sigmund Freud's relationship with his most famous analysand, Dora (Gustar, 2004, p. 353).[1]

Masculine textual authority is privileged over the feminine voice – there is a similar division of power in the quotation from *The Bostonians* discussed above – and this desire to translate an inscrutable woman's voice into a quantifiable textual document is also an important theme in Atwood's representation of the proto-psychoanalyst Dr Jordan. Walser ponders: 'who or where is all this business was the Svengali who turned the girl into a piece of artifice, who had made of her a marvellous machine and equipped her with her story?' (Carter, 1985, pp. 28–9). Walser clearly cannot imagine a woman in possession of her own narrative voice and can only construct Fevvers as an automaton-like dummy, an objectification that echoes the revelation of Trilby as being a 'singing machine' at the end of Du Maurier's novel. It is also worth noting that Walser's opinion of Fevvers' 'artifice' suggests an essentialist understanding of gender roles, as he implies that a 'natural' woman could never have such command over their voice. In Walser's world view it is only men who might appropriate the ventriloquial role of influence, manipulation and possession.

The limitations of Walser's presumptions are exposed when he experiences the powers of Fevvers' voice during the interview:

> Her voice. It was as if Walser had become a prisoner of her voice, a voice made for shouting about the tempest, her voice of a celestial fishwife. Musical as it strangely was, yet not a voice for singing with [...] Her dark, rusty, dipping, swooping voice, imperious as a siren's. Yet such a voice could almost have had its source, not within her throat but in some ingenious mechanism or other behind the canvas screen, voice of a fake medium at a séance. (Carter, 1985, p. 43)

Walser's equation of Fevvers' voice with that of a 'siren's' is telling. The Sirens appear in various incarnations but perhaps most famously in Homer's *Odyssey* where they are depicted as a group of bird-women who live by the sea and lure sailors to their doom through the influence of their irresistibly seductive singing voices.[2] Odysseus is only able to survive the Sirens' deadly oral seduction by having his crew block their ears with wax and having himself bound to the mast of his ship (Warner, 2000, p. 272). The myth of the Sirens tends to be interpreted in distinctly sexualized terms; as Charles Segal notes, the power of this gendered voice is linked with the body on a fundamental level considering that the Siren's power is only effective if physically experienced (Segal, 1996, p. 18). More generally however, the Siren myth can also be understood as representing and perpetuating a central tenet of patriarchal culture through the association of femininity with the body:

> The anchoring of the female voice in the female body confers upon it all the conventional associations of femininity with bodily fluids (milk, menstrual blood) and the consequent devaluation of feminine utterance as formless and free-flowing babble, a sign of uncontrolled female generativity. Such associations further point to the

identification of women's vocality with her sexuality: like the body from which it emanates, the female voice is constructed as both a signifier of sexual otherness and a source of sexual power, an object at once of desire and fear. (Dunn and Jones, 1996, p. 3)

The link drawn between Fevvers and the Sirens thus has complicated implications for thinking about the ways in which her voice 'talks back' to the Victorian script of ventriloquism. Although there is a certain degree of agency implied by Fevvers' ability to exercise a penetrative influence over her auditors – this manifestation of oral/aural manipulation is typically the preserve of male ventriloquist figures – the presentation of her extraordinary voice is apparently shackled to essentialist fears and fantasies about the connections between women's sexuality, voices and the body. Verena and Trilby also possess influential voices, but this does not prevent them from being reduced to the dummy role by their masculine manipulators.

Even as such a trope is invoked, however, it is troubled by the admission that Fevvers' voice is 'not [...] for singing with', denying the classical Siren connection, and also by the suggestion that there is something ventriloquial about her utterances. Like Trilby's and Verena's voices, Fevvers' voice inspires doubt as to its source. Walser does not experience it as a 'natural' woman's voice but as displaced, mechanical, artificial. In the Victorian texts discussed in Chapter 2 such connotations are mired in misogynistic ideas about the female speaker's lack of agency, yet the construction of Fevvers' voice could have an alternative interpretation. Fevvers' voice might sound 'fake' (and the novel consistently engages with the quandary of her 'authenticity') but, unlike James' and Du Maurier's texts, there is no Svengali figure voicing Fevvers. Her 'artificiality' is her 'reality', undermining the notion that there is a finite origin or essence to Fevvers' performance and questioning the assumption that voices can always be located to stable sources. Fevvers is her own Svengali; she ventriloquizes her self. This exposure of the 'real' voice as ventriloquial has crucial implications for conceptualizing *Nights at the Circus* as giving 'voice to the historically silenced' (Kohlke, 2004, p. 155). If the 'voice' of this subject is always already artificial then surely the use of 'giving voice' as a metaphor for imbuing social agency must also acknowledge that voices are not repositories of souls, selves or finite identities but are always displaced, in construction, and in flux. Fevvers' voice can teach us that neo-Victorian ventriloquisms – thematic and metatextual – are not a straightforward process of 'giving voice' to the silenced Victorians or simply speaking in Victorian tongues. When freed from a dichotomy that privileges the 'real' over the 'artificial', or the 'original' over the 'copy', ventriloquial utterances can elucidate the construction of social subjectivity and agency as a multi-voiced negotiation.

The influence of Fevvers' voice has an uncanny effect upon Walser in the course of the interview as 'he continued to take notes in a mechanical fashion' (Carter, 1985, p. 40). It is now Walser who is forced into the Trilby-esque role of automaton. Magali Cornier Michael has noted: 'The interview reduces Walser rather than Fevvers to a passive state' (Michael, 1994, p. 496), but I want to suggest that it is something more complex than a role-reversal which takes place between Fevvers and Walser. A strange doubling occurs between these two characters. When Walser first interviews Fevvers we learn that although 'sandpaper his outsides as experience might, his inwardness had been left untouched' (Carter, 1985, p. 10). Walser is apparently impenetrable, a trait which correlates with the status of the Victorian ventriloquists, but so is Fevvers, for she is famously a virgin: 'Her inaccessibility was also legendary' (Carter, 1985, p. 10).[3] Whilst performing as a clown in Colonel Kearney's circus Walser takes the part of the chicken in the clown's dinner routine. Avoiding the homicidal rage of Buffo the clown, 'Up Walser rose out of his garnish like Venus from the foam' (Carter, 1985, p. 176). His performance as a bird is an obvious connection to Fevvers, but the reference to 'Venus' also connects him to Fevvers' billing as the 'Cockney Venus' (Carter, 1985, p. 7). The most striking example of doubling between Fevvers and Walser occurs when an explosion on a train leaves the circus performers stranded in the Siberian wilderness and Walser suffers a blow to the head inducing amnesia. As fragments of his former life haphazardly return, Walser begins to speak using Fevvers' cockney dialect: 'Eel pie and mash, me old cock' (Carter, 1985, p. 256).

As Karl Miller has suggested, the relationship between ventriloquist and dummy is frequently interpreted as representing a split between self and other, or the motif of the double or doppelgänger (Miller, 1985, pp. 49–50).[4] In a twentieth-century ventriloquist/dummy performance the audience is presented with the illusion of a dummy (thus a simulacrum, a copy of a human) who possesses a life of its own beyond its human counterpart. The ventriloquist will frequently fulfil the role of stooge in a comic exchange with the dummy for the dummy will generally have a more charismatic 'personality' than that of the ventriloquist (Goldblatt, 2006, p. 36). In spite of the 'copy' of the ventriloquist being imbued with a sense of superiority to the 'origin(al)' voice, the dummy's agency is ultimately dictated by another and the subversion of 'original'/'copy' is a temporary illusion (Schwartz, 1996, p. 136). Although this balance of power ostensibly should be questioned in the nineteenth-century ventriloquist narratives where the 'dummy' role is fulfilled by a human subject as opposed to an object, we saw in Chapter 2 that the feminized dummy is generally depicted as unable to transcend the manipulations of her master. In neo-Victorian representations of ventriloquism, however, the 'dummy' can 'talk back' to her ventriloquist. Walser's plan to make Fevvers' story 'copy' for his editor – to take her voice and supplant it with his own – is thwarted by her oral/aural influence upon him and he will ultimately learn to speak with her voice. Furthermore, Fevvers' vision is not that their roles should reverse and she should exercise ultimate power over him. Instead, she imagines them working together, and in a conversation with her adoptive mother Lizzie she explains: 'Think of him as the amanuensis of all those tales we've yet to tell him, the histories of those women who would otherwise go down nameless and forgotten, erased from history as if they had never been' (Carter, 1985, p. 285). They will dictate their stories to him and he will write a new script of women's lives. Fevvers does desire to ventriloquize Walser – to speak through him – but Walser-as-dummy will have a crucial role in this process. He will help the women to redress the balance of patriarchal history and include women's voices in this record. Fevvers' and Walser's double-act will offer a microcosm of neo-Victorian authorship; a multi-voiced exchange that does not privilege 'his master's voice'.

There is another Trilby-esque figure in *Nights at the Circus* in the form of the abused young woman Mignon. She has a beautiful singing voice and yet initially she only sings songs with words that she does not understand. As she bathes in a St Petersburg hotel, Fevvers, Lizzie and Walser are struck by the quality of her voice: 'All three who listened felt the hairs rise on the napes of their necks, as if that lovely voice were something uncanny, its possessor either herself as sorceress or under some spell' (Carter, 1985, p. 132). Again, the double meaning of 'possess' comes into play, as Mignon can be figured as either the agent behind the voice – the 'sorceress' – or as an empty vessel to be filled with songs taught to her by a boy who used to work in the circus. It is as if the songs 'shone through her, as though she were glass, without the knowledge of what she heard' (Carter, 1985, p. 134). Like Trilby, at this stage Mignon is a dummy for the voice of another; the intention and agency behind her song is located elsewhere. Fevvers introduces Mignon to the Princess of Abyssinia, the big cat trainer in the circus. The Princess has chosen not to speak because the human voice troubles her animals and yet her voluntary silence has left her vulnerable to being spoken for by others. Various speculations about her life abound in the circus, and 'Since she said nothing, she never denied these stories. The Colonel spread them freely' (Carter, 1985, p. 149). The Princess is thus another woman whose lack of an independent voice leads her life narrative to be scripted and dictated by men. Mignon joins the Princess's act and a relationship blossoms between the women, united by their love of music. After the train crash a group from the circus stumble across the derelict Conservatorie of Transbaikalia, where the Princess finds a piano to replace her instrument lost in the wreck and Mignon sings to reassure the solitary music teacher at the Conservatorie. Fevvers relates the effect of this new voice:

> When we first heard her song [...] it sounded as if the song sang itself, as if the song had nothing to do with Mignon and she was only a kind of fleshy phonograph, made to transmit music of which she had no consciousness. That was before she became a woman. Now she seized hold of the song in the supple lasso of her voice and mated it with her new-found soul. (Carter, 1985, p. 247)

This is a Trilby singing without a Svengali; no longer an objectified singing machine, her ownership of her new voice is articulated by her ability to 'seize hold of the song' and utilize her performance to gain the trust of a fellow musician. At this textual moment, the Princess of Abyssinia also recovers her power of speech (Carter, 1985, p. 248). The lovers form a happy working relationship with the music teacher to such an extent that when the time comes for the circus party to leave the Conservatoire, Mignon and the Princess choose to stay. The only audience for their new music and song will be the music teacher and the wild tigers roaming around the house, 'for which the women must make a music never before heard on earth' (Carter, 1985, p. 275).

Unlike the queer ventriloquist Olive Chancellor of *The Bostonians*, who cannot transcend the script of heteronormative ownership and objectification of her puppet Verena, the relationship between Mignon and the Princess represents a queer coupling that allows both women to find and possess voices of their own. M. L. Kohlke understands this relationship as a depiction of 'idealized lesbianism' (Kohlke, 2004, p. 161), though the novel's voicing of same-sex love as an antidote to heteronormative ventriloquism does have problematic elements. For how challenging could Mignon's and the Princess's new voices actually be when they are located explicitly in a marginal realm beyond social interaction? Is it even possible to disregard the scripts which have dictated women's social silencing? Fevvers' ventriloquial ambitions for Walser, engaging him as the scribe who will help her 'talk back' to the patriarchal construction of history, might be an ambivalent enterprise as Walser initially sought to speak for Fevvers and reduce her fabulous voice to journalistic 'copy'. It is significant that the novel stops short of telling us how Fevvers' and Walser's relationship – and, indeed, Mignon's and the Princess's songs – develop. There is the promise of new voicings yet we do not hear them and in this sense Carter's neo-Victorian ventriloquism does not offer a wholly liberatory solution to the gendered power dynamics of Victorian ventriloquist narratives.

'There are always those that will supply you with speeches of their own': problematizing ventriloquial agency in *Alias Grace*

In her collection of essays meditating on the practice and process of authorship, Margaret Atwood considers the ethical issues surrounding authorial voice: 'writers can be accused of appropriating the voices of others. A socially conscious writer can quite easily be charged with exploiting the misery and misfortune of the downtrodden for their own gain' (Atwood, 2002, p. 119). Atwood's remark demonstrates that she is attuned to the power politics of voicing/silencing in literary production, and the concept that appropriating the voice of the other might be perceived as an 'accusation' or 'charge' associates the practice of narrative ventriloquism with morally dubious behaviour. Atwood's anxiety surrounding 'voice' is relevant to *Alias Grace*, for this novel can be understood as a narrative of ventriloquism in several ways. *Alias Grace* is based on the historical events of an infamous Canadian murder case about the brutal killing of Thomas Kinnear and his housekeeper Nancy Montgomery in 1843. James McDermott and Grace Marks, servants in the household, were tried and convicted of the murders. McDermott was hung and Marks served nearly thirty years in jail before her conviction was overthrown and she was released to begin a new life in New York. Atwood's retelling and reimagining of the events of the case can thus be understood as a form of metatextual ventriloquism, a strategy for providing a 'voice' for Grace's story.

However, how might Atwood negotiate the 'accusation' of appro-priating Grace's voice for her text? Fiona Tolan's reading of the novel comments on the trope of 'voice' being equated with social agency in second-wave feminism and hence the movement was interested in 'creating a history and a voice for a silenced feminine experience' (Tolan, 2007, p. 222). Nevertheless, she identifies that Atwood's novel takes a cautious approach to such an enterprise:

> *Alias Grace* seemingly enters into this same project of recovering lost female histories and giving voice to the silenced woman of the past. But Atwood [...] challenges, not just the assumption that there is a stable subject to be recovered from the historical record, but also the systems of power and desire that can be unwittingly exposed in the attempted construction of another person's identity. (Tolan, 2007, pp. 222–3)

To develop Tolan's analysis, I suggest that through using the theme of ventriloquism within *Alias Grace* Atwood refuses to reduce Grace's voice to a finite location, offering a metatextual reflection on the layers of voices that must contribute towards a narrative and utilizing Simon Jordan's frustrating experience of attempting to give his authoritative voice to Grace's story as an allegory for the ambiguity of neo-Victorian ventriloquial authorship.

Simon Jordan, Atwood's fictional addition to the Marks case history, is a young doctor with specific interest in mental health and the burgeoning discipline of psychology. He begins to visit Grace in an attempt to unlock her apparent amnesia surrounding the events at Kinnear's house, using proto-psychoanalytic methods of free association and suggestion, encouraging Grace to speak of her life to uncover the 'truth' behind the murders.[5] Grace has several supporters in the local community who are confident of her innocence and believe that Dr Jordan's investigations will exonerate Grace. In this sense, Jordan's interest in 'voicing' Grace has some element of benevolence; she will finally be allowed to speak for herself and his assistance will lead to her release. However, Jordan has ambitions to establish himself as a leading name in the field of mental illness and to open a private asylum. His dealings with Grace are thus motivated by an agenda of personal and professional success. Jordan's situation comes perilously close to Atwood's vision of the ventriloquial author who might be accused of exploiting vulnerable subjects for his own gain. The motif of an authoritative man inciting a woman's speech – and taking notes to provide a script of her life – echoes the Victorian ventriloquist narratives in which 'voice' must always be generated by men, and also Jack Walser's desire to fix Fevvers' voice in a defamatory exposé of the 'truth'. Jordan articulates his work with Grace in a vocabulary of penetration. In a letter to his friend

Dr Murchie, he remarks: 'I approach her mind as if it is a locked box, to which I must find the right key' (Atwood, 1997, p. 153). As Jeannette King has observed, his language is gendered and sexualized; he is the patriarchal penetrator, she is the permeable vessel (King, 2005, p. 74) and in my terms he is positioned as a typically masculine Victorian ventriloquist. Giving Grace a voice is associated with penetrating her mind.

Grace has become inured to silence during her incarceration. During her time in an asylum she learns that her speech can be used to condemn her, and so 'stopped telling them anything' and admits: 'At last I stopped talking altogether, except very civilly when spoken to' (Atwood, 1997, pp. 35–6). Her muteness might be interpreted as symptomatic of her oppression and yet can also be perceived as a strategy of self-preservation, for she knows that her words might be used against her. Prior to her session with Jordan which will discuss the day of the murders, Grace contemplates the multiple voices that were imposed upon her in the trial: her lawyer reporting what she has said and telling her what she should say; McDermott's testimony on what she said; the reporters speculating on what she must have said:

> What should I tell Dr. Jordan about this day? [...] There are always those that will supply you with speeches of their own, and put them right into your mouth for you too; and that sort are like the magicians who can throw their voice, at fairs and shows, and you are just like their wooden doll. And that's what it was like at the trial, I was there in the box of the dock but I might as well have been made of cloth, and stuffed, with a china head; and I was shut up inside the doll of myself, and my true voice could not get out. (Atwood, 1997, p. 342)

Grace overtly aligns the process of being voiced with the practice of ventriloquism and she recognizes that she is positioned in the role of doll or dummy. Her acknowledgement of this objectification is important when compared to the dummy-women of the Victorian ventriloquist narratives; Verena and Trilby are repeatedly represented as dummies, puppets and automata in their attempts to produce a voice, but the novels never disclose what their opinions on this might be, let alone if they are even aware of this process. Grace's invocation of the ventriloquist/dummy trope prior to her interview with Jordan might imply that she fears her session with him will be a further instance of being ventriloquized and yet the key difference is that she is pondering which voice she will use with Jordan. This hints that she actually has a choice/sense of agency through her conversations with him, an unexpected consequence of Jordan's desire to manipulate and voice Grace. Her commentary implies that there is a 'true voice' that might be uncovered, but the extent to which Jordan is able to access this becomes increasingly questionable.

Jordan's ability to make sense of Grace's tangled narrative is compromised by the influence of her voice; like Walser, this would-be ventriloquist finds himself to be increasingly confounded by her utterances. Her speech has a disorientating effect upon him:

> For a moment he thinks he's gone deaf [...] he can see her lips moving, but he can't interpret any of the words [...] The trouble is that the more she remembers, the more she relates, the more difficulty he himself is having [...] It's as if she's drawing his energy out of him [...] In his notebook he has pencilled the word *whisper*, and underlined it three times. Of what had he wished to remind himself? (Atwood, 1997, pp. 338–9)

His 'deafness' represents the failure of his ventriloquial powers; rather than an image of his immunity to her speech, it suggests his loss of control over the meaning of Grace's story. The more she speaks, the deeper his confusion becomes. A colleague has previously warned him of the 'siren' powers of Grace: 'you would do well to stop your ears with wax, as Ulysses made his sailors do, to escape the Sirens' (Atwood, 1997, pp. 81–2). Grace is imbued with comparable powers to Fevvers in terms of her ability to exercise an aural seduction and Jordan's description of her as 'drawing the energy out of him' indicates the extent to which he is penetrated and drained by Grace's voice. The word '*whisper*' is significant. Whispering is an activity related to secret speech, almost inaudible and easily misheard, a set of connotations that pertinently reflect the difficulty Jordan has in defining and transcribing Grace's voice.

Grace's investment in whispering takes a ventriloquial turn when she dwells on the implications of her appellation of 'murderess':

> *Murderess* is a strong word to have attached to you. It has a smell to it, that word – musky and oppressive, like dead flowers in a vase. Sometimes at night I whisper it over to myself: *Murderess, Murderess* [...] I would rather be a murderess than a murderer, if those are the only choices. (Atwood, 1997, p. 25)

Grace literally recites the script that has been assigned to her and she actually finds a sense of identity and even glamour in this label. This is hardly very liberating, underscored by her latter comment on the lack of options that she has for owning her identity: 'if those are the only choices'. However, we should note that these whispers are repeated later in the text. Fantasizing about Grace, Jordan echoes her words: '*Murderess, murderess*, he whispers to himself. It has an allure, a scent almost. Hothouse gardenias. Lurid, but also furtive. He imagines himself breathing it as he draws Grace towards him, pressing his mouth against her. *Murderess*. He applies it to her throat like a brand' (Atwood, 1997, p. 453). Jordan's desire to 'brand' Grace's throat is doubly symbolic; her throat is a location of erotic allure and also the source of her voice. We could interpret this as a sadistic image of Jordan's wish to silence the voice that he finds so disturbing but as opposed to stopping Grace's voice, Jordan is compelled to repeat it. If the dummies of *Trilby* are haunted by the chant 'Svengali, Svengali, Svengali', then *Alias Grace* offers us a female ventriloquist who can put her words in the mouth of her auditor. As Walser becomes a double of Fevvers, there is also a process of doubling between Jordan and Grace. He becomes increasingly like her, repeating her words, obsessed with her story, forgetting his train of thought and this comes to fruition at the end of the novel when we learn he is suffering amnesia as a result of an injury in the Civil war. His mother and fiancé resort to showing him 'little homely objects' in an attempt to restore his memory (Atwood, 1997, p. 499) and so ironically he is ultimately subjected to the speech-inciting methods he used in an attempt to restore Grace's memory.[6]

This is not to suggest, of course, that Grace has ultimate agency over her voice in the novel. There is another female ventriloquist presence in the text in the form of Mary Whitney, Grace's friend who dies after a botched abortion. Mary's voice repeatedly surfaces in the passages of Grace's first-person narration and her interviews with Dr Jordan. Recounting the story of her mother's death on board a ship from Ireland to Canada, she remarks that the doctor was 'of no more use – if you'll excuse me, Sir – than tits on a rooster, as Mary Whitney liked to say' (Atwood, 1997, p. 138). Mary's voice is even more prominent when Grace is describing McDermott's actions after the murders; he attempts to have sex with her but 'as Mary Whitney would say, he'd mislaid the poker' (Atwood, 1997, p. 386) and she reflects on his increasingly erratic behaviour: 'I thought him as mad as a moose in heat, as Mary Whitney used to say' (Atwood, 1997, p. 386). In her personal narrative, Grace describes the lewd comments and abuse she receives at the hands of the men that escort her from her prison cell to her employment in the house of the Governor, and confides:

> I try to think of what Mary Whitney would say, and sometimes I can say it. If you really thought that of me you should hold your dirty tongues, I said to them, or one dark night I'll have them out of your mouths roots and all, I won't need a knife, I'll just take hold with my teeth and pull. (Atwood, 1997, p. 72)

Mary's voice is most conspicuous when Grace is discussing sexualized situations and, more specifically, when she is defending herself from unwanted sexual attention. Mary/Grace's voice demands silence from the men in the above quotation and the image of biting out their tongues represents a symbolic castration. Grace recognizes that the tongue/voice has a resonance with the phallic power the men exercise over her, and it is significant that she states that it will be her *mouth* that will enact this silencing. Holly Blackford has conceptualized Mary's emergence in the narrative as 'the crass voice that "talks back" in a way Grace would not' (Blackford, 2006, p. 254) and the ventriloquial dynamics of this process bear consideration. To project the desired image of herself as an innocent victim to Jordan – for she recognizes that the authority of his voice might facilitate her exoneration from involvement in the murders – Grace must recite the script of appropriate nineteenth-century femininity: chastity, decorum, passivity. Her use of Mary's voice to express the more sexualized and knowing moments of her story displaces the origin and intention of such utterances on to her dead friend, a young woman who has already transgressed in having sex before marriage and has already been punished by a painful death. Grace's ventriloquizing of Mary allows her to surreptitiously subvert the script of Victorian femininity – to 'talk back' – without calling the integrity of her own 'voice' into question. Esther Saxey interprets Mary as Grace's double (Saxey, 2010, p. 68) and this relationship knowingly echoes a standard trope of the dummy/ventriloquist performance in which the dummy/double is given license to say the unspeakable, to articulate 'our dreams of defiance, of talking and acting from the gut' (Schwartz, 1996, p. 136).

However, such a reading of the ventriloquial exchange between Mary and Grace depends upon understanding Grace as being possession of her own autonomy, yet a key question raised by the novel is whether Grace is ventriloquizing Mary, or Mary is ventriloquizing Grace. After Mary dies, Grace admits that she begins to hear her voice and the most dramatic manifestation of Mary's voice comes when Grace is hypnotized by Jerome DuPont. She begins to speak in a 'new thin voice' (Atwood, 1997, p. 466), making outrageous comments about the assembled audience, admitting to seducing Kinnear and McDermott and finally confessing to the murders. The voice explains its manipulations of the men in puppet-inflected imagery: 'I had him on a string [...] I had the two of them dancing to my tune!' (Atwood, 1997, p. 465). However, this voice denies Grace's agency: 'I'm not Grace! Grace knew nothing about it!' (Atwood, 1997, p. 467). The implication is that Grace has become possessed by the spirit of Mary Whitney, who has compelled her to commit murder. In effect, Grace is still being ventriloquized – manipulated and reduced to the condition of a dummy – but by a female figure. The other characters offer various explanations: the Reverend Verringer remarks that historically speaking, it would seem like a case of possession and would have necessitated an exorcism, and psychological explanations of a split personality are debated (Atwood, 1997, pp. 470–1). Jordan is not convinced that the scene isn't a performance on behalf of Grace. There is the possibility that a conscious performance would generate agency for Grace, but if she is possessed by Mary – either supernaturally or psychologically – then the liberatory implications of Mary ventriloquizing Grace are still rather limited. 'Mary' might be a successful female ventriloquist, talking back to the Victorian script of femininity and the script of Victorian ventriloquism discussed in Chapter 2, but Grace fulfils the role of dummy and has suffered terribly for her receptivity to possession and manipulation. Either way, the voice complains that it is rarely listened to by others: '"You're all the same, you won't listen to me, you won't believe me, you want it your own way, you won't hear..." It trails off, and there is silence' (Atwood, 1997, p. 468). Whether we understand the female ventriloquist to be Grace and/or Mary, the ultimate silencing of the voice is haunting. Atwood's novel has offered a more potent version of a female ventriloquist figure than *The Bostonians* and yet acknowledges that women's voices are still more easily disregarded.

Stephanie Lovelady discusses the various possible explanations for Mary's voice in the hypnotism scene but concludes that Grace as a knowing agent behind the voice is 'improbable' (Lovelady, 1999, p. 57). Jeannette King is more willing to contemplate that Grace might be in control of her performance, noting that the hypnotist Jerome DuPont appears genuinely shaken after the event (King, 2005, p. 80). Nevertheless, it is important to remember that Jerome is a consummate performer; when Grace first sees him in the home of the Governor she recognizes him as Jeremiah, the travelling peddler who has been a friend to her during her position in service with Mary and her fateful time at Kinnear's residence. During this time, he entertains the domestic staff with brilliant impersonations of a gentleman, 'with the voice and the manners and all' (Atwood, 1997, p. 179). Jeremiah is thus presented to us in the trappings of an early nineteenth-century ventriloquist; his powers of imitation and itinerant lifestyle align him with the ventriloquists performing at fairs discussed in Chapter 2. Indeed, he tries to persuade Grace to join him in a medical clairvoyant act at these fairs. Jeremiah explains that the performance is worked in pairs – a man and a woman – and that the woman has a veil cast over her face, speaks in 'a hollow voice' and diagnoses the audience's ailments (Atwood, 1997, pp. 309–10). He tells her he will 'instruct you in what to say' (Atwood, 1997, p. 311), underscoring the ventriloquial component to the performance, but implying that the act will be a ruse. Of course, his subsequent hypnotism of Grace as Jerome Dupont is an alternative version of this act yet the crucial ambiguity is in the extent to which Grace is a willing participant in the scene.

Grace is initially delighted by her recognition of Jeremiah/Jerome, but then remembers that he 'really did know the art of such things, and might put me into a trance. And that brought me up short, and gave me pause to consider' (Atwood, 1997, p. 356). I argue that Jeremiah/Jerome is the most potent ventriloquizer of Grace, and the closest echo the novel contains of the fantasy of the all-powerful Victorian ventriloquist. Jerome/Jeremiah's powers of hypnotism associate him with Svengali, and Grace also describes him as having the appearance of a Jew or gypsy (Atwood, 1997, p. 177). He even suggests that women are more suggestible to hypnotism, associating his hypnotic/ventriloquial abilities with the gendered script of masculine penetration/feminine permeability (Atwood, 1997, p. 350). The scene of Grace's 'hypnotism' represents four potential ventriloquists: Simon, who has tried, unsuccessfully, to incite Grace's confession; Grace herself, who might be posing as a dummy but producing Mary's voice under her own volition; Mary, the spirit or alternative personality that might be manipulating Grace; and Jerome/Jeremiah. Simon's experience of Grace's hypnotism exposes the limitations of his influence over Grace, and his own susceptibility to ventriloquial manipulation. As Grace walks into the room, he notices that her eyes are fixed upon Jerome with 'the pale and silent appeal, which Simon – he now realises – has been hoping for in vain' (Atwood, 1997, p. 460). DuPont has usurped his ventriloquial role over Grace, emphasized by the way in which Jerome explains how the trance will occur: 'all she has to do is listen to me, and then go to sleep' (Atwood, 1997, p. 460); the hypnotism is enacted by verbal instruction. Jerome/ Jeremiah also orchestrates the speech/silence of the others present, requesting that the assembled party must remain quiet until Grace is in the trance and then may speak quietly (Atwood, 1997, p. 461). Simon is vulnerable to the influence of Jerome/Jeremiah's voice, 'the back of his neck creeps' as the performance begins (Atwood, 1997, p. 462) and also is profoundly challenged by Grace/Mary's utterances. He tries to question Grace, to regain some semblance of ventriloquial mastery, and yet: 'For Simon this whole occasion is reeling out of control. He must seize the initiative, or at least try to seize it; he must keep Grace from reading his mind' (Atwood, 1997, p. 465). Jordan is feminized by the influence of Grace/Mary's voice and his loss of control over the voice is equated with the symbolic penetration of his mind by Grace/Mary.

But what if the voice does not belong to Mary or Grace, and is in fact Jerome's? Some time after the hypnotism Grace is finally acquitted of her involvement in the murders. She sends a letter to Jeremiah, but it is addressed to '*Signor Geraldo Ponti, Master of Neuro-Hypnotism, Ventriloquist, and Mind-Reader Extraordinare*' (Atwood, 1997, p. 492). The ventriloquial implications of Jeremiah/Jerome are highlighted by his adoption of this new role and we are left to consider whether it was really Jeremiah/Jerome who produced Grace/Mary's voice. When Grace sees Jeremiah/Jerome at the Governor's house he gestures that she should not reveal his identity: 'I was to button my lip, and not to say anything, or give him away' (Atwood, 1997, p. 354). This image of silencing returns in Grace's letter to the master of ventriloquism, as she explains that she received a button in the post. It has the same pattern as the one Jeremiah gave her when she worked at the Parkinson's residence but she also recognizes the command it exercises over her voice: 'you might have been telling me to keep silent, about certain things we both know of' (Atwood, 1997, p. 496). Although this suggests that there might have been some complicity between Grace and Jeremiah in the hypnotism/ventriloquism scene, we can see Jeremiah's message that Grace should 'button it' as an ultimate signifier of Jeremiah's ventriloquial prowess, for he can still dictate the terms under which she will speak. If the voice at the hypnotism was Jeremiah's, then the penetrative effect it exercised upon Jordan is a distinctly queer moment.

There is a sense of doubling between Grace and Jeremiah in the novel; both have multiple identities, both have voices of indeterminate origin, both can exercise the power – in Grace's case, either consciously or unwittingly – of ventriloquial influence. If Grace is Trilby to Jeremiah's

Svengali, then the balance of power in the ventriloquial relationship is made more ambivalent by the potential of the female ventriloquist and the ultimate uncertainty as to the origin of Grace's voice. To an extent, the Victorian script of ventriloquism is altered in *Alias Grace*, for Simon Jordan is a failed ventriloquist whose patriarchal entitlement to voice is challenged by Grace's influence. But Jordan is also challenged by Jeremiah/Jerome. Coral Ann Howells, one of the few commentators on the novel to recognize Jeremiah's role as a ventriloquist, argues that Jeremiah succeeds in silencing both Grace and Jordan, 'who cannot write his medical report [on the events of the hypnotism] for fear of being professionally discredited' (Howells, 2003, p. 36). There is only one significant moment of Jeremiah/Jerome's silencing in the text; in a letter addressed to Dr Bannerling, the Reverend Verringer elides Jerome's role in the hypnotism scene, and attributes the agency wholly to Jordan (Atwood, 1997, p. 501). This offers us a brief glimpse into the vulnerability of this ventriloquist; in this instance, Jeremiah is a liminal character, operating at the margins of speech/silence and liable to vanish into obscurity. However, in Chapter 2's outline of the fears and fantasies surrounding Victorian ventriloquists there is evidence to suggest that ventriloquists run the risk of being exposed as fraudulent, ridiculous, impotent. Although Simon is certainly subjected to this fate, Jeremiah/Jerome escapes such condemnation; he remains elusive, ambivalent, sinister. Atwood's novel mutes this aspect of the nineteenth-century script of ventriloquism.

3.3 'His voice cracked': the vulnerable ventriloquists of *Clara*

In Janice Galloway's article, 'Silent Partner', written for the *Guardian* to coincide with the publication of *Clara*, she discusses her motivation for writing about the virtuosa pianist Clara Schumann. The novel focuses on Clara's early years under the tutelage of her father, Friedrich Wieck, and her tempestuous marriage to the composer Robert Schumann. She explains: 'History works against the accomplishments of most of us [...] and against the truer accomplishments and priorities of women especially' (Galloway, 2002, p. 16). Such a statement apparently aligns Galloway's novel with the process of 'talking back' to patriarchal history in neo-Victorian texts such as *Nights at the Circus* and *Alias Grace*. This was certainly a theme in the critical reception of *Clara*, demonstrated by Rosemary Goring's review which champions the novel's feminist reappraisal of the construction of history: 'In taking a woman who has hitherto been relegated to a footnote and reinstating her to her rightful position, Galloway has at the same time struck a blow for silent, and silenced women of all generations' (Goring, 2002, p. 4). However, Galloway's Clara does not emerge as being particularly verbose and, although we have access to her inner thoughts at some points in the novel, she is not represented as being as overtly challenging to patriarchal authority as Fevvers or as an accomplished a ventriloquist as Grace Marks might be. *Clara* is unusual for the way in which it focuses on the men who have silenced Clara and attempted to install her in the feminized dummy role. I argue that Galloway's 'talking back' to the Victorian script of ventriloquism becomes manifest in its exposure of the precariousness of the masculine ventriloquist role; Clara is not a female ventriloquist that challenges patriarchal voicing, but the very authority of the patriarchal ventriloquist is revealed to be vulnerable, fragile and riddled with insecurities in the first place.

The figure of the silenced woman is still an important trope in the novel. As a child, Clara does not speak until she is four years old: 'Some people say she's deaf or simple; others that she's both' (Galloway, 2003, p. 13). Like the Princess of Abyssinia, the silent female runs the risk of being spoken for and spoken about; her family's friends are eager to position her in a script of marginalization and disability, and her muteness affords her no opportunity to redress this balance. Her father, however, sees promise in Clara and even praises her lack of speech: 'That the girl-child says nothing has its good side' (Galloway, 2003, p. 14). Wieck evidently prefers women to be seen and not heard, and he is initially presented as being secure in his verbal dominance over his family: 'If she can't hear or comprehend, what's the loss? He can speak enough for a household, the voice of one trained to know and disseminate the will of God, so who need add or interrupt? He speaks because he speaks. He does it well' (Galloway, 2003, p. 17). Wieck's slippage between his role as a patriarch and God seems to conveys the extent of his omnipresent authority. The phrase 'he speaks because he speaks' implies that he does not reflect on his vocal mastery, he takes it for granted, yet it subtly undermines any sense of meaning or thought behind his utterances. Wieck speaks for the sake of speaking and his verbosity appears excessive, unchecked in comparison to his reserved family.

Wieck does try to compel Clara to speak. He sits in front of her, swinging a watch on a chain: '*Clara. Say it. Clara*' and his actions are explicitly related to Mesmer (Galloway, 2003, p. 24). We are reminded of the mesmeric/ventriloquial abilities of Svengali and Jerome/Jeremiah, but also Selah Tarrant of *The Bostonians*, another ventriloquist-patriarch who is able to 'start up' the voice of his daughter. Wieck is a music teacher, and his lessons always begin with the incitement of his students to '*Sing!*' and Clara reflects: 'She has never heard anyone refuse. The very idea' (Galloway, 2003, p. 15). Sure enough, Clara's first use of her voice is in response to this ventriloquial instruction; she finally repeats her master's voice and her formation into a piano virtuosa, at the hands of her father, is under way (Galloway, 2003, pp. 20–1). Although Clara imagines her father to be able to command speech and silence, outside of the sphere of his family his authority is questionable. Wieck is mocked by his students, he hears a group of them shouting in the street:

> *Sing!* one shrieks, and they laugh again. But two of their number have lessons with him tomorrow [...] You might laugh, taking the gamble he doesn't recognise your voice disguised and in the dark [...] Inside his house, though, the teacher hears every word. What's more, he can identify the timbre of voices through walls with near medical accuracy, and that without even trying; he knows who they are all right (Galloway, 2003, p. 46)

Friedrich's identification of voices, even that are displaced and disguised, suggests his ventriloquial ability to capture voices and use them against the speakers, although it also conveys the limitations of his power over his ostensible dummies. The students repeat his voice, but this a parodic, mocking recitation of their master, surreptitiously challenging his authority. His female students clearly are not as in awe of him as Clara: 'They speak even when they are told not to and on occasion, rare occasion, when Papa is out of the room, Clara speaks back' (Galloway, 2003, p. 47). The powers of his influence are thus subjective; not everyone, particularly outside of the family circle, is in thrall to his commands for speech/silence and furthermore even his otherwise silent protégé can be encouraged to 'talk back'.

The most striking manifestation of Wieck's control over his daughter's voice comes in the description of her diary, yet even this is ambiguous. As Clara begins to find success with her musical performances, Wieck makes the decision that he will keep a diary on her behalf: 'Now the decisions have been made that this life will be remarkable, someone must record it. It stands to reason. And who better than her father/ teacher/her guiding light [...] Whom does she belong to, after all? Whom? My diary. His own hand. *Mine*' (Galloway, 2003, p. 61). There is a crucial uncertainty as to who is speaking the phrase: 'My diary. His own hand. *Mine*', and though Wieck might appear to steal Clara's voice, he also loses his own voice in her. The motif of doubling between father and daughter is limiting for the latter, but surely also for Wieck and it is almost as if he begins to lose control of the division between ventrilo-quist-patriarch and dummy-daughter:

> After a while he can't stop. *Father deserves my greatest devotion and gratitude for his ceaseless efforts on my behalf*, he writes – no sense of irony at all [...] After he's gone – by which he means dead – people will cite him as her voice, read this telling as though it's her own. (Galloway, 2003, p. 61)

This is his-story in the making; Wieck transcribes her diary, and this is depicted as a process of narrative ownership. He will provide the voice for her life and his writing/dictation of the script of her life offers a pertinent microcosm of the way in which histories are scripted by patriarchal authority. Wieck imagines it will be *his* voice that will be recited but this will still be refracted through Clara; does he thus run the risk of losing his own voice in his 'dummy'? This ventriloquial dynamic does not imbue Clara with any agency yet ironically exposes the vulnerability of the ventriloquist. This passage brings to light an unresolved question that haunts the nineteenth-century dream of mas-culine ventriloquial ubiquity: does the ventriloquist steal the voices of others because he lacks a voice of his own?

A further facet of the vulnerability of ventriloquists is addressed in the novel's recounting of a public execution of a murderer which is attended by Clara and her father. The details of the crime offer an uncanny echo of *Wieland*, for the killer, Woyzeck, was compelled to murder a woman he loved due to hearing disembodied voices: 'they found him talking out loud about what he had done [...] Voices did it, he said. They had incited him; angels and devils beneath the ground. He was misunderstood, the world despised him, and the voices told him the source of his misery and how to put it right' (Galloway, 2003, pp. 27–8). Woyzeck is known as 'the whispered-to', and Clara reflects: 'she knew that words had been the cause. Something had spoken in his ear and he had listened' (Galloway, 2003, p. 28). The narrative hints that Clara understands the dangers of ventriloquial voices, for 'words' are not always a source of agency and power but madness and death. His last words on the scaffold are *'Think of me on your wedding day'*, and their effect upon Wieck is strange: 'Woyzeck's last words [...] amused him and he repeated them often' (Galloway, 2003, p. 28). Friedrich is compelled to recite the words of the already ventriloquized Woyzeck. A continuum between ventriloquizing/ventriloquized men has been established and on occasion Wieck will also manifest the symptoms of Woyzeck's delusions. Whilst he rants at Clara about the importance of remaining independent (which is ironic, considering her father's desire to control her career), 'Clara listened and said nothing, which was what she was meant to do. He was not talking to her now, in any case, but to himself' (Galloway, 2003, p. 71). The trope of a man talking to himself – the trait of ventriloquial madness – forms a connection between Woyzeck and Wieck. Although Woyzeck is not mentioned on the day of Clara's wedding his plight will return in Clara's marriage to Robert.

Robert enters the Wieck household as Friedrich's student. The two men have a difficult relationship, as Wieck makes hurtful comments about his playing and also 'personal things about his *lack of manliness*' (Galloway, 2003, p. 89). He 'endures' this treatment, however, because of Wieck's abilities, but also: 'Because Robert could never find the words when he needed them [...] He felt ashamed and pitiable suddenly, unable to speak' (Galloway, 2003, p. 90). Wieck has the ability to silence Robert, and this is associated with being emasculated. As a relationship develops between Clara and Schumann, Wieck vehemently objects to the proposed marriage. When he discovers their engagement he declares: 'he had a pistol, a *pistol* – his voice cracked on an accelerating crescendo – and he'd shoot him like a dog if he came near their house again!' (p. 122). We should note the image of the father's 'voice cracking'. If we consider that Wieck's mastery over his household – and Clara in particular – has been so dependent upon the exercise of his voice, the 'crack' suggesting weakness when his control is wavering symbolizes the usurpation of his power by another ventriloquist.

The struggle over who will possess Clara – her father or her lover – takes a ventriloquial turn when Wieck insists: 'Clara was already spoken for [...] Art had spoken for her' (Galloway, 2003, pp. 136–7). This statement implicitly links her possession to her father, for, as we have already seen via her diary, he has also 'spoken for' her. Despite Friedrich's desire to keep Clara under his control, he still recognizes that her life with Robert might curtail her agency: 'he had not raised a daughter to this pitch for her to play like a clockwork doll only for cliques of her husband's friends, for the applause of a few' (Galloway, 2003, p. 137). The 'clockwork doll' image positions the woman in the domestic sphere as being like an automaton. Robert does have such intentions for Clara which are along strictly gendered lines:

That she is a woman out in the world while he stays at home, writing, is pure accident; things will fall differently when they are – he catches his breath even thinking it – man and wife. Not that he will stop her playing – not at all! She will play endlessly, he hopes, but suitably, appropriately, at home. (Galloway, 2003, p. 156)

Robert's wish to dictate the terms under which Clara will perform echoes Basil's plan to only allow Verena to exercise her vocal abilities in their home in *The Bostonians*. The chief difference between the texts is that Robert is unable to do this, not because Clara is unwilling, but due to his own mental illness.

Robert's mental disturbance links him to Woyzeck, for he repeatedly hears voices and also has periods of aphasia; he loses the ability to speak. However, it also forms a connection between Schumann and Wieck as both display increasingly irrational behaviour. Whilst Clara is away on tour Robert sends her paranoid missives: '*Never forget*, he wrote. *I see you always. I know everything you do.* Her father had always said the same. Her father and Robert' (Galloway, 2003, p. 174). It is obvious that neither man really does have this ability, but it offers another example of the way in which they desire to possess Clara, to penetrate her mind in an impossible way. As a young man Robert conceptualizes himself as having a split identity, a double self containing the calm and destructive sides of his personality (Galloway, 2003, pp. 87–8). I posit that Friedrich Wieck can also be perceived as Robert's double in the novel. They are united by their need to possess and manipulate Clara and yet there is also evidence to suggest that Wieck holds a ventriloquial power over Schumann. Whilst the couple struggle against Friedrich's disapproval, Robert tells Clara: '*He has read all my letters to you, Clärchen. He knows everything, he will do anything.* Horribly, his words, or something like them, slipped into Robert's mouth, surfaced like drowned heads in Robert's letters' (Galloway, 2003, p. 177). The 'slipping' of Friedrich's words into Robert's mouth represents the insidiousness of Wieck's control of Schumann, and, as in the case of Woyzeck, the manifestation of another's voice within the self is associated with death; Wieck's words surface like corpses in Robert's writing.

One of the last confrontations between Clara's father and husband comes when Robert is in the midst of an episode of depression. Wieck enters their marital home and finds Robert 'refusing to speak or sleep'. His reaction is violent:

Her father had begun to help, declaiming and pointing with his stick, sure if he spoke loudly enough his orders would be obeyed [...] From nowhere he reached and began hauling, pulling Robert's arm and *screaming*. Manliness, Self-respect, the need to Pull Oneself Together, a great jumble of words formed in bites, burst of horrible meaning. (Galloway, 2003, pp. 287–8)

Robert has retreated to the dummy role of silence and passivity, and Wieck's behaviour demonstrates his belief that speech – specifically *his* speech, articulated at a volume that will be able to penetrate Robert's confused mind – will be able to restore Robert's voice. When the patriarch-ventriloquist realizes that he cannot control the emasculated dummy, Wieck loses control over his own voice: the description of his 'great jumble of words' represent hysterical babble, a form of utterance that is traditionally associated with femininity. Both would-be ventriloquists are confronted with the limitations of their powers; Robert's aspirations to replace Wieck as the possessor of Clara actually leave him vulnerable to possession by Wieck, and Friedrich's frustrated efforts to control Robert's speech culminate in an eruption of near-incomprehensible rage which ironically align him with the mental instability of his disobedient dummy. The men's mutual desire to control their woman locks them into a relationship of ventriloquial doubleness and gender-crossing.[7] *Clara* re-cites the heteronormative script of masculinity represented by the more powerful Victorian ventriloquists such as Basil Ransom and Svengali, offering us a vision of ventriloquial masculinity in crisis.

3.4 Conclusion

The neo-Victorian narratives of ventriloquism explored in this chapter all feature men who attempt, unsuccessfully, to provide a definitive 'script' of the history of individual women. In *Nights at the Circus*, Jack Walser is confident that he will be able to reveal Fevvers' incredible life story as fraudulent. *Alias Grace*'s Simon Jordan seeks to incite Grace's voice and manipulate her speech into a neat case history that will bring him personal satisfaction and professional acclaim. Friedrich Wieck plans to exercise narrative control over his daughter's diary to ensure that Clara's life will be told in his voice. Each character can be considered as desperate to have the power to 'speak for' their subject, aspiring towards Svengali-esque powers of influence, manipulation and penetration. What emerges, however, is that the origin and agency behind 'voice' is unstable and often negotiable. If in *The Bostonians* and *Trilby* the origin of influential female voices is finally fixed in ultra-masculine ventriloquist figures, then the gendered inflection of

Victorian ventriloquists are recited but also transformed in Carter's and Atwood's novels. Walser and Jordan find themselves captivated by the 'siren' voices of their subjects; they are both liable to being ventriloquized by the women they seek to possess.

The concept of ventriloquism also encourages the reader to reflect upon the neo-Victorian process of 'talking back' to the nineteenth century. The ambiguity of Fevvers' voice – a paradoxically genuine fake voice – leads us to question whether Victorian 'voices' can ever be considered as having a fixed origin or authenticity. *Nights at the Circus* suggests that voices are always already ventriloquial: displaced, performed, and possessed by echoes of other utterances. It is worth being aware of these factors when invoking the metaphor of 'voice' to express agency and identity, particularly considering the rather casual way this concept is sometimes used in neo-Victorian criticism. *Alias Grace* similarly problematizes the wish to 'give voice' to the socially marginalized or silenced; the search for the origin of Grace's voice is thwarted, and the novel's subversive potential lies in this very uncertainty. Ventriloquism becomes an ambivalent strategy of subversion, for Grace must pose as a passive dummy even as she 'talks back' to her manipulators. The agency behind Grace's challenging speech is divided amongst various subjects: Mary, Jeremiah, and Grace herself. Which version of Grace's voice does the neo-Victorian reader want to hear? Do Grace/Mary/Jeremiah 'talk back' to us when the possessed woman accuses her audience of 'wanting it our own way' in attempting to quantify the 'truth' of her life? *Clara* offers an alternative critique of 'speaking for' the silenced subject, as Friedrich's attempts to make a ventriloquial double of his daughter and preserve his own voice in the historical record comes perilously close to him losing his own voice/identity. We are provoked to consider the vulnerability of the ventriloquist figure and to recognize that ventriloquial authors must negotiate multiple voices in their (re)scripting of history.

Although these novels can be interpreted as opening up the power exchanges of Victorian ventriloquisms, there are also issues that remain problematic. *Nights at the Circus* offers the possibility of queer partnerships away from the ventriloquist/dummy relationship of Olive and Verena in *The Bostonians* and yet ironically echoes the marginalization of same-sex desire in James' novel. Mignon's and the Princess's new voices, freed from patriarchal manipulators, must remain in the Siberian wilderness instead of being heard in mainstream society. Although Simon Jordan and Jack Walser both learn that masculine ventriloquists are subject to manipulation by the voices of their ostensible 'dummies', Carter's and Atwood's novels are not attuned to the ways in which

Victorian ventriloquists might already be vulnerable characters: we should remember that Selah Tarrant, Basil Ransom and Svengali struggle to produce their own voices before they alight upon suitable vessels for their utterances, whereas Walser and Jordan initially have strong voices in their own right. In *Alias Grace*, Jeremiah/Jerome retains much of the potency of his Victorian forebears, but little of the vulnerability. In this sense, Galloway's *Clara* provides a more thoughtful reflection on the role of the nineteenth-century ventriloquist by amplifying the fragility of the would-be ventriloquizers of Clara. If Clara is spoken for and silenced, the men who aspire to do this are fraught with fits of voice-related insecurity, feminized hysteria and split identity. The next chapter will return to the Victorian script of ventriloquism in the work of Oscar Wilde to highlight and elaborate upon the *queer* currencies of desire that are hinted at in the Victorian and neo-Victorian texts discussed so far.

4
Queering the Dummy/ Ventriloquist Dichotomy: Oscar Wilde and Ventriloquial Influence

At first glance, Oscar Wilde's poem 'The Harlot's House' (1885) seems to replicate the association between women and puppets that is so prevalent in nineteenth-century narratives of ventriloquism. The poem's speaker and his female companion are described as walking along a moonlit street and pausing outside a brothel. They hear the strains of music playing inside, and witness the shadows of dancers against the blinds: 'Like strange mechanical grotesques' (Wilde, 2003, p. 867). The speaker continues:

> Sometimes a clockwork puppet pressed
> A phantom lover to her breast
> Sometimes they seemed to try to sing. (Wilde, 2003, p. 867)

The 'clockwork puppet' has a female pronoun, and we might be tempted to assume that the poem therefore aligns women with the artificiality, objectification and susceptibility to manipulation of the dummy. Coupled with the apparent failure of voice of the puppets – they only 'try' to sing, but seemingly remain inaudible – Wilde's poem is ripe for accusations of misogyny.[1] However, such a reading is belied by the ambiguity of gender in the poem. For although 'The Harlot's House' depicts the occupants of the brothel as 'wire-pulled automatons' and even describes a 'horrible marionette' coming outside to smoke a cigarette on the house's steps, it is not stated whether these puppets are male or female. Indeed, it is worth bearing in mind that although by the nineteenth century the word 'harlot' was used as a derogatory appellation for a woman, historically the term has also been applied to men.[2] In Wilde's terms, 'puppets' can be either men or women, and the dichotomy between female object and male manipulator is blurred.

Although sexual desire might turn subjects into objects, what further complications between the role of puppet and master – or dummy and ventriloquist – could arise in Wilde's work?

Various commentators on neo-Victorian literature have instilled caution against constructing 'the Victorians' as a monolithic signifier of a stable set of cultural values.[3] Bearing such a warning in mind, this chapter seeks to explore the work of Oscar Wilde as offering an alternative 'voice' in the script of Victorian ventriloquism. I suggest that although Wilde's use of ventriloquial tropes in texts such as *The Picture of Dorian Gray* and *De Profundis* finds resonance with some aspects of the novels discussed in Chapter 2, Wilde's work also interrogates the relationship of power between 'ventriloquist' and 'dummy' and the gendering of these respective roles. As Chapter 2 identified, the figure of the queer ventriloquist haunts *The Bostonians* and *Trilby* and yet the machinations of would-be ventriloquists such as Olive Chancellor and Little Billee tend to be thwarted by the superior powers of the heteronormative manipulator. This chapter argues that the trope of ventriloquism emerges as a queer practice in Wilde's work and also that the role of 'dummy' is not restricted to women.

The Picture of Dorian Gray tells the story of a gorgeous young man painted by his admirer, the artist Basil Hallward. In the final sitting for the picture Dorian is introduced to Lord Henry Wotton, a languid aristocrat whose theories on aestheticism, art and beauty exercise such a profound effect upon Dorian that he wishes he could stay as lovely as the portrait whilst the picture ages in his place. Under the mentorship of Wotton, Dorian embarks upon a life of sensual pleasure and decadence. The portrait bears the signs of his sins, which include the callous rejection of an actress, Sibyl Vane, resulting in her suicide, murder, blackmail, and a myriad of other indiscretions on which the novel generally remains silent. Dorian's desire to be rid of the portrait's record of his secret life ultimately results in his death. My analysis of *Dorian Gray* situates Lord Henry Wotton as a ventriloquist figure whose desire to manipulate/possess Dorian is expressed through the powers of oral/aural influence. Dorian is figured within the feminized 'dummy' role, learning to recite his 'master's' voice and perform a social script dictated by Henry. I propose that Dorian also exceeds Henry's expectations, 'talking back' to his ventriloquist in ways that belie the prescribed roles of master/puppet to generate a sense of agency and render the process of ventriloquial influence unstable. As a counterpoint to such a reading, however, I will also highlight how the alternative vision of ventriloquial power dynamics offered in relationships between men in *Dorian Gray* do not wholly extend to Sibyl Vane. My analysis will demonstrate the ways in which 'artificiality' or 'mimicry' are desirable qualities for Dorian, strategies for constructing multiple personae, yet are invoked as limiting traits for Sibyl. Sibyl is ultimately condemned to be a mere 'copy' or 'mimic' of Dorian's passions and her attempt to alter the 'script' of her performance is punishable by death.

The next section of the chapter examines *De Profundis*, the letter written to Lord Alfred Douglas whilst Wilde was in prison. I suggest that *De Profundis* is a performative re-construction of Wilde's persona, a process of 'talking back' to his silencing at the hands of the British justice system. My analysis highlights Wilde's use of puppet/ventriloquial imagery throughout the text. I explore how Wilde blurs the boundaries between the roles of puppet and master and maps this concept onto his relationship with Douglas, articulating the queer currencies of desire and power struggles that define their partnership. I argue that *De Profundis* provides a re-evaluation of the use of ventriloquism in previous Victorian texts. Even a compelled performance of the 'dummy' role can generate agency, a theme that I have identified as also being key to neo-Victorian uses of ventriloquial motifs.

4.1   Influentially speaking: negotiating ventriloquial influence in *The Picture of Dorian Gray*

The word 'influence' resonates throughout *The Picture of Dorian Gray*.[4] It is often prefixed by the terms 'good' or 'bad' and so is morally conceptualized in a way that appears to support the dubious connotations of the practice of influence explored in Chapter 2. In his first meeting with Dorian, Lord Henry Wotton dwells on this moral definition:

> There is no such thing as a good influence, Mr Gray. All influence is immoral [...] Because to influence a person is to give him one's own soul. He does not think his natural thoughts or burn with his natural passions [...] He becomes an echo of someone else's music, an actor of a part that has not been written for him. (Wilde, 2003, p. 28)

Wotton's explanation could be interpreted as a clear commentary on the negative implications of influence. His speech indicates that there is a static boundary separating such terms as 'natural / unnatural' and the statement 'to influence a person is to give him one's own soul' is particularly ominous, reminding us of influence's etymological heritage of spiritual imposition or penetration. Wotton implicitly refers to acting under influence as the subject losing control of her/his autonomy. The analogy of 'an actor of a part that has not been written for him' casts the influenced individual in the role of the puppet or 'dummy' in relation to the influencer's role as ventriloquist; the 'origin' of the script of the performance lies elsewhere. Influence is equated with manipulation that transgresses 'natural' boundaries and the reference to the influenced being 'an echo of someone else's music' equates this process with aural perception. Removed from the broader context of the novel, Henry's commentary appears to be profoundly moralistic, preaching the need to retain an 'authentic' or 'original' sense of self.

However, Henry's previous conversation with the painter Basil Hallward radically undermines such a reading. Basil remarks: 'You never say a moral thing, and you never do a wrong thing. Your cynicism is simply a pose', to which Henry responds: 'Being natural is simply a pose, and the most irritating pose I know' (Wilde, 2003, p. 20). Henry's comment suggests that he does not subscribe to the concept of an essential self that is vulnerable under influence, as 'naturalness' is a social construct. Basil's criticism of Henry's incongruity installs a disjuncture between 'saying' and 'doing'. The 'voice' is evidently not the expression of a coherent internal subjectivity, as Basil implies that his friend will say things that he does not really mean and so the connection between 'voice' and self is destabilized.

Of course, the irony of Henry's speech on influence is that it is during this first meeting with Dorian that Henry's words exercise a profound influence upon the young man. As he listens to Henry's beautiful voice, Dorian wonders: 'Words! Mere words! How terrible they were! How clear, and vivid, and cruel! One could not escape from them. And yet what a subtle magic there was in them! They seemed to be able to give a plastic form to formless things' (Wilde, 2003, p. 29). His account invokes the invasive properties of oral suggestion and also emphasizes the manipulative influence of verbal utterances: the spoken word is imbued with the power to construct or create. Henry possesses this power, a trait that aligns him with the master ventriloquists of James' and Du Maurier's novels. We subsequently discover that it was Henry's intention to possess Dorian with his voice:

> There was something terribly enthralling in the exercise of influence [...] To project one's soul into some gracious form, and let it tarry there for a moment; to hear one's own intellectual views echoed back [...] He was a marvellous type, too, this lad [...] or could be fashioned into a marvellous type, at any rate [...] He could be made

a Titan or a toy [...] He would make that wonderful spirit his own. (Wilde, 2003, pp. 39–40)

Henry's musings on his intentions towards Dorian resonate with the language of possession and his ventriloquial agenda is boldly stated through his desire to hear Dorian echo his words. Wotton wants the boy literally to speak with his voice. Henry's commentary suggests that the effect of influence becomes manifest through explicitly vocal resonance: 'echoed back'. Dorian is imagined as a quasi-dummy figure that can be manipulated at will, and later in the novel he does come to emulate Henry's speech. On meeting Dorian, Victoria Wotton remarks: 'Ah! That is one of Harry's views, isn't it, Mr Gray? I always hear Harry's views from his friends. It is the only way I get to know of them' (Wilde, 2003, p. 46). Dorian eagerly obeys his master's voice as Henry will express an opinion and Dorian will behave accordingly: 'I don't think I am likely to marry, Henry. I am too much in love. That is one of your aphorisms. I am putting it into practice, as I do anything that you say' (Wilde, 2003, p. 46). Dorian's interest in echoing Henry takes the form of acting under verbal influence. It is Henry's utterances to which Dorian responds. Henry's use of the word 'domination' seemingly articulates his lust for utter control over Dorian but their relationship cannot be reduced to a dichotomy of ubiquitous power and complete passivity. Henry's statement of influence reveals this unpredictability. Dorian could become a 'Titan or a toy' and thus the scope and results of Henry's influence are not quantifiable.

The unstable quality of ventriloquial influence is exposed in the scene of Dorian's awakening. As he listened to Henry:

He was dimly conscious that entirely fresh influences were at work within him. Yet they seemed to him to have come really from himself. The few words that Basil's friend had said to him – words spoken by chance, no doubt, and with wilful paradox in them – had touched some secret chord that had never been touched before, but that he felt was now vibrating and throbbing to curious pulses. (Wilde, 2003, p. 29)

Henry's words are figured as powerful and Dorian is represented as subject to specifically aural influences. The phrases 'secret chord' and 'vibrating and throbbing' resound with the vocabulary of musicality, and also erotic sensation. Dorian is positioned as a quasi-instrument of Henry's mastery – we are reminded of Trilby's relationship with

Svengali – yet his own sense of agency is not negated by this process but enhanced.[5] The above quotation emphasizes Dorian's conviction that these ostensibly external influences are actually emanating from within his own self; ironically, Henry's 'few words' are repositioned as being a mere medium for Dorian's awakening. A role-reversal is at work as Henry is represented as simply echoing Dorian's own internal thought processes, providing a voice for desires that potentially originate from the younger man.

Several critics have remarked that Dorian's fate in the novel is largely due to the negative influence of Henry Wotton. Jean M. Ellis D'Alessandro, for example, posits that Dorian is wholly good and inno-cent prior to his 'corruption' by Henry (D'Alessandro, 1994, pp. 72–3) and implies that the process of 'influence' is solely outward. Camille Paglia also argues that Henry has complete power over Dorian: 'Dorian, like the Delphic Oracle, is under the mediumship of a hidden god [...] Dorian *becomes* Lord Henry' (Paglia, 1990, p. 518). Paglia's invocation of Dorian as a 'medium' is suggestive but does not account for the plu-rality of oracular utterances discussed in Chapter 1. Henry does 'speak through' Dorian yet this act of ventriloquial influence is not an eradica-tion of Dorian's own voice but an ambiguous blurring of subjectivity and agency. The quest to identify who or what 'really' influences Dorian is surely fruitless and as Pamela Thurschwell also notes, the currencies of influence coursing through the text cannot be reduced to a finite source (Thurschwell, 2001, pp. 61–2). As the etymology of the word reveals, 'influence' is associated with contamination and the influencer cannot be deemed immune from similarly falling under influence. Henry confesses that he is enthralled or, in other words, enslaved to the pleasures of influence and his speculations on the practice reveal that he has been so influenced by Basil's relationship with Dorian that he wishes to imitate it. Influence can 'flow in' from one individual to another and so can also flow back, as Henry's behaviour at a dinner party demonstrates:

> He felt the eyes of Dorian Gray were fixed upon him, and the con-sciousness that amongst his followers there was one whose tempera-ment he wished to fascinate, seemed to give his wit keenness [...] He was brilliant, fantastic, irresponsible. He charmed his listeners out of themselves, and they followed his pipe laughing. Dorian Gray never took his gaze off him, but sat like one under a spell, smiles chasing each other over his lips, and wonder growing grave in his darkening eyes. (Wilde, 2003, p. 43)

The theme of Henry's oral/aural influence is reiterated as he is positioned in a quasi-Pied Piper role. Chapter 3 considered the spell-binding voice of the Siren as a gendered image that associates dangerously seductive utterances with the sexualized female body. Henry's possession of a similarly captivating voice queerly re-cites this script, demonstrating that the trope of the seductive voice can also be appropriated by a man for the purpose of influencing his male object of desire. Furthermore, there is a currency of influence flowing through this scenario. Henry is compelled to perform under the influence of his dummy; he must fulfil the role in which he has been cast and in turn be manipulated by the subject he wishes to possess.[6]

The double motif is of obvious significance in *Dorian Gray* and Linda Dryden positions Wilde's text as being part of a continuum of fin-de-siècle narratives of the double (Dryden, 2003, p. 18), most overtly represented through Dorian's relationship with his painting but also through the relationship between Henry and Dorian and even Basil and Dorian. Although the painting is ostensibly a copy of the 'original' Dorian, Basil confesses that the picture is 'a portrait of the artist, not of the sitter. The sitter is merely the accident, the occasion. It is not he who is revealed by the painter, it is rather the painter who, on the coloured canvas, reveals himself' (Wilde, 2003, p. 20). The painting thus has an indeterminate identity: is it just Dorian or a representation of Basil's adoration of Dorian? Basil's confession that the secret of his own soul is revealed in the portrait suggests that there is an authenticity in the work that runs much deeper than its apparent status as a mere 'copy'. Similarly, the painting comes to function as a moral barometer of Dorian's own soul, as the 'original' of the painting maintains the unblemished appearance that should have been the trait of the 'copy'. Dorian also becomes a 'double' or 'copy' of Henry, a 'dummy' who echoes his epigrams but additionally provides action to Henry's thoughts. At an early stage in the novel Henry informs Dorian that he represents 'all of the sins you have never had the courage to commit' (Wilde, 2003, p. 67) and yet Basil has already told us that Henry never actually *does* anything wrong. As Linda Dryden has argued, Dorian comes to enact Henry's aesthetic ideals in a way that the older man never actively fulfils (Dryden, 2003, p. 121). Henry's 'dummy' is imbued with a dangerous life of his own.

Dorian's actions also have the power to influence his portrait and yet as the novel progresses, it is the portrait that dominates Dorian's existence. He is tortured by the possibility of its discovery and when he reveals the disfigured work to its painter: 'Dorian Gray glanced at the picture, and suddenly an uncontrollable feeling of hatred for Basil

Hallward came over him, as though it had been suggested to him by the image on the canvas, whispered into his ear by those grinning lips' (Wilde, 2003, p. 117). In his quest to become the controller of his own destiny, Dorian is ultimately dictated to by the portrait. The object comes to ventriloquize the subject, to utter the words that will compel his murderous actions. If the image of the dummy as a double of the ventriloquist must always be thwarted by the superior agency of the latter, Wilde's novel offers the vision of a subject that can house multiple voices and identities. The roles of ventriloquist and dummy, or original and copy, will shift and blur.

Although *Dorian Gray* represents a world dominated by currencies of ventriloquial desire where the gendered power relationships between puppet and master might be queered, the fate of actual women in the novel does not significantly deviate from the conclusions of *The Bostonians* and *Trilby*. Henry Wotton's misogyny is notable and is directed at women's access to speech in the social world of the text. He informs Dorian that women 'never have a thing to say, but they say it charmingly' (Wilde, 2003, p. 47) and this gendered division between utterance and meaning is reiterated by the comparisons drawn between women and parrots in the novel. Basil tells us that the party where he meets Dorian is filled with 'elderly ladies with gigantic tiaras and parrot noses' (Wilde, 2003, p. 21) and in the scene where Sibyl Vane tells her mother of her love for Dorian, Mrs Vane chastises her daughter in a 'parrot-phrase' (Wilde, 2003, p. 55). Both Hillel Schwartz and Paul Carter have identified a thematic connection between parrots and ventriloquists' dummies, considering the typical understanding of parrots as possessors of displaced voice and, more specifically, as copiers of the human voice (Schwartz, 1996, p. 143; Carter, 2006, pp. 109–10).[7] Carter's book pursues the gendered implications of 'parroting', detailing how there is an entrenched cultural patriarchal association between femininity and parrots in terms of gaudy appearance, narcissism (the captive bird who bonds with the mirror) and women's predilection for chatter/gossip; the meaningless repetition of another's speech (Carter, 2006, pp. 78–84). Wilde's use of parrot imagery to describe the women of *Dorian Gray* has an investment in this ventriloquial continuum, and Sibyl Vane – whose name also has narcissistic implications – possesses psittacine qualities: 'The joy of a caged bird was in her voice' (Wilde, 2003, p. 55).

Initially Sibyl is a contender for Henry's role as the ventriloquizer of Dorian, for, like Henry, she possesses a beautiful and influential voice. Dorian elucidates this similarity between the two characters: 'You know how a voice can stir one. Your voice and the voice of Sibyl Vane are two things that I shall never forget. When I close my eyes, I hear them, and each of them says something different. I don't know which to follow' (Wilde, 2003, p. 49). Dorian does not elaborate on what the 'different' messages from Henry's and Sibyl's mellifluous tones might be; perhaps this is the tension between the queer and heterosexual impulses that influence him, or is it that Sibyl's voice offers Dorian an alternative vision of the connections between gender, voice and agency? Kerry Powell has suggested that the purported power of Sibyl's voice echoes the challenge that Victorian actresses posed to the gendered expectations that women should be 'seen and not heard', as the nineteenth-century theatre offered a 'reversal of Victorian standards [...] a place where women could speak powerfully while men sat mute in the darkness' (Powell, 1997, p. 186). Sibyl's first name connects her to the Delphic oracle and the ambiguous ventriloquial exchanges outlined in Chapter 1, but her potential as the ventriloquial influencer of Dorian is thwarted by Henry's superior abilities. Dorian is drawn to the actress because of her capacity, through performance, to encompass multiple identities: 'She is all the great heroines of the world in one. She is more than an individual' (Wilde, 2003, p. 51). At first, then, she might be interpreted as another 'double' for Dorian, considering his own investment in cultivating alternative personae. However, we should note that Sibyl's relationship to her performance is expressed in ventriloquial terms. When eulogizing her charms, Dorian explains: 'Lips that Shakespeare taught to speak have whispered their secrets in my ears' (Wilde, 2003, p. 65). Though Dorian might fall under the influence of this voice, it has its source in another man; Sibyl is the dummy of Shakespeare, condemned to recite his script.

Sibyl's siren sway over Dorian is compromised when he, Basil and Henry witness her inferior performance as Juliet, and it is via the medium of Sibyl's voice that the men realize that her ability to perform has been affected by Dorian's love. She speaks 'in a thoroughly artificial manner [...] the voice was exquisite, but from the point of view of tone it was absolutely false. It was wrong in colour. It took away all the life from the verse. It made the passion unreal' (Wilde, 2003, p. 69). She is relegated to the role of an imperfect feminine mimic. Ironically this was the source of Dorian's original attraction to her; Sibyl, like Dorian, is a work of art come to life, but her acknowledgement of her ventriloquial relationship to art negates her influence over Dorian. Justifying her poor performance, Sibyl remarks: 'What have I to do with the puppets of a play?' (Wilde, 2003, p. 71). Her recognition of her 'dummy' role inaugurates Sibyl's 'talking back' to Dorian, her plea that she does not want to remain a 'copy' doomed to repeat scripts but to experience the 'reality' of life. However, the transgression of the boundaries between art and life, or copy and original, is only available to the men of *Dorian Gray*. It is Henry's voice that triumphs in the struggle to influence Dorian, and Sibyl must remain a 'copy' or die. Women cannot succeed as either ventriloquists or unruly dummies in this text, and Dorian's dismissal of Sibyl's attempt to voice her desire results in her ultimate silencing by suicide orchestrated by Dorian's callousness.

4.2 Speaking through silence and rewriting history in *De Profundis*

Despite *The Picture of Dorian Gray*'s inability to imagine the woman-as-dummy with a subjectivity and voice of her own, the novel does offer an alternative rendering of the roles of queer ventriloquist and dummy to its nineteenth-century counterparts. Sibyl's silencing from the world of the text elicits no tangible sympathy from Wilde, but in his later work he does appear to become more attuned to the dynamics of speech/silence and the implications this might have for social agency. In the text that has become known by the title of *De Profundis*,[8] Wilde mentions an exchange that happened in the exercise hour during his time at Wandsworth prison:

> the poor thief who, recognising me as we tramped round the yard at Wandsworth, whispered to me in the hoarse prison-voice men get from long and compulsory silence: *'I am sorry for you: it is harder for the likes of you than it is for the likes of us'*. (Wilde, 2003 pp. 1044–5)[9]

According to several of Wilde's biographers, this initial contact instigated a series of surreptitious conversations between the two prisoners but, as André Gide recounts Wilde's remark: 'I still didn't know how to talk without moving my lips' and the men were discovered and punished (Gide, 1951, p. 37).[10] In other words, to communicate in an environment where speech is forbidden one must engage in a practice typically associated with ventriloquial prowess; the production of voice cloaked by an illusion of silence.[11]

The condition of being a prisoner is equated with enforced mute-ness. If we accept that the ability to 'give voice' is a requisite of social agency, then the silence imposed upon the prisoners signifies their utter powerlessness. The men are literally 'dummies' who should only speak when compelled by a higher authority. Nevertheless, the prisoner who communicates through this act of ventriloquial speech is simultaneously fulfilling the roles of both dummy and ventriloquist. He is masquerading as a dumb body whilst producing a covert voice that not only confirms his own status as a social subject but also inaugurates another ostensible 'dummy' into subjectivity. An unexpected voice/agency is produced to 'talk back' to the constraints of extreme social marginalization and we see that the subject placed in the role of a 'dummy' does not stay in his prescribed position. The boundaries between ventriloquist and dummy, or puppet and master, are transgressed. Although this ventriloquial voicing does afford an instance of self expression, we must also remember that this transgression is temporary as the rebellious prisoners are punished and their powerless status is ultimately reiterated.

De Profundis has an ambiguous textual status and prior to exploring the letter's relationship to ventriloquial voice, agency and history it is worth considering the conditions of its production. Richard Ellmann understands the text as being primarily a love letter (Ellmann, 1988, p. 483) and one should not lose sight of the intended recipient of the text, Lord Alfred Douglas. Many commentators have suggested, however, that this 'letter' was aimed at a broader audience. Jonathan Dollimore, for example, perceives the text as Wilde's unfortunate renunciation of his transgressive aesthetic in relation to art and life (Dollimore, 1991, p. 95) whereas Claude J. Summers argues that the letter is an expression of Wilde's 'authentic' homosexual self: '[Wilde] exemplifies the political realities of gay oppression and symbolises both gay vulnerability and gay resistance' (Summers, 1990, p. 21). Wayne Koestenbaum also focuses on the autobiographical content of the text and suggests that Wilde's epistle is a self-conscious construction of proto-gay subjectivity, a call-to-arms for gay liberation (Koestenbaum, 1998, p. 235). Ian Small and Josephine Guy offer convincing manuscript evidence to posit that the letter was composed with eventual publication in mind (Small and Guy, 2006, pp. 46–76). There is therefore a tension between readings of *De Profundis* that understand the document as an intensely personal revelation of Wilde's identity and interpretations of the text that suggest it functions as a performative self-(re)construction that was ultimately intended for publication.

Critical assessments that favour a performative, quasi-fictional reading of the 'Wilde' of *De Profundis* still must acknowledge the disparity between the material conditions of Wilde's pre-conviction writings and the environment in which the letter was produced. The precise date of composition is unknown but the general consensus is that Wilde started to write the letter towards the end of 1896 or early in 1897 and that it was completed during March of the same year.[12] Unsurprisingly, the text frequently refers to the conditions of prison life and thus has a tangible autobiographical component. As Regenia Gagnier has suggested, it is surely impossible for the vast majority of critical commentators to imagine the extent of Wilde's suffering throughout the public humiliation of the trials and the degradation of his imprisonment, and so in some ways it could seem callous to label the epistle as 'fictive' (Gagnier, 1986, pp. 180–1). Despite the validity of Gagnier's argument, we should also remember that Wilde had a life-long interest in the production of performed, constructed and 'artificial' personae and a profound distaste towards 'earnestness', 'truth' and 'authenticity'. Jerusha McCormack, amongst others, states that Wilde self-consciously and consistently blurred the boundaries between 'art' and 'life' as both a man and artist (McCormack, 1997, p. 96) and this impulse is still apparent in the prison letter. As other critics have argued, Wilde's life is always situated at a vexed site between 'fact' and 'fiction'.[13] Although I recognize that this text is very different to the others considered in this book and biographical information will inform my reading of Wilde's letter, I also understand the 'I' of *De Profundis* as a partially fictional narrative persona that reflects the perpetual ambiguity of Wilde's 'original' life in relation to the 'copies' of his work.

As the above commentary on the connection between prison life and silencing suggests, Wilde's experiences as a prisoner placed him in the role of 'dummy' to be manipulated and voiced by others, and his position as puppet-prisoner is a direct result of his conviction for 'acts of gross indecency'. There is a story related in Ellmann's biography that has a symbolic resonance in highlighting the moment of Wilde's passage from being the master of his own voice to being a silenced prisoner. As his third trial concluded with a guilty verdict and the sentence of two years hard labour, Wilde allegedly asked: 'And I? May I say nothing, my lord?'. The presiding judge merely waved his hand to dismiss Wilde's presence and his voice (Ellmann, 1988, p. 449). Wilde had a reputation as a fabulous speaker,[14] but at this moment he lost access to his own voice and he was transported to Holloway prison, the first of various institutions where Wilde served his time. His remaining personal possessions were taken from him. He was stripped, ordered to bathe and given his prison uniform (Ellmann, 1988, p. 450). Ruth Robbins has commented that Wilde's prison experience constituted a process of stripping away the signifiers through which he had constructed his artistic and social persona. Aside from the imposition of silence, compulsory isolation meant that he was denied access to social interaction. A number was substituted for his famous name and his beautiful clothes were replaced with a prison uniform (Robbins, 2005, p. 118). Wilde's situation as a prisoner, condemned for his queerness, therefore denied him access to 'voice' in terms of utterance and also in relation to social expression.

Several other factors can be understood as motivating the writing of the letter, reflecting the text as a process of Wilde's 'talking back' to his persecutors and the outside world at large. The addressee of the letter Lord Alfred Douglas, his erstwhile lover and friend, inadvertently played a central role in Wilde's imprisonment.[15] Douglas was not to stand trial or to be accused of any incriminating behaviour by Wilde's prosecutors, despite the evidence to implicate the young aristocrat in Wilde's 'crimes'.[16] The perception of Wilde as a pernicious influence upon youth was repeatedly discussed in the trials and was consolidated by his eventual conviction. After the trials he had no further opportunity to reject this label. In this sense, the queer influence of Wilde was silenced. In *De Profundis*, Wilde addresses the attitude of Douglas' mother towards their relationship, commenting on her desire to blame Wilde: 'I hear of it, not from people who know you, but from people who do not know you, and do not desire to know you. I hear it often' (Wilde, 2003, p. 1048). The repetition of the word 'hear' is important, suggesting a state of passivity when coupled with Wilde's status as 'silenced'. Wilde had cleverly and provocatively manipulated his appearances in the popular media and yet after the trial the press had the freedom to celebrate the jury's decision and to deride and condemn the disgraced playwright without consideration of Wilde's response. Although there were exceptional voices of dissent, the general public opinion appeared to be that Wilde's punishment was deserved and just.[17] Wilde was in a position of apparent powerlessness in relation to the attitudes, both public and private, towards him at this time as he was unable to mediate in the debates surrounding his incarceration. The letter written whilst in prison can therefore be understood as an act of 'talking back' to Douglas, of regaining a voice not only with regards to their personal relationship but also in relation to broader public attitudes towards this partnership.

During the August of 1895 Wilde heard of Douglas' plans to have an article published in the *Mercure de France*, providing details of their relationship and quoting from several of the private letters that had passed between the men. Some months later he discovered that Douglas also intended to publish a volume of poems dedicated to his former lover. Wilde was outraged at Douglas' presumption and his anger and disappointment at this appropriation of his name is a significant theme in the letter. He subsequently elaborates on this perceived imposition:

> The letters that should have been to you things sacred and secret beyond anything in the whole world! These actually were the letters you proposed to publish for the jaded *décadent* to wonder at, for the greedy *feuilletoniste* to chronicle, for the little lions of the *Quartier Latin* to gape and mouth at! (Wilde, 2003, p. 1007)

The use of the words 'gape and mouth' is an evocative statement of the uselessness of any commentary that the public could provide upon these letters. Speech is reduced to a mere bodily motion as 'mouthing' suggests the attempt to speak without producing a meaningful voice or, put another way, the motions of a dummy without a ventriloquist to provide voice. This quotation also suggests that there are several versions of history – that which should have happened, that which is said to have happened and that which has actually happened – and yet subjects such as Douglas that have access to the power of an artistic 'voice' are only fuelling a meaningless version of a biased history.

The subjectivity of historical perception is also addressed in relation to the public's understanding of the Marquis of Queensberry, Douglas' father and the man who instigated the private investigations into Wilde's relationships with men. At the time of the letter's composition the narrative of Wilde's history could only be voiced by his persecutors and Wilde's understandable personal despair at such bias highlights a broader problem about how history is constructed, chronicled and disseminated. Queensberry is now considered to be 'the hero of the hour': 'That version has now actually passed into serious history: it is quoted, believed, and chronicled: the preacher has taken it for his text [...] such was the irony of things that your father would live to be a hero of a Sunday-school tract' (Wilde, 2003, p. 1008). The letter proceeds to meditate on the power politics of speech:

> I remember as I was sitting in the dock on the occasion of my last trial listening to Lockwood's appalling denunciation of me [...] Suddenly it occurred to me, *'How splendid it would be, if I was saying all this about myself!'* I saw then at once that what is said of a man is nothing. The point is, who says it. (Wilde, 2003, p. 1050)

Moral assessments are necessarily subjective and have an arbitrary relationship to 'truth' or 'reality' but if there is enough authoritative power behind such an assessment it will come to be accepted as 'fact'. This formative power is associated with verbal utterance in the above quotation. It is Queensberry's version of Wilde that has come to dominate the opinion of the contemporary public. Although Queensberry can hardly be considered to be a reliable authority, fuelled as he was by bigoted rage and warped sensibilities, it is individuals such as Queensberry that have the power – or 'voice' – to create a viable version of history. His sex, heterosexuality and class status all enabled Queensberry to have a profound influence upon Wilde's fate and to silence the queer desire between Wilde and his son. This quotation emphasizes the speaker's identity over the content of a statement and thus an authoritative voice becomes associated with social power. Wilde's suggestion that Queensberry was the sole orchestrator of his downfall is an act of hyperbolic construction; ironically, Wilde imbues both Queensberry and his own self with a much greater social significance than was actually the case. *De Profundis* represents Wilde's rearticulation of his diminished social status. Through bemoaning the subjectivity of history, he ingeniously creates another version of events in which he is elevated to the status of 'one who appealed to all the ages' (Wilde, 2003, p. 1008). The silenced prisoner has the opportunity to 'talk back' to the machinations of history, and we can see that Wilde's act of ventriloquism recognizes the privileging of some narrative voices over others in a foreshadowing of neo-Victorianism's desire to 're-voice' the historical record.

The ventriloquial currencies of *De Profundis* are not solely metatextual; the relationship between influence, desire and agency manifest in *Dorian Gray*, and the ability of puppets to 'talk back' to their manipulators, is also a thematic concern of the letter. The material conditions of Wilde's imprisonment have cast him into the role of a dummy or puppet as not only must he remain silent and be spoken for but his physical actions are also controlled. Relating the circumstances of having to attend a bankruptcy hearing orchestrated by Queensberry, he informs Douglas that his father 'was able not merely to put me in prison for two years, but to take me out for an afternoon and make me a public bankrupt' (Wilde, 2003 p. 1004). Wilde's statement focuses on the extent to which his status as a prisoner has left him vulnerable to being physically manipulated by others. Queensberry is cast as puppet-master, instrumental in placing Wilde at the mercy of the legal and penal system and now able to dictate the circumstances under which Wilde will appear in public.

However, Wilde asserts his agency as a ventriloquist in another way in the course of *De Profundis*, as the letter is explicitly motivated by the absence of Bosie's voice. He begins by stating that he is writing to Bosie because he has heard no word from him (Wilde, 2003, p. 980). The letter is therefore not only a response to Wilde's own literal and symbolic silencing but also to Douglas' 'silence'. The letter functions as an incitement to dialogue and Wilde ostensibly expects a reply, concluding: 'Write to me with full frankness about yourself: about your life: your friends: your occupations: your books. Tell me about your volume and its reception. Whatever you have to say for yourself, say it without fear' (Wilde, 2003, p. 1058). This statement notably dictates the terms under which Douglas should respond. Wilde desires to hear a specific type of narrative voice from his friend and is instructing him as to how this should be articulated. The form of a letter typically implies the absence of the addressee but Wilde's narrative voice is also a process of imagining the appropriate responses that his addressee should make. In other words, he constructs a dialogue and yet necessarily speaks all the parts himself. Rhetorical questioning permeates the text: 'You must surely realise that now?' (Wilde, 2003, p. 982); 'Do you think I exaggerate?' (Wilde, 2003, p. 983). Melissa Knox has argued that *De Profundis* conjures the figure of Bosie making his responses (Knox, 1994, p. 115) and the form of this ostensible dialogue has a distinctly ventriloquial feel as Wilde constructs the voice of the respondent and imposes it upon him.

As mentioned above, Wilde was generally considered to have exercised a dangerous influence upon the young and impressionable Douglas but the narrative voice of the prison letter vehemently refutes this assumption:

> I blame myself for allowing an unintellectual friendship, a friendship whose primary aim was not the creation and contemplation of beautiful things, to entirely dominate my life [...] The basis of character is will-power, and my will-power became absolutely subject to yours [...] I had allowed you to sap my strength of character. (Wilde, 2003, pp. 981–5)

Contrary to the construction of Wilde as influencer and Bosie as influenced, this quotation stages a reversal of their respective positions. Wilde casts his self in the role of the utterly dominated. His comment resounds with a master/slave imbalance of power that is reminiscent of Basil's obsession with Dorian Gray, leading him to be uncannily 'possessed' by the young man's personality. Wilde portrays his self as completely enthralled by Douglas and his former companion is figured as quasi-vampiric in this exercise of influence, 'sapping' his partner's character and artistic abilities. Despite such claims, Wilde's turn of phrase shrewdly reinstates his own sense of agency. This process of domination/subjection only occurred, according to Wilde, because *he* allowed it and the dichotomy between activity/passivity is startlingly unravelled. Although Douglas can play the role of manipulator to Wilde's position of puppet-prisoner, these roles can be constructed in alternative ways. Wilde's gloss of their relationship can be understood as the 'puppet' of the relationship rebelling against its ventriloquial master and taking on a voice and role of its own.

Wilde's narrative retells an unpleasant scenario in his relationship with Douglas in which Bosie apparently refused to tend to Wilde on his sick-bed. A specific phrase in a previous letter exchanged between the men resonates throughout *De Profundis*: '*When you are not on your pedestal you are not interesting. The next time you are ill I will go away at once*' (Wilde, 2003, pp. 993–4). Wilde explains the effect of his statement: 'How often have those words come back to me in the wretched solitary cell of the various prisons I have been sent to. I have said them to myself over and over again, and seen in them, I hope unjustly, some of the secret of your strange silence' (Wilde, 2003, p. 994). Wilde finds himself haunted by the words of his beloved and compelled to repeat them. Douglas' words function as a judgement on Wilde's current predicament and his compulsion to duplicate Douglas' voice constitutes a form of recitation; Bosie has succeeded in imposing his voice upon Wilde. Wilde's repetition is also a transformation as he uses the phrase not to indict himself but to reconstruct and thus demonstrate his lover's cruelty. Through transcribing these words, Wilde immortalizes his erstwhile friend's failings and punishes Douglas for his silence. In a slippage between self and other, the possessed Wilde becomes the possessor, and the dummy becomes the ventriloquist.

There is an important motif of doubling in *De Profundis*. Wilde recounts his reaction to the death of Bosie's brother, and explains: 'I opened to you my house, my home, my heart. I made your sorrow mine also, that you might have help in bearing it' (Wilde, 2003, p. 995). This statement suggests that the motivation for Wilde's emotional identification with Bosie is selflessness as he bore the burden of Bosie's grief as an expression of love. He subsequently continues this theme:

> Do you think that I would not have let you know that if you suffered, I was suffering too: that if you wept, there were tears in my eyes also: and that if you lay in the house of bondage and were despised of men, I out of my griefs had built a house in which to dwell until your coming. (Wilde, 2003, p. 1015)

Wilde imagines himself engulfing his lover's suffering through the process of doubling. This is, of course, a hypothetical amalgamation of self and other. Wilde uses the imagined example of his own emotional connection to Douglas to castigate the younger man for his callous silence with regards to Wilde's sorrow. Bosie is thus figured as an unruly double, an alternative self who has accepted Wilde's transgressions of the boundaries of subjectivity without reciprocation. Wilde provides an example of doubling marred through unequal affection, leading to an imbalance of power between the ostensible 'doubles'. The double motif is a utopian vision of an ideal relationship that is ultimately thwarted by the unanticipated behaviour of the beloved, but unruly, other.

In the process of berating Douglas with memories of his bad behaviour, Wilde pauses momentarily:

> It makes me feel sometimes as if you yourself had been merely a puppet worked by some secret and unseen hand to bring terrible events to a terrible issue. *But puppets themselves have passions.* They will bring a new plot into what they are presenting, and twist the ordered issue of vicissitude to suit some whim or appetite of their own. (Wilde, 2003, p. 997, my emphasis)

Wilde's invocation of the puppet with an uncanny desire of its own is significant, emphasizing the tension between agency and subjection that permeates the text. Although *De Profundis* utilizes the former connection between Wilde and Douglas as an attempt to exercise an influence upon the intended recipient and to reinstate Wilde's own agency in the relationship, here his words acknowledge the limitations of control that the self can have over the other. Wilde's letter frequently articulates his sense of powerlessness and manipulation at the hands of others – his own 'puppet' status – and yet also positions Douglas in a 'puppet' role through his imposition of voice and persona upon his lover. The statement 'But puppets themselves have passions' expresses the perpetual instability of the respective roles of ventriloquist/dummy, master/puppet. The results of an attempt to assert individual agency or to control the beloved subject are never wholly predictable.

4.3 Conclusion

This chapter has sought to demonstrate the centrality of ventriloquial imagery in the work of Oscar Wilde, and the ways in which Wilde's understanding of ventriloquism highlights the queer potential of ventriloquists and dummies that is frequently suppressed in nineteenth-century ventriloquist narratives. My opening reading of 'The Harlot's House' outlined a theme of gender ambiguity in the presentation of puppets which resurfaces in *The Picture of Dorian Gray* and *De Profundis*. Although Henry Wotton appears to adhere to the characteristics of the masculine Victorian ventriloquist, his desire to influence his dummy Dorian via the medium of a seductive voice also echoes the traditionally feminine role of the Siren. Furthermore, the practice of ventriloquial influence is revealed to be fluid and negotiable; the ostensible dummy can in turn influence his master and the ventriloquist might lose control of his possession. Ventriloquism in *Dorian Gray* has the potential to engender multiple identities and voices which transgress the static dummy/ventriloquist dichotomy of power and imbue the puppet with an agency of his own. My reading of *De Profundis* focused on Wilde's prison letter as a ventriloquial strategy of producing voice when it has ostensibly been denied. Wilde recites the script of his silencing, manipulation and objectification – the condition of the dummy – and yet the very process of recitation re-constructs the queer voice that has been muted. Like *Dorian Gray*, *De Profundis* articulates the ways in which the influencer might become influenced; through positioning himself as the puppet of Bosie's desires, Wilde constructs an alternative subjectivity via his former lover and this process of ventriloquial doubling reiterates the trope of the unruly dummy which exposes the relationships of influence in *Dorian Gray* as being unpredictable.

Crucially, ventriloquism emerges as an ambivalent strategy for generating agency for 'passionate puppets'. The problem with ventriloquial negotiations of agency and desire resides in the very malleability of these roles. Dorian might exceed the expectations of his master but still finds himself enthralled to the influence of his 'copy' in the form of the portrait. Wilde as a silenced 'puppet' of the prison system might reposition his self as the queer ventriloquial manipulator of Douglas and yet there are limits to his control over such a 'passionate puppet'. The manipulator is still subject to manipulation. Despite the way in which both texts allow the role of feminized dummy to be performed by men, challenge the heteronormative masculinity of the ventriloquist and thus trouble the gendering of Victorian ventriloquism to an extent, the representation of women in *Dorian Gray* is still dependent on misogynistic scripts of women's susceptibility to 'copying'. The novel cannot imagine Sibyl Vane as a serious threat to Wotton's ventriloquial prowess and Sibyl is punished for being a 'puppet' with too much passion. There is a marked absence of women from *De Profundis*. It is only Bosie's mother who has a brief voice in the letter, but this voice is conceptualized as an oppressive force which will 'speak for' the silenced Wilde. Interestingly, Wilde's understanding of how the historical record will privilege some voices over others, and his palpable desire to 're-voice' history, anticipates the compulsion of some neo-Victorian texts to similarly recover the silenced subjects of the nineteenth century. Chapter 3 identified a selection of novels that engage in such neo-Victorian ventriloquisms, and this chapter has suggested a queered script of Victorian ventriloquism. I want to turn now to two of Sarah Waters' neo-Victorian novels – *Tipping the Velvet* and *Affinity* – to consider how this queer script will in turn be re-cited in Waters' dialogue with Victorian gender and ventriloquism.

5
Sexual Re-scripting: Ventriloquial Repetitions and Transformations in Sarah Waters' *Tipping the Velvet* and *Affinity*

Academic criticism on the work of Sarah Waters often approvingly lists her intertextual allusions to Victorian authors,[1] and yet Waters has occasionally expressed concern about her sense of indebtedness to prior authorial voices. In an interview with John O'Connell for *Time Out* magazine, she remarks: 'I've got a slight anxiety that all I can do as a writer is ventriloquize, that I haven't got a voice of my own' (O'Connell, 2006, p. 18). Interestingly, Waters' invocation of the term 'ventriloquism' seems to hint at the pejorative connotations of the metaphor discussed in the Introduction and Chapter 1. She is either figured as a dummy-author, spoken through by the voices of her forebears and reciting a script that is not her own, or as a ventriloquist-author condemned to mimic or even steal the voices of others in a manner reminiscent of the distant voice ventriloquy considered in Chapter 2. However, Mark Wormald's chapter on Sarah Waters' neo-Victorian novels comments upon 'the literary and cultural paradigms of a period Waters knows well enough to ventriloquize and thus to test' (Wormald, 2006, p. 187). His remark echoes this book's sustained argument that ventriloquial repetition has the potential to be interpreted as a form of critique or transformation. Indeed, elsewhere Waters has conceptualized her interest in Victorian authors, specifically Oscar Wilde, as a way of 'talking back' to the silencing of same-sex desire from patriarchal versions of history. In an interview about her first novel *Tipping the Velvet*, she explains: 'A lot of work has been done on Oscar Wilde and his milieu [...] I wanted to steal it for a lesbian agenda' (Cohu, 2002, p. 23) and in a later article in *The Times* she again draws a contrast between the respective histories of gay men and lesbian women:

> Gays have such an obvious historical record – think about Oscar Wilde [...] I think it is because male homosexuality was illegal; men

114

were arrested for it, executed for it. Whereas women were under the radar a little. In a way, it was always easier for the mainstream to ignore them. (Millard, 2008, p. 5)[2]

Waters' distinction between the histories of queer men and women is significant, for, as I explained in the last chapter, the queer recasting of ventriloquial relationships in Wilde's *The Picture of Dorian Gray* does not address the patriarchal assumption that the origin and agency of 'voice' cannot be located in a female speaker. In this chapter, I argue that Waters' *Tipping the Velvet* and *Affinity* are not only addressing the silencing of women in Victorian ventriloquist narratives such as *The Bostonians* and *Trilby* but also producing a critical repetition of Wilde's male-centred queer script of ventriloquial power relationships.

I position *Tipping the Velvet* as engaging in a dialogue with *The Picture of Dorian Gray* and, in part, *Trilby*, whereas *Affinity* 'talks back' to both *De Profundis* and *The Bostonians*; metatextually, as a form of neo-Victorian ventriloquism, and also in relation to the theme of ventriloquism in these texts. Although I emphasize the ways in which Waters' re-voicings offer a subversion of the heteronormative and patriarchal aspects of Victorian ventriloquism, I will also remain attuned to Waters' ambivalence about the extent to which ventriloquial repetition can operate as a liberatory transformation. A key theme of this chapter is whether Waters' neo-Victorian ventriloquisms challenge patriarchal history or ultimately repeat and reiterate the tropes of her Victorian precursors. As I emphasized in Chapter 4's discussion of Oscar Wilde, queer ventriloquism is not necessarily subversive. *Tipping the Velvet*, in Emily Jeremiah's words, is a queer bildungsroman (Jeremiah, 2007, p. 136). The novel tells the story of Nancy Astley's journey from Whitstable oyster girl, to male impersonator on the music hall stage with her partner Kitty, to 'rent-boy' on the streets of London, the 'kept woman' of her wealthy lover Diana to socialist convert with her lover Florence. A Butlerian gender trouble repeatedly emerges as Nancy re-cites and subverts the heteronormative script of gender to express the development of her queer subjectivity. More specifically, my reading concentrates on the ventriloquial imagery that permeates this text to articulate the tension between subversion and reiteration of patriarchal, heteronormative gender in the novel. At times, the women of the novel might be figured as an 'unruly dummies' that exceed the manipulations of the script of heteronormative, patriarchal gender and thus the gendered imbalance of ventriloquist/dummy is challenged. However, Nancy can never wholly free herself from the machinations of gendered scripts and is repeatedly returned to a 'dummy' role which constrains her agency and autonomy. It is during Nan's time as a 'renter' – both on the streets of London and in the household of Diana – that Waters' ventriloquial dialogue with Wilde's *Dorian Gray* becomes most apparent. Waters 'talks back' to the homosocial world of *Dorian Gray* by giving a voice to female coteries of same-sex desire. My analysis of the text questions the extent to which such a re-voicing actually constitutes a transformation, for Nancy's relationship with Diana begins to emulate that of Svengali and Trilby and ironically retains some of the misogyny of Wilde's novel. I suggest this is a self-conscious strategy on the part of Waters, articulating her anxieties about the subversive potential of repeating Victorian scripts.

My reading of *Affinity* considers the novel's use of a central trope in the history of ventriloquism and gender – nineteenth-century spirit mediumship – to articulate the ambivalent agency produced through the social performance of displaced voice. *Affinity* is set in London during 1870s, telling the story of the relationship between Margaret Prior, a lonely, middle-class, single woman, and Selina Dawes, a disgraced medium serving time in jail for fraud, via a series of diary extracts. The women meet when Margaret volunteers as a 'lady visitor' at Millbank prison, and a distinctly queer partnership blossoms as Margaret becomes drawn into Selina's shadowy world of séance rooms and spirit voices. Selina is not all that she seems, however, and Margaret is unwittingly manipulated by the prisoner and Selina's lover, Ruth Vigers, who conspires to assist in Selina's ultimate escape from jail. Revisiting Chapter 2's commentary on *The Bostonians*, I suggest that *Affinity* is in various ways an overtly queer recasting of this ventriloquism narrative. Margaret struggles to produce a 'voice' beyond the influence of her father (and mother) and her burgeoning relationship with Selina offers a parallel to Olive Chancellor's desire for Verena Tarrant. *Affinity* thus echoes *The Bostonians'* themes of influence, possession and control. The role of the patriarchal puppet-master is supplanted by the character of Ruth Vigers, a queer reappropriation of the manipulative impulses of Basil Ransom. I also emphasize *Affinity*'s dialogue with *De Profundis*, for both texts engage with images of manipulation, doubling and imprisonment. Despite the centrality of desire between women in *Affinity*, we see that the ventriloquial dynamics of puppets and possession express the limitations of the potential relationships between these women. Ventriloquism emerges as a strategy of agency within constraints, dramatized by Margaret's simultaneous emulation/undermining of her father's voice and Selina's performance of passivity that masks her own agenda yet still leaves her vulnerable to manipulation. The ventriloquial exchanges of *Affinity*, whether through mediumship, prisoner/visitor relationships or erotic power games, suggest that the roles of 'ventriloquist' and 'dummy' are available for appropriation and resignification. Margaret, Selina and Ruth each find ventriloquial strategies for expressing their desires in arenas where it is ostensibly silenced and utilize the fluidity of ventriloquist/dummy, master/puppet relationships to articulate personal autonomy. Such moments of autonomy do not necessarily translate into a substantial challenge to gendered inequalities. The women manipulate each other, emulate patriarchal discourses and run the risk of being returned to the 'dummy' role that they have attempted to subvert.

Speaking sexual silences in *Tipping the Velvet*

It has become a critical commonplace to note the influence of Judith Butler's theories of gender as performance on the music hall world of male impersonation as depicted in *Tipping the Velvet*. Even the name of the male impersonator that captures Nancy's heart – Kitty Butler – offers a knowing tribute to the presence of queer theory in the novel. Kitty's performance recites the script of Victorian masculinity in her clothes, gestures and voice, but also incorporates her female body in the shape of her 'rounded' bosom, stomach and hips and her feminine gender in her 'two inch heels' (Waters, 1999, p. 13). She represents the dissonance between the performer's sex, the performer's gender and the gender of the performance which Judith Butler recognizes as drag performance's parodic exposure of the lack of 'originary' sex/gender (Butler, 1999, p. 175). Furthermore, it is fissures in Kitty's act, the incoherence of sex, gender and performance, which allow queer desire to become manifest and 'speak' to Nancy in the audience. It is this concept of corporeal acts as a form of language which is interesting from a ventriloquial perspective, as in the first section of *Tipping the Velvet* we can understand onstage gender performance as a way of producing a queer speech which ostensibly has no 'voice' in late Victorian society. Nancy's attempt to articulate her attraction towards Kitty generates a negative response from her sister Alice and our narrator acknowledges: 'I knew at once that I shouldn't have spoken; that I should have been as dumb and cunning with her as the rest of them [...] I had said too much' (Waters, 1999, p. 20). Here Nancy recognizes that there is protection in silence; to speak same-sex desire is dangerous in this context and she must remain an ostensibly heterosexual 'dummy'.

It is only when Nancy and Kitty become lovers and Nancy becomes part of Kitty's act that she can find a covert way of speaking her desire. She equates making love to Kitty with their exchanges onstage:

> beyond our songs, our steps, our bits of business with coins and canes and flowers, there was a private language, in which we held an endless, delicate exchange of which the crowd knew nothing. This was the language not of the tongue but of the body, its vocabulary the pressure of a finger or a palm, the nudging of a hip, the holding or breaking of a gaze, that said, *You are too slow – you go too fast – not there, but here – that's good – that's better!* (Waters, 1999, p. 128)

Public performance is doubled with private sexual performance; there is a bodily script to be repeated in both scenarios and the body becomes a substitute for the voice, for even in the throes of passion the lovers must be 'in silence, [...] with an ear half-cocked for the sound of footsteps on the stairs' (Waters, 1999, p. 127). The silence – countered with the language of the body – imbues the women with a degree of protection and even agency, for the 'doubleness' of their stage act becomes a strategy of queer ventriloquism, of displacing the vocal declaration of desire into a script of masculinity to which the women 'talk back' via their subversive repetitions. Their performance does communicate to certain members of the audience. Nancy perceives that some of their female fans respond to the secret voicings: 'These girls sent letters – letters, like their stage door manners, full of curious excesses or ellipses; letters that awed, repelled and drew me, all at once' (Waters, 1999, p. 128). Even the girls who are susceptible to the influence of their performance cannot find words to articulate their interest; these utterances are either too frank, 'excessive', or muted. The effects of Nancy's and Kitty's act are unpredictable in this way; the queer potential lies in the eye/ear of the beholder/auditor and yet leaves the dichotomy between heterosexual speech/queer silence intact.[3]

Kitty is particularly resistant to a queer interpretation of their act. At one fateful performance a drunk man 'reads' (or hears) something more in the show:

> 'Why, they're nothing but a couple of – a couple of *toms!*' He put the whole force of his voice into it – the word that Kitty had once whispered to me, flinching and shuddering as she said it! It sounded louder at that moment that the blast of a cornet – seemed to bounce from one wall of the hall to another, like a bullet from a

sharp-shooter's act gone wrong. *Toms!* At the sound of it, the audience gave a great collective flinch. There was a sudden hush; the shouts became mumbles, the shrieks all tailed away [...] Kitty had stiffened; and then she had stumbled [...] her mouth flew open. Now it shut. Now it trembled. Her voice – her lovely, shining, soaring voice – faltered and died. (Waters, 1999, pp. 140–1)

The perils of articulating queer desire via performance are amplified at this moment. The voice of patriarchal oppression which equates gender dissonance with sexual dissidence resounds with a violent power – the man's utterance becomes a phallic gun – and steals the sound of not only the audience, but also Kitty. Her ventriloquial 'talking back' to the script of gender is silenced by this interpellation and she is reduced to the role of mute dummy, opening and shutting her mouth with no response. This scene represents the limitations of the subversive potential of male impersonation in the context of the Victorian music hall; the bodily language, the coding of same-sex desire, must remain muted, as speaking this script will expose the women to ridicule, scrutiny and danger. Kitty's repetitions engender the unexpected repetition of the word 'toms!' as it echoes around the music hall. She has lost control of her performance and must be spoken for by a hostile heteronormative audience, and the fine line between subversive performance and restrictive performativity is expressed by the ventriloquial dynamics of gendered speech and silence.

It is thus telling that shortly afterwards Kitty will seek the cover of a heterosexual relationship with their manager, Walter. On discovering Kitty's deception Nan leaves the world of the music hall and finds protection by wearing her men's clothes on the streets of London. This strategy of off-stage performance inaugurates her entry into another silenced world of covert desire. Dressed as a young man, she is propositioned by a man who, despite his non-heterosexual predilections, reminds her of Walter: 'I spoke – but it was as if someone else were doing the speaking, not me. I said: "All right. I'll do it. I'll – touch you; for a sov"' (Waters, 1999, p. 198). Nancy's response is couched in ventriloquial terms. She is distanced from her utterance, the agency behind her voice is understood as coming from elsewhere. Aside from reiterating the performative aspect of Nancy's new role – she is repeating a script over which she has limited control – the displacement of Nancy's voice might also remind us of the metatextual ventriloquism at play in this section of the novel. This is the Wildean world of customers and renters, the script that Waters has 'stolen' for a women-centred queer agenda. Nancy explains her motivation behind her life as a renter: 'I first donned trousers to avoid men's eyes; to feel myself the object of *these* men's gaze's, however, these men who thought I was like them, *like that* – well, that was not be pestered; it was to be, in some queer way, *revenged*' (Waters, 1999, p. 201, emphasis in original). Nancy's performance as a male renter challenges the heteronormative male gaze, but also the economy of the queer male gaze. Although she is cast into the role of 'object', this 'dummy' has an ulterior agenda; to deceive all men who would make objects of vulnerable subjects on the streets of the city, heterosexual or otherwise. As my above reading of Waters' recognition of the differences between male and female queer history demonstrates, same-sex desire between women is doubly silenced by both heteronormativity and patriarchal privilege. Nancy's 'revenge' through reciting a male-authored script offers an allegory for Waters' own appropriation of this subculture for her re-voicing of the Wildean underworld that includes the women who have been silenced as sexual agents. Ironically, however, Nancy's subversion appears to operate only on a personal and individual basis. She bemoans the lack of an audience for her queer performance: 'a bold and knowing eye that saw how well I played my part, how gulled and humbled was my foolish, trustful partner' (Waters, 1999, p. 206). Again, subversion can only be in the eye of the beholder, and hence Nancy's 'talking back' to her sexual objectification falls on deaf ears.

However, there actually is an audience in the form of Diana Lethaby, whose cruising of the renters from the elevated position of her carriage is reminiscent of Dorian's nocturnal escapades that are hinted at in Wilde's novel. Louisa Yates remarks that Diana Lethaby has 'a queer sexuality reminiscent of Oscar Wilde – modern, yet subject to resolutely Victorian morals, while being allowed to flourish in the underworld' (Yates, 2009/2010, p. 194). In contrast to the silence that must cloak Nancy's relationship with Kitty, Diana is explicit about her intentions towards Nancy and yet, as Yates' comment suggests, her queer 'voice' can only be heard within the secretive confines of the underworld of same-sex desire. Nancy ponders the performative inflection of their sexualized conversation on the way to Diana's opulent home: 'Here we were, this strange lady and I [...] playing whore and trick so well we might have been reciting a dialogue from some handbook of tartery!' (Waters, 1999, p. 235). Diana's acknowledgement of Nan's performance seems to highlight the transgressive potential of Nan's gender-crossing and affords her the opportunity to resignify the heteronormative and patriarchal script of 'whore' and 'trick' from a queer perspective. Or does it? Nancy acknowledges that they are 'reciting', which implies that there is no other way to express this desire than through the trappings of traditionally patriarchal power imbalances. In this sense, Diana might be understood as being just as dictated to and manipulated by patriarchal discourse as her 'whore' and yet the inequality of power in their relationship becomes increasingly marked.

Nancy accepts the role of being Diana's mistress, to be dressed as a young man and presented to the knowing audience of her 'Sapphic' friends. Diana and her coterie are all wealthy, leisured women and the vocabulary of their desire has various Wildean echoes. When first introduced to Nancy, Maria Jex quizzes her about the night she met Diana: 'She herself will tell us nothing – only [...] that the moon was reeling through the clouds like a drunken woman looking for lovers. Tell us, Miss Nancy, tell us, do! *Was* the moon really reeling through the clouds, like a drunken woman looking for her lovers?' (Waters, 1999, p. 273–4). This is a reference to Wilde's play *Salomé*, a direct echo of the words of the insane patriarch Herod (Wilde, 2003, p. 592). Nancy also dresses up and performs as Salomé at one of Diana's all-women parties (Waters, 1999, p. 281). Furthermore, another friend of Diana's, Dickie, comes to her costume party dressed as Dorian Gray (Waters, 1999, p. 307). The text performs an act of neo-Victorian ventriloquism as Wilde's words and characters are re-cited, manipulated into signifiers of queer women's sexual pleasure.[4] Emily Jeremiah has suggested that 'Waters's novel [...] eroticizes gender, but queerly, in opposition to heterosexism' (Jeremiah, 2007, p. 137). Jeremiah's comment rests on the assumption that queer eroticism is necessarily in opposition to heterosexism, but on examining the power dynamics of Diana's relationship with Nancy the repetition of gendered scripts comes to represent a reiteration of social inequalities instead of a subversive opposition.

The character of Diana provides the most recognizable repetition of the script of the Victorian ventriloquist, and Nancy's commentary on their relationship emphasizes Diana's manipulative powers:

I could help none of it. It was all Diana's doing [...] When she spoke, they listened. It was her voice, I think, that snared them – those low, musical tones which had once lured me from my random midnight wanderings into the heart of her own dark world. Again and again I heard arguments crumble at a cry or a murmur from Diana's throat; again and again the scattered conversations of a crowded room would falter and die, as one speaker after another surrendered the slender threads of some anecdote or fancy to catch at the more compelling cadences of hers. Her boldness was contagious. Women came to her, and grew giddy. She was like a singer, shivering glasses. (Waters, 1999, pp. 281–2)

Like Henry Wotton, Diana's voice is the instrument of her ventriloquial influence. It possesses the same 'musical tones' that prove so pervasive and persuasive in Dorian's manipulation and it has the same penetrative abilities. Diana is a queer Siren, Trilby and Svengali all in one, able to 'snare' and seduce her auditors, perform with the verbal dexterity of an opera singer and to silence those who listen. This is a compelling voice, but also malignant – 'like a cancer' (Waters, 1999, p. 282) – and it is significant that Diana's version of ventriloquism is actually represented as being more pernicious than Wotton's. She will not allow multiple voices/influences to exist in her presence and her voice exercises a violence upon the listeners; the utterances of others must 'crumble' or even 'die'. The alteration of the script of Victorian ventriloquism comes in the absence of men; the world of Felicity Place is dominated by a queer female ventriloquist but one whose ventriloquial prowess is dictated by forebears such as Svengali and Wotton.

Of course, a ventriloquist in this mould must have her dummy, and it becomes progressively clearer that it is Nancy who is cast in this role. Diana dictates the terms of her existence: when she will perform sexually, how she will dress, when she will appear in public. As Diana dresses her for her first public outing, Nancy admires her new costume in the mirror: 'I looked not like myself at all, but like some living picture, a blond lord or angel whom a jealous artist had captured' (Waters, 1999, p. 270). The allusion is clear; Nancy has become Dorian to Diana's Henry, the object of desire, but also of manipulation. Although Nancy's performance under the tutelage of Diana imbues her with a sexual confidence that was lacking in her relationship with Kitty, her agency in this situation is constantly in question. When Nancy responds wittily to Maria's introduction, the latter is surprised: '"But it speaks! [...] All this" – she gestured to my face, my costume – "and the creature even speaks!"' (Waters, 1999, p. 273). Speech is seemingly not required from this dummy, but when she does answer back to Maria it affords Nancy no reprieve from her objectification at the hands of Diana and her friends. Maria does not even grant Nancy a gender; she is 'it', a 'creature' to be admired, desired, but certainly not listened to. Queer ventriloquism in Diana's world only serves to underscore inequalities of class, and the callous use of working-class female performers such as Sibyl in *Dorian Gray* is reiterated by Maria's dehumanizing appraisal of Nancy's charms.

The consequences of Nancy's attempt to 'talk back' to Diana's machinations – she insults her guests at her puppet-mistress's birthday party, ending up in bed with Diana's maid – are abrupt. She is expelled from Felicity Place, semi-clothed and bleeding from a wound inflicted by her former lover. Nancy seeks refuge in the home of a woman she briefly met during her renter days: Florence Banner, a committed socialist living with her brother and the child of her dead friend. In attempting to appeal for shelter, Nancy finds herself slipping into an alternative performance. Florence asks whether she is 'in trouble', euphemistically wondering whether she is pregnant: '"In trouble? I –" I couldn't help it; it was as if she was handing me the play text, for me to read it back to her. "I *was* in trouble [...] but the gent fixed that when he beat me"' (Waters, 1999, p. 355). Nancy's recital of the script of battered, abused woman does have some element of truth considering her exploitation at the hands of Diana, but it also demonstrates her predilection for copying or repetition. She readily responds, almost involuntarily, to the opportunity to repeat the words of another and although this will secure her pity and protection it still underscores her dummy-like condition. In a crucial passage, Nancy expresses her burgeoning desire for Florence in explicitly ventriloquial terms: 'With every step I took away from her, the movement at my heart and between my legs grew more defined: I felt like a ventriloquist, locking his protesting dolls into a trunk' (Waters, 1999, p. 403). In Nancy's attempt to master her queer passion and adhere to a script of heterosexuality, she positions her queer 'voice' as being like an unruly dummy that refuses to be silenced. Although she has been in various ventriloquial scenarios throughout the novel, it is only with Florence that Nancy recognizes that queer voices can be heard and do not have to be confined to coded performances at the music hall or puppet poses behind locked doors.

Towards the end of the novel, Florence has organized a socialist rally in a local park and her brother is required to give a speech to the assembled crowd. He stumbles over his words, and Nancy assists in the recitation, providing yet another powerful performance. Flo is unimpressed: 'I should like it very much [...] if I thought that Nancy really meant her speeches, and wasn't just repeating them like – a dam' parrot!' (Waters, 1999, p. 461). As explored in Chapter 4, the ventriloquial image of parrot repetition has misogynistic connotations in *The Picture of Dorian Gray* but Florence's usage is an expression of anxiety over whether Nancy actually possesses a 'true' voice. This quandary is not easily answered. In response to this condemnation, Nancy responds: 'you were right, what you said before, about that address I gave with Ralph. It wasn't mine,

I didn't mean the words – at least, not then, when I said them [...] Oh! I feel like I've been repeating other people's speeches all my life. Now, when I want to make a speech of my own, I find I hardly know how' (Waters, 1999, p. 471). Nan realizes that her previous performances – which are intrinsically bound up with her previous relationships – have always been following a script authored by another. She is revealed to have been a perpetual dummy and even when seemingly creating her own 'performances' she has been subject to performative scripts of gender and sexual behaviour. Is this the moment when this unruly dummy will finally realize an agency of her own, will create her own script to articulate her desire for Flo? As the lovers reunite, 'there came a muffled cheer, and a rising ripple of applause' (Waters, 1999, p. 472) and Jeannette King's gloss of the novel offers an optimistic interpretation of this final scene, as the cheers 'are a symbolic acknowledgement that she can now act as herself in public, and use her own voice' (King, 2005, p. 153).[5] Significantly, however, we do not quite hear this voice, for this is where the novel ends. As in the promise of Mignon's and the Princess' unheard songs in *Nights at the Circus*, Waters stops short of offering us an example of what Nancy's 'real' voice will be when it is freed from ventriloquial influence. Waters' strategy of 'talking back' to Victorian ventriloquism by repeating the 'master' voices of this script highlights the uncertainty of repetition as a subversive strategy, but, like the absence of Nancy's new voice at the end of *Tipping the Velvet*, also recognizes that stepping outside of this system is not an option. We must recite the scripts or roles that we have inherited and the liberatory potential comes in the audience's interpretation.

Power in passivity? Queer female ventriloquism in *Affinity*

The concept of mediumship has proved to be a generative discourse in neo-Victorian literature, and Sarah Waters' *Affinity* is one of a cluster of texts which utilizes the figure of the female spirit-medium to consider issues such as gender, agency, sexuality and class in the Victorian era.[6] Furthermore, spiritualism and mediumship have received a considerable amount of attention in neo-Victorian criticism, most notably in Tatiana Kontou's monograph which figures the neo-Victorian author as a medium herself, channelling the voices of the dead but also constructing a Victorian 'afterlife' and thus 'alter[ing] our relationship with the past' (Kontou, 2009, p. 5). Such an enterprise clearly has similarities with my ventriloquial metaphor; indeed, Diana Wallace has argued that 'the female medium becomes a suggestive figure for the historical novelist herself, ventriloquizing the voices of the past' (Wallace, 2005, p. 208) and Kontou also identifies the connection between mediumship and ventriloquism (Kontou, 2009, p. 99). As neither critic offers much explanation of what 'ventriloquism' might mean in the context of nineteenth-century mediumship and gender, I want to pause to consider the ventriloquial dynamics of mediumship before pursuing this theme in relation to *Affinity*.[7]

As outlined in Chapter 1, the medium at a séance is apparently spoken through by spirits and the appellation 'medium' is, of course, appropriate in terms of articulating the role of passivity that the medium must fulfil; s/he is apparently only a conduit or instrument for the spirit utterances. Despite this ostensible submissiveness, the medium does not completely lose her own voice as she must direct the messages that she receives and offer them to the séance participants. The attendees at the séance must also impose their own understandings of these 'spirit' messages upon the medium and so we see that there are multiple voices at work in this supposedly passive/active exchange. The medium, posing as a mere dummy for the voices of others, potentially produces a spectrum of voices and is therefore performing the roles of both 'dummy' and ventriloquist. Alex Owen notes that although there were male mediums in the nineteenth century, mediumship was generally considered to be a feminine accomplishment; women were recognized as being especially gifted in this area (Owen, 1989, p. 1). Owen explains the paradoxical power/passivity embodied by the figure of the female medium:

> It promoted a species of feminine power whilst at the same time interacting with contemporary concepts of acceptable womanhood [...] Spiritualist mediums became the 'repositories', the 'vessels' [...] and what is vital here is that spiritualists assumed that it was innate femininity, in particular female passivity, which facilitated this renunciation of self and cultivation of mediumistic powers. Passivity, or the lack of masculine will-power, might have been construed as that which made women the gentle, retiring creatures of prescriptive literature – but it was also, for spiritualists, the very quality which facilitated spirit communication. They therefore privileged passivity and sought to develop it. *Passivity became, in the spiritualist vocabulary, synonymous with power.* (Owen, 1989, pp. 9–10, my emphasis)

Owen's concluding sentence is important. The agency of the female medium is inaugurated by a denial of agency. Mediumship, for the female subject, is founded upon the patriarchally-prescribed values of 'natural' femininity, colludes with the Victorian status quo and therefore would appear to have limited potential for thinking about the development of voice/agency. Owen's analysis posits, however, that female mediumship can be associated with an, albeit paradoxical and covert, assertion of social power:

> During any séance led by a female medium it was a woman who directed the proceedings and acted as communicator and interpreter. This was a direct contravention of the female role in polite society, that of the dutiful woman whose required 'stillness' ensured strictly controlled conduct and limited and contained access to speech. Within spiritualist circles this same woman became the medium of spirit intercourse, the pivot of spiritualist practice through and with whom the spirits spoke. Utterance was central to mediumship whether it occurred in a séance circle, vicariously through passive writing, and via an inspirational address at the spiritualist gathering, and it effectively confounded the prescriptive virtue of silence. (Owen, 1989, p. 210)

This aptitude for mediumship could imbue a woman with significant social status and financial rewards and thus afforded women a degree of influence in a widely patriarchal society. Owen's emphasis on the centrality of 'voice' and its simultaneous displacement and production underscores the link between mediumship and ventriloquism in relation to gender and agency. Marlene Tromp has championed the nineteenth-century spiritualist movement as offering its female participants the opportunity for subversion of traditional feminine roles (Tromp, 2006) and yet we should be attuned to the ambivalence of mediumship as a strategy for women's 'talking back' to the script of Victorian gender. I want to turn now to *Affinity* to consider how the tension between ventriloquial repetition and transformation is articulated as a theme within the novel and also the Victorian 'voices', in the form of the Victorian script of ventriloquism, which become manifest in Waters' re-citations.

The impulse to produce voice/agency, even when it appears to be silenced, becomes apparent in the opening pages of Margaret's diary when she addresses the disparity between gendered versions of history:

> Pa used to say that any piece of history might be made into a tale: it was only a question of deciding where the tale began, and where

it ended [...] And perhaps, after all, the histories he dealt with were rather easy to sift, like that, to divide up and classify – the great lives, the great works, each one of them neat and gleaming and complete, like metal letters in a box of type. (Waters, 2000, p. 7)

Margaret's statement pluralizes history, suggesting that there is more than one account existing in this academic discipline. The patriarchal weight of the conventional version of history is rendered literal through the invocation of the words of her father. Margaret still does desire the authoritative guidance of her father's voice: 'I wish that Pa was with me now. I would ask him how he would start to write the story I have embarked upon to-day. I would ask him how he would neatly tell the story of a prison – of Millbank prison' (Waters, 2000, p. 7). M. L. Kohlke's interpretation of this passage provides a justifiably pessimistic reading of Margaret's apparent inability to produce her own narrative 'voice':

The female voice [...] lacks the masculine social status to comment authoritatively on historical events [...] Margaret's first diary entry begins not with the autobiographical 'I' but with 'Pa'. Her would-be-historical subjectivity stages itself in the shadow of the dead historian-father. (Kohlke, 2004, p. 157)

Kohlke's juxtaposition of the words 'historian-father' is pertinent, as she relates Margaret's personal relationship with her 'Pa' to the broader social context of the suppression of women's voices in patriarchal history. The conventional narrative of history, for Margaret as a woman living in the 1870s, is inscribed by the word of the 'Father'; his master's voice. She is an intelligent, educated woman and yet her access to learning materials has been mediated by her father. Margaret is known in the British Museum's reading room, for example, as 'Mr George Prior's daughter' (Waters, 2000, p. 58). Margaret's gender erodes her ability to speak authoritatively as her approach to history must be mediated by her father and her social status in the form of a name is defined by the patriarch.

On the other hand, this notion of mediation is ambiguous considering the novel's subsequent focus on spiritualism and mediumship. Kohlke's remarks implicitly suggest that Margaret is cast in the role of medium to the authority of her dead father, allowing the voice of patriarchal history to speak through her and thus position her as 'dummy' to the ventriloquist of his-story. Margaret is keen that she should remain objective in her new diary and suppress her personal, emotional narrative voice (Waters, 2000, p. 70). In spite of Margaret's intentions, as her narrative develops the reader becomes aware that Margaret's subjective, personal voice does emerge. Like a passive dummy-medium she channels the objective, logical voice of the father-historian and yet her own narrative perspective does ultimately manifest. The 'dummy' role in which she initially casts her narrative persona 'talks back' to the reader in unexpected ways. An example of this tension between 'Pa's' and Margaret's voices, or contrasting versions of history, is provided by Margaret's hesitation as to where to begin her account of Millbank prison. She wonders whether her father would approve of starting with her getting dressed in the morning, but quickly dismisses this idea: 'no, of course he would not start the story there, with a lady and her servants, and petticoats and loose hair' (Waters, 2000, p. 7). The value system of 'appropriate' history in opposition to 'irrelevant' details is outlined and this classification is again overtly gendered. As Kohlke notes, the domesticated, feminine sphere of women's fashions and servants is deemed inappropriate and is accordingly suppressed (Kohlke, 2004, p. 157) but, almost inadvertently, *is* provided with a voice. Margaret may dismiss these details but she still does not excise them. The voicing of a personal, feminized version of events is articulated even as it is undermined. There is also a potential double meaning in this image of 'petticoats and loose hair', charged as it is with sexualized connotations. Placed in the private domestic forum of matters that take place between women, these apparently unintentional signifiers of sexuality are imbued with nuances of covert same-sex relationships, a dominant theme of the novel. Silenced history rises, uncannily, to the surface of Margaret's narrative; though denied the authority of paternal sanction, it is still transmitted. Through her attempts to echo the voice of George Prior, Margaret produces a voice that surreptitiously reveals itself to be at odds with the status quo of patriarchal history.

The father-ventriloquist has had a significant role in script of Victorian and neo-Victorian ventriloquism outlined in this book so far; we are reminded of Selah Tarrant who must 'start up' his daughter Verena in *The Bostonians* and also Friedrich Wieck, the Svengali-father who will orchestrate Clara's life. Even when the patriarchal puppet-master is not literally the 'dummy's' father – as in the case of Svengali, Jack Walser, Simon Jordan – there has still been a recurring pattern of men who have the authority to dictate the terms under which women will speak. Although *Affinity* does begin with the voice of the father, I argue that it is Margaret's mother who is soon established as the ventriloquial controller of her daughter. Mrs Prior is an oppressive force in Margaret's life. She encourages Helen, Margaret's former lover and now sister-in-law, to ignore Margaret's stories of Millbank prison (Waters, 2000, p. 29) and similarly dismisses Margaret's voice in a discussion with a family friend about servants (Waters, 2000, p. 32). When Margaret's sister leaves the family home to begin married life, Mrs Prior insists that her older daughter will now read to her at night, thus only permitting her daughter to recite a script that she has approved. Furthermore, Margaret has internalized her mother's dictation of her life to such an extent that it shapes her understanding of her own history. Mrs Prior has generated a heteronormative version of Helen and Margaret's 'friendship'; the women first met at Mr Prior's lectures and 'it was all on Stephen's account that she came here' (Waters, 2000, p. 102). The bonds between women are conveniently substituted for Helen's more appropriate interest in Margaret's brother, and Margaret reflects: 'I have heard the story told that way so many times, I am half-way to believing it myself' (Waters, 2000, p. 103). It is Mrs Prior's voice that has almost convinced Margaret and caused her to also repeat the script of heterosexual love that silences desire between women. The subsequent depiction of Mrs Prior playing with 'a little black doll upon a wire that she was making dance' (Waters, 2000, p. 290) provides an allegory for her role as the puppet-master of Margaret's domestic life.

As Ann Heilmann has suggested, the surveillance, restriction and manipulation of Margaret within her mother's domestic sphere is 'as persistent and relentless as that experienced by the prisoners in Millbank' (Heilmann, 2010, p. 122) and yet Margaret's role in the context of Millbank prison is initially very different. On her first visit to Millbank as a 'Lady visitor' she is allowed to watch the inmates come out into the yard for their exercise time: 'I don't think I ever saw such a queer and impressive sight as they made then, for we watched them from our high window and they looked small – they might have been dolls upon a clock, or beads on a trailing thread' (Waters, 2000, pp. 13–14). The reference to the doll-like qualities of the prisoners is important, emphasizing the extent to which inmates might be manipulated by Millbank's rules and regulations and echoing Wilde's image of his self as a puppet-prisoner in *De Profundis*. The women are objectified, made into puppets of the prison system and this is reiterated by Margaret's reference to a woman she subsequently visits as being 'stiff as a mannequin' (Waters, 2000, p. 21). The process of institutional objectification and the role that Margaret might play in this is emphasized by Mr Shillitoe's remarks: 'If I encounter a difficult woman, he said, I must "make her my special object"' (Waters, 2000, pp. 50–1). Margaret's role as lady visitor places her in a role of power over the prisoners' access to speech. The women are condemned to silence 'unless at the express request of a matron or Visitor' (Waters, 2000, p. 14). Margaret's own 'silencing' is therefore relative; though she fulfils the role of 'dummy' in relation to her mother, she in turn has the power to impose speech upon these women as and when she sees fit. From a gendered perspective, Margaret has the opportunity to appropriate the role of ventriloquist/puppet-master yet this privilege is dependent upon the silencing/manipulation of other women.

Margaret's status as a visitor to the prison is explicitly linked to the exercise of ventriloquial influence: 'Let them see the miserable contrast between her speech, her manners, and their poor ways, and they will grow meek, they will grow softened and subdued [...] It is a matter of influence, of sympathies, of susceptibilities tamed' (Waters, 2000, p. 12). The potential for the prisoner to emulate the visitor's speech patterns and style is emphasized. However, as Jeannette King has also noted, Margaret gradually finds that Selina comes to exercise an influence upon her (King, 2005, p. 83; pp. 85–6). Lying in bed at home, Margaret begins to think of the mysterious medium reciting her prison lessons:

> Dawes is murmuring the queer verses of the wards. Now my mind has caught the words up – I think I shall recite them with her, all night long. What sort of grain best suit stiff soils? What is that acid which dissolves silver? What is *relief*, and how should shadows fall? (Waters, 2000, p. 71)

In a similar way to Wilde's recitation of Bosie's speech in *De Profundis*, Margaret finds herself haunted by the utterances of Selina and thoughts of the prisoner's voice pervade Margaret's most intimate sanctuaries: her bedroom and her diary. It is also notable that Margaret is so focused upon Selina that she wishes to recite the same speech as her. In a ventriloquial motif, she comes to speak in the same voice as her beloved. Nevertheless, this seeming 'repetition' is still a construction of Margaret's narrative and she imposes both a 'voice' and scenario upon Selina. Margaret's dummy-style repetitions are thus actually an enactment of ventriloquial power and Selina is doubly ventriloquized by the dictated speech of the prison education system and Margaret's fantasy.

The depiction of Selina as dummy-medium relies on the abnegation of agency and voice which Owen identifies as symptomatic of the female medium's power: 'It was like losing her self, like having her own self pulled from her' (Waters, 2000, p. 166). Selina's denial of possessing the voices she transmits appears to echo the oratory performances of Verena Tarrant, who repeatedly insists that the voice she produces 'is not *me*' (James, 1998, p. 51). Even so, the dynamics of Selina's 'possession' are more complicated. In a demonstration of her ventriloquial abilities, she gives Margaret a message from her dead father expressing his sorrow at Margaret's suicide attempt. Selina reports his direct speech, and her performance is permeated by the phrase 'He is saying' (Waters, 2000, p. 88). Selina, emulating Margaret's earlier repetition of her father's voice, seemingly recites a script of patriarchal authority and she is penetrated by the ghost of the dead father. However, Margaret's reaction to this act of displaced speech is odd: 'I was terribly afraid that [...] she would begin to speak – would speak of Pa, or *for* him, or *as* him' (Waters, 2000, p. 89, emphasis in original). The slippage between speaking 'of', 'for', or 'as' encapsulates the multiple possibilities of agency behind Selina's utterance but does not locate the source of voice as being simply Mr Prior. Perhaps we can understand Margaret's confusion as the recognition that Selina is not a passive dummy but has a voice of her own. Crucially, the source is not Selina; we ultimately discover that Ruth Vigers, Margaret's servant, Selina's lover and co-conspirator in her ventriloquial deceptions, has been reading Margaret's diary and feeding Selina with information to repeat. In a sense, Margaret herself is the source of this speech, for Selina ventriloquizes Margaret's own private voice in this poly-vocal exchange.

A process of ventriloquial doubling takes place between the women, as Selina comes to speak in Margaret's voice and the boundaries between self and other are transgressed. The roles of prisoner and visitor are clearly demarcated at the beginning of Margaret's diary and yet when she hears of Selina's apparent lack of friends, both inside and outside of prison, she speculates on their comparable isolation: 'what I thought was: *You are like me.* (Waters, 2000, p. 82). Margaret equates Selina's condition of being silenced as a prisoner to her own lack of interaction and social silencing in the outside world. Her supposition, articulated through an imposition upon Selina's identity, is echoed by Selina's subsequent comments: 'We are the same, you and I. We have been cut, two halves, from the same piece of shining matter [...] our flesh is the same' (Waters, 2000, p. 275). Their 'affinity' is expressed as a process of doubling or a shared subjectivity that stands for the supposed perfection of the relationship between the women.

Chapter 4 discussed the trope of the queer double in Wilde's *De Profundis* and the acknowledgement of an alternative self has comparable benefits for Margaret and Selina, allowing Margaret a fantasy identity that is not dependent on her socially prescribed and inhibiting roles of 'daughter' or 'spinster' and providing Selina with a prospective subjectivity beyond the confines of 'prisoner'. As a result of her increasing sense of connection with Selina, Margaret rejects her role of dutiful daughter at her mother's dinner party, informing the group of the harshness of Millbank's regime: 'the words came from me, I seemed to feel the shape and taste of them as they left my mouth [...] they could not have silenced me' (Waters, 2000, p. 255). Her utterances transgress the social propriety of the occasion and Margaret's emphasis on the corporeal experience of her voice – the 'taste' of the words emanating from her body – underscores her ownership of her speech; there is no question as to the origin of voice, 'the words came from me'. However, after agreeing to assist Selina in her escape from prison, the agency behind Margaret's voice becomes more complicated. When her mother pesters her about their impending visit to Margaret's sister's marital home, she responds and 'perhaps it was Selina, speaking for me! [...] "I'm not a serving-girl, to be reprimanded and dismissed"' (Waters, 2000, p. 295). Margaret refuses the agency behind her rebellious speech; she imagines that Selina must be the ventriloquial force behind her words. Margaret is beginning to lose her sense of independent subjectivity under Selina's influence, becoming her mouth-piece and the puppet that will be used to orchestrate the prisoner's escape from Millbank. Her dismissal of 'serving-girls' as being subject to verbal instruction is of great consequence considering the way in which she has unwittingly been manipulated by her own servant, and indicates her class-based sense of entitlement to agency which is undermined dramatically as the novel progresses.

Selina has an ambiguous status as both dummy and ventriloquist in the novel. Her performance as the 'passive' medium of the spirits is a covert way of producing voice and influence, but there is another, more material, presence which dictates the terms of her mediumship. Her spirit guide is named 'Peter Quick' and the following excerpt is taken from Selina's diary, recounting an incident where Selina and 'Peter' are tutoring a young woman, Miss Isherwood, to develop her spiritualist abilities. 'Peter' dictates the order of the events:

'You must [...] be a servant of the spirits, you must become a plastic instrument for the spirits' own hands. You must let your spirit be *used*, your prayer must always be *May I be used*. Say that, Selina'. I said it, then he said to Miss Isherwood 'Tell her to say it'. She said 'Say it Miss Dawes' & I said again 'May I be used'. He said 'Do you see? My medium must do as she is bid. You think she is awake but she is entranced. Tell her to do another thing'. I heard Miss Isherwood swallow, then she said 'Will you stand up, Miss Dawes?' but Peter said at once 'You must not ask Will you, you must command her'. Miss Isherwood said then *'Stand up Miss Dawes!'* and I stood, & Peter said 'Say another thing' [...] I did all these things & Peter laughed, his voice growing higher. He said 'Tell her to kiss you'. She said 'Kiss me Miss Dawes'. He said 'Tell her to kiss me!' & she said 'Miss Dawes, kiss Peter'. (Waters, 2000, pp. 261–2)

If 'Peter' is in fact a spirit and Selina is 'entranced', she is merely a passive puppet to be manipulated by his commands and yet note that Selina's ostensible 'trance' does not preclude her ability to 'hear Miss Isherwood swallow'. We subsequently realize that 'Peter' is in fact Ruth Vigers, Selina's lover, who performs the role as her spirit guide to facilitate the deception of séance audiences. Selina is still cast in the part of 'dummy' made to speak and act at the will of another but it is Ruth who manipulates her as opposed to spirit forces. The scene is permeated by vocal directions: 'He said/she said' and it is through Ruth/Peter's voice that Selina is seemingly possessed. The reference to the medium acting as the 'servant' of the spirits is telling as this is Ruth's role in both Selina's and subsequently Margaret's home where she has access to Margaret's diary, the words that she will feed to Selina to facilitate the deception of her 'affinity'.

In the representation of Ruth's ability to manipulate both Selina and Margaret, the text poignantly demonstrates that servants are not wholly subjected to their mistress' desires and have their own agenda. If Selina can also be positioned as a 'servant', this implies that she too has a will of her own. Selina may be aurally manipulated by Ruth/Peter yet she is a willing participant in the role of 'puppet', echoing Wilde's statement in *De Profundis* of his conscious collusion with Douglas' 'domination'. It is also notable that as the scenario takes a more salacious turn, 'Peter's' voice changes, 'growing higher'. The closer the spiritualist display comes to same-sex desire, therefore, the more feminine 'Peter' becomes. Viewed through the lens of queer desire, this séance room becomes an arena for erotic power games.[8] 'Peter's' reference to the medium becoming a 'plastic instrument' for the spirits is suggestive, implying malleability or the ability to slide between roles and boundaries. The exchange between Selina, 'Peter' and Miss Isherwood demonstrates the fluidity of roles in ventriloquial/mediumistic exchanges. The conventional power relationship between 'dummy' and 'ventriloquist' breaks down and the roles become interchangeable.

The above scene, and the triangulation of desire between Margaret, Selina and Ruth, performs a notable re-scripting of the depiction of ventriloquial manipulation in Henry James' *The Bostonians*. Miss Isherwood is also a pale, red-headed American, and her evident interest in learning to develop her mediumistic abilities is perhaps reminiscent of Verena Tarrant. More significantly, Margaret can be considered to be a neo-Victorian version of Olive Chancellor; a lonely, intellectual single woman who seeks to make a connection with a mysteriously gifted young women to provide a 'voice' for women's rights, and, indeed, desires. If James stopped short of offering the reader the opportunity to hear Olive's 'voice', then Waters' novel redresses this silencing by giving Margaret an extended narrative of her own through which we can identify her isolation and her need to connect with other women. Ann Heilmann and Mark Llewellyn have also recognized *Affinity*'s intertextual debt to *The Bostonians*: 'as in James a "masculine" intruder intervenes in the "romantic friendship" between a repressed lesbian middle-class hysteric and her feminine-spiritualist object of desire; the difference is that Waters' triumphant lover is a lesbian servant' (Heilmann and Llewellyn, 2010, p. 189). In these terms, Basil Ransom's position of master ventriloquist is usurped by Ruth but Heilmann and Llewellyn imply that this re-scripting offers a limited respite from the unequal currencies of ventriloquial influence in James' novel: 'Verena is as much under Basil's spell and command as Selina is under Ruth's' (Heilmann and Llewellyn, 2010, p. 281). I feel that the representation of Selina actually offers a more complex recitation of Verena's role of dummy than Heilmann and Llewellyn suggest, for she is imbued with a greater ability to influence Margaret than her Victorian counterpart can exercise upon Olive and she is in possession of a narrative 'voice' – via her diary extracts – that is consistently denied to Verena in James' novel. However, the implication that the gendered dynamics of the ventriloquial power imbalance remain ultimately untroubled is convincing. Ruth's performance as 'Peter' in the séance room demonstrates that the masculine ventriloquist role is not shackled to biological sex as it can be fulfilled by a woman reciting the script of masculinity for her own agenda, and yet this queer agency still remains entrenched in patriarchal mastery and control. Rachel Carroll reads 'Peter's' role in the séance as a reiteration of gender roles in which Ruth and Selina enact 'heterosexual rituals of desire' (Carroll, 2006, p. 140). Altering the sex of the ventriloquist does not change the script of objectification and manipulation of women.

Paulina Palmer has interpreted Ruth as the supreme mastermind of the novel, authoring the roles that the other characters will perform

(Palmer, 2008, pp. 75–6) and this ventriloquial image of Ruth as puppet-master, or mistress, has also been invoked by Tatiana Kontou (Kontou, 2009, p. 197). These readings are justified by the ostensible power imbalance between Margaret, Selina and Ruth, and yet we should remember Wilde's vision of the 'passionate puppet' in *De Profundis* that will bring its own desire to the required performance. Selina might be manipulated but she colludes with Ruth by performing the role of medium for her own gains. Should we therefore consider Margaret to be an innocent victim in this currency of influence, cruelly duped as she is by the other women's machinations? It is important to recognize that, like Olive Chancellor, Margaret also articulates the desire to 'possess' her beloved, to hear her protégé speak in her voice. In a conversation between the women, Selina does not understand Margaret's literary allusion and Margaret comments: 'There came a movement in my breast – part dismay, part fear, part simple love. Then I thought, Why should she know? Who was there ever, to teach her things like that? I thought, *That will come*' (Waters, 2000, p. 300). The women are speaking in incompatible cultural languages due to the differences in their class, and Margaret hints that she will eradicate this difference by taking on the role of Selina's educator. The expression of 'simple love' is not straightforward, articulating an urge to mould the speech of the beloved other. Margaret anticipates projecting her own cultural values upon Selina, regardless of the prisoner's willingness to accept this role. On realizing that Selina has indeed escaped from Millbank and absconded with Ruth, Margaret moves to accost a policeman outside the house:

> Seeing him, I thought one thing – it was my mother's voice rising in me. *I have been robbed*, I thought, *by my own servant!* Only let me tell that policeman, and he will stop her – *he will stop her train! I'll have them both at Millbank! I'll have them put in separate cells, and make Selina my own again!* (Waters, 2000, p. 342)

The statement on being 'robbed' is telling. Ruth has certainly taken the travelling clothes and accessories that Margaret had bought for Selina but she has also taken Selina – Margaret's 'special object', to use the words of Mr Shillitoe. Margaret does not conceptualize Selina as an autonomous subject but an object or possession and this desire to possess her at all costs breaks through into Margaret's thoughts of having her re-incarcerated, returned to the role of a puppet-prisoner to be dominated by Margaret's will. Significantly, Margaret has returned to being ventriloquized by her mother's voice. Selina might previously have helped Margaret 'talk back' to her oppression by her mother, but at this moment her influence has been usurped by Mrs Prior, the matriarch-ventriloquist who will silence desire between women and manipulate them into speaking a patriarchal, heteronormative script.

It is not until the last pages of the novel that Margaret realizes the extent of her deception at the hands of Selina and Ruth. She learns of the letters that have passed between the women, providing Selina with the information she needs from Margaret's own diary: 'she had written the words to Selina, and the words had become her own' (Waters, 2000, p. 342). This statement refers to Ruth's letters, and yet the use of pronouns becomes ambiguous; do these 'words' ultimately belong to Ruth, Selina, or Margaret herself? Both Selina and Ruth have repeated Margaret's private script of the relationship, but have made her passion their own. Margaret has become the dummy of their desire, temporarily animated but now rendered empty. The final words of Margaret's journal are ambiguous, suggesting suicide. Ironically, this is an ultimate act of futile agency. It is never revealed whether Selina and Ruth anticipated that this would be the result of their plan but perhaps Margaret's tragic act can be understood as an unexpected consequence of the lovers' plot. Margaret, who has been placed in the role of manipulated puppet, does, albeit fruitlessly, express autonomy in her final acts. Kym Brindle, Mark Llewellyn and Tatiana Kontou have all noted that Ruth's voice is largely absent from the novel (Brindle, 2009/2010, p. 76; Llewellyn, 2007, p. 199; Kontou, 2009, p. 190) but she has succeeded in stealing Margaret's voice and the last sentence of the text – 'Remember [...] whose girl you are' (Waters, 2000, p. 351) represents the triumph of one queer ventriloquist at the expense of another. Olive Chancellor's voice has, yet again, been silenced.

Conclusion

This chapter has explored the way in which Sarah Waters' novels address a muted aspect of the Victorian script of ventriloquism; the queer female ventriloquist. Significantly, Waters herself identifies with this role in terms of her repetition of prior Victorian authorial voices and recognizes the ambivalent tension between the reiteration of nineteenth-century scripts and the potential for subversively 'talking back' via re-citation. I demonstrated the ways in which ventriloquial repetition is a key trope in Waters' novels, and I argue that it is deployed as a strategy to dramatize the problematic aspects of ventriloquism as subversion. In *Tipping the Velvet* the world of the male impersonation on the Victorian music hall stage offers Nancy the opportunity to produce a covert 'voice' for female same-sex desire through the language of corporeal recitations of the script of gender. The liberatory potential of her performance is subject to audience interpretation, however, and if the act 'speaks' too loudly of her queerness she runs the risk of being silenced by regulatory patriarchal voices. Waters' representation of gender as performance can therefore be understood as 'talking back' to Judith Butler's work, as she indicates that the subversive intentions of queer theory do not necessarily translate into a Victorian context. Through a succession of performances throughout the course of the novel Nancy attempts to generate a sense of queer agency and subjectivity, but she repeatedly finds herself manipulated by the scripts of patriarchal, heteronormative gender and sexuality. Although the novel concludes with the promise that Nancy will finally take ownership of her voice and renounce her dependence upon repetition, we are left to speculate how her independent voice might sound. Perhaps this absence represents Waters' refusal to ventriloquize Nancy any further, but it also provides a pertinent neo-Victorian allegory for the impossibility of producing a wholly 'original' voice.

Several critics have noted Waters' refusal to represent same-sex desire as a utopian space beyond heteronormative and patriarchal power struggles (Armitt and Gamble, 2006, p. 141; Kaplan, 2007, pp. 111–12) and this caution becomes manifest in *Tipping the Velvet*'s characterization of Diana and her Sapphic friends and the currencies of ventriloquial influence between Margaret, Selina and Ruth in *Affinity*. Diana's articulation of woman-centred eroticism finds a script in the work of Oscar Wilde, specifically the ventriloquial seductiveness of Lord Henry Wotton, but it is also dependent on the misogynistic objectification of working-class women. *Affinity* recasts the love triangle of *The Bostonians* and temporarily grants Margaret/Olive Chancellor a voice and Selina/Verena the status of unruly dummy. However, Ruth's emulation of Basil Ransom's role of master-ventriloquist changes only the sex of the ventriloquist; the gendered script of objectification, possession and influence remains the same. The ultimate irony in both novels is that ventriloquial strategies of producing agency for individual women which are dependent on the silencing and manipulation of others actually end up repeating the Victorian scripts which are supposed to be challenged. Metatextually, we see that women such as Ruth, Diana, Selina, Margaret are returned to the dummy role, reciting without transformation the master discourses of Victorian ventriloquism. Waters' novels do offer an alternative understanding of ventriloquism which encompasses multiple voices, agencies and intentions. Subversion through ventriloquial repetition might occur, but it is often localized, individualized and temporary if it relies upon silencing the voice of the other as opposed to negotiation. Waters' talent as a neo-Victorian ventriloquist resides in her ability to include multiple textual voices and in her staging of the dangers in privileging some utterances over others. To return to Mark Wormald's comment at the beginning of this chapter, Waters not only deploys ventriloquism as method of 'testing' Victorian discourses, but also as a self-reflexive strategy to interrogate ventriloquism as a practice in itself. The next chapter will consider neo-Victorian ventriloquisms in a broader context, contemplating the role that the 'voice' of the critical reader plays in contributing to the multi-voiced discourse of neo-Victorianism.

6
Talking to Ourselves? Ventriloquial Criticism and Readership in Neo-Victorian Fiction

In Tatiana Kontou's study of the role of mediumship in neo-Victorian fiction, she ponders the dynamics of voice and agency that are raised by the neo-Victorian fascination with the séance room:

> To what extent do these author-mediums *ventriloquize* the dead? If the dead speak through the medium, then surely we can argue that the medium also speaks through them? How do we distinguish between these new and old voices? [...] What is added and what is taken away? What is lost forever in transmission? (Kontou, 2009, p. 2, emphasis in original)

Kontou's speculations invoke the uncertainties of the ventriloquial exchanges in mediumship that were outlined in Chapter 5's discussion of *Affinity*. Her understanding of the 'author-mediums' of neo-Victorian literature also has significant parallels with this book's discussion of the neo-Victorian author-ventriloquist. In a comparable way to Kontou, I have identified the tensions between speech and silence in neo-Victorian 're-voicings' of Victorian discourses of ventriloquism; if the neo-Victorian authors of my study can be understood as providing voices for the 'dummy' women of nineteenth-century script of ventriloquism, then, as Chapter 3's reading of *Nights at the Circus* and *Alias Grace* demonstrated, they can also be perceived as muting or even silencing some aspects of this script.

Aside from the voices of Victorian and contemporary authors, however, there is a further set of voices that need to be accounted for in neo-Victorian ventriloquial exchanges: those of the critical readers of these texts.[1] Louisa Hadley's commentary on the popularity of tropes of detective fiction in neo-Victorian literature suggests that neo-Victorian fiction: 'presents the process of recovering the Victorian past as similar to that of a detective solving a case; "clues" from the past need to be interpreted in order to make sense of "what really happened"' (Hadley, 2010, p. 59). The reader is thus encouraged to take an active role in identifying the 'textual remains of the past' (Hadley, 2010, p. 59); put another way, we listen to the Victorian voices that have been rearticulated, hear the ventriloquial transformation of such voices and, in the case of literary critics, might be stimulated to bring our critical voice to the texts. Neo-Victorian ventriloquisms do not end with the author-ventriloquist, then, but also draw critical readers into a multi-voiced dialogue. This ventriloquial role of the critical reader is implied in Kontou's comment on how 'we' might distinguish between 'new and old voices' but, as Kontou also notes, this is never an unbiased process. What will be spoken, and what will be silenced? To what extent does critical interpretation take on a ventriloquial role in relation to both Victorian and neo-Victorian texts and authors? Although this study has made the case for understanding ventriloquism as more than an active/passive exchange between ventriloquist and 'dummy' and argued that ostensible 'dummies' might talk back to their manipulators, I have also underscored that the agency of the dummy is often precarious. In what ways might the critical reader be manipulated or 'voiced' by neo-Victorian texts? To what extent is neo-Victorian criticism reciting a script dictated by prior voices, both Victorian and neo-Victorian?

This chapter seeks to address such questions by considering the role that critical ventriloquism plays in three neo-Victorian novels: A. S. Byatt's *Possession: A Romance* (1990), Sarah Waters' *Fingersmith* (2002), and Kathe Koja's *Under the Poppy* (2010). There is necessarily a certain degree of self-consciousness in my analysis, for as a critical reader writing about Victorian and neo-Victorian ventriloquisms I am also implicated in the politics of 'giving voice' to texts, to silencing some voices, amplifying others, but also reciting the voices of other critics. Indeed, in making this statement I am in turn echoing Cora Kaplan's remarks on her own position to 'Victoriana': 'I am as implicated in the contradictory sets of feelings that the Victorian provokes as any other writer and reader, and my intention in analysing such emotions is not to rationalise or depoliticise them, or to suggest that I or anyone else can finally stand outside them' (Kaplan, 2007, p. 5). It is a truism to note that a critical response to a text involves the individual's subjective voice, but it bears repeating when the politics of ventriloquism runs the risk of being occluded; this is my starting point for considering ventriloquial exchanges in Byatt's work. Byatt's understanding of the term 'ventriloquism' in her own critical reflections on *Possession* is curiously apolitical, failing to acknowledge the slipperiness of the power relationships of ventriloquism, and this supposedly politically neutral interpretation of ventriloquial dynamics has serious implications for the position of the critic-ventriloquist in relation to the novel and also the representation of gender and sexuality in the text.

Possession tells the story of a group of contemporary academics searching to solve the mystery of the relationship between a famous Victorian poet, Randolph Henry Ash, and a lesser-known poet, Christabel LaMotte. Roland Michell, a young scholar who is struggling to find an academic post and works on a research project producing an edition of Ash's collected works, discovers an unusual letter during routine archive research. The draft letter is from Ash to an unknown woman, and in a moment of 'possessiveness' Roland takes the manuscript. His investigations lead him to enlist the help of Maud Bailey, a beautiful and intimidating feminist critic who specializes in the work of LaMotte. The novel consists of both Victorian and contemporary narrative perspectives, punctuated by extracts from the work of Ash and LaMotte. The word 'ventriloquism' resonates throughout the text and is regularly discussed in critical accounts of Byatt's work but, as we shall see, is generally considered as either a demonstration of Byatt's accomplishment as an author or sometimes as an aesthetic anxiety of neo-Victorian authorship. In contrast, my reading of *Possession* will argue that the theme of ventriloquism is deployed to demonstrate the anxiety of *critics* rather than authors, positioning the academics within the world of the novel as dummies who belatedly mouth prior scripts but also metatextually manipulating the critical reader into the role of dummy. Moreover, Byatt's performance of the role of Victorian ventriloquist ironically leads her to replicate some of the more troubling gendered power imbalances of nineteenth-century ventriloquism narratives, and the politics of speaking about (neo)Victorian ventriloquism, gender and sexuality will be further interrogated.

The plot of *Fingersmith* is located in the 1860s and is organized around two narrative voices: Susan Trinder, a young woman who lives in the bosom of a criminal network in the underworld of London, and Maud Lilly, a young lady who lives a secluded life in her uncle's home, acting as a scribe for the bibliography he is producing of his comprehensive library of pornographic texts. Their life stories become irrevocably entwined as a plot is hatched to claim the inheritance Maud will receive on her marriage which pits the women against each other, blurs their identities, and ultimately reveals that Susan is the daughter of Christopher Lilly's sister whereas Maud is the progeny of Mrs Sucksby, the woman who has been priming Susan to fulfil Maud's proposed fate in the madhouse whilst the inheritance which Susan's mother intended to be shared by the girls falls into the hands of Maud and her mother. Sensational plot twists aside, my reading of *Fingersmith* will focus on the function of pornography within the novel and as a metatextual device to reflect on women's agency in relation to sexual 'scripts'. Maud is repeatedly figured as a doll or puppet in her manipulations at the hands of others. Her exposure to pornographic texts inflects and, to an extent, conditions her burgeoning sexual desire towards Susan. I will explore the extent to which Maud's engagement with the patriarchal script of pornography provides an outlet for a women-centred articulation of desire. Maud becomes a passionate puppet that comes to life to rebel against her master's desires; via authorship she 'talks back' to the discourses by which she has been ventriloquized. My reading explores the ways in which *Fingersmith*'s pornography theme also 'speaks' to debates about the erotic representation of women; does Waters manipulate her readers' desires to be titillated by tales of those 'other' Victorians, or is a more critical ventriloquial agenda at play? Waters' neo-Victorian novels have a significant cultural afterlife in the form of adaptations for television, and this chapter considers how the additional 'voices' that such adaptations have generated extend and complicate the reflections on neo-Victorian ventriloquism in Waters' text.

Under the Poppy tells the story of a nineteenth-century European brothel and a charismatic ventriloquist, Istvan, who uses his puppets to perform alongside the girls at The Poppy. Although Koja's novel makes some attempts to reflect upon the power relations of ventriloquism and gender, *Under the Poppy* graphically reiterates the masculine potency of the Victorian ventriloquists discussed in Chapter 2. Considering the ambiguous historical context of the novel, I suggest that Koja's text actually discourages critical reflection on neo-Victorian ventriloquism by producing a version of 'the Victorians' which recites salacious stereotypes rather than engaging in a dialogue with nineteenth-century literature or culture. Providing a 'voice' for 'Victorian sexuality' is a fraught enterprise and this chapter is concerned with exploring the ways in which neo-Victorian ventriloquism incites, manipulates or even silences critical voices in the process of 'talking back' to the nineteenth century.

Her master's voice: Byatt and Victorian ventriloquism in *Possession*

In an essay entitled 'Forefathers', A. S. Byatt makes the claim that *Possession* is a novel about 'ventriloquism, love for the dead, the presence of literary texts as the voices of persistent ghosts or spirits' (Byatt, 2001, p. 45). She is thus drawing a connection between ventriloquism and mediumship, a link which indicates that she has some knowledge of the historical development of displaced voice. However, she also remarks that she terms 'historical writing' as '"ventriloquism", to avoid the loaded moral implications of "parody", or "pastiche"' (Byatt, 2001, p. 43). Byatt does not clarify what these 'moral implications' might actually be, or elaborate upon how she might define parody and pastiche, yet her coupling of these terms is surely reminiscent of Fredric Jameson's critique of pastiche as a postmodern form:

> Pastiche is, like parody, the imitation of a peculiar or unique, idiosyncratic style, the wearing of a linguistic mask, speech in a dead language. But it is a neutral practice of such mimicry, amputated of the satiric impulse, devoid of laughter and of any conviction that alongside the abnormal tongue you have momentarily borrowed, some healthy linguistic normality still exists. Pastiche is thus blank parody, a statue with blind eyeballs. (Jameson, 1991, p. 17)

Jameson's condemnation of pastiche is, as mentioned in the Introduction, informed by ventriloquial imagery and attendant value judgements. Both parody and pastiche apparently have ventriloquial impulses – typified by a borrowed, copied voice which is dependent upon a prior original – and yet pastiche is associated with sickness; 'amputated' from the mockery which Jameson perceives as characteristic of parody and in opposition to the 'healthiness' of the 'normal' use of language. There is certainly a moral judgement at work in these loaded terms. In fact, Jameson's indictment of pastiche has notable parallels with the unhealthy etymology of 'influence' discussed in Chapter 2, so it is perhaps unsurprising that Byatt would want to reject the word. Nevertheless, it is still ironic that she favours 'ventriloquism' when historically speaking it has such resonance with the dirtiness, sickness or moral dubiousness implied by Jameson's definition. I concur with Diana Wallace's criticism of Byatt's 'ventriloquism' as depoliticized (Wallace, 2005, p. 218), for Byatt's insistence on the neutrality of ventriloquism not only silences its gendered and sexualized connotations but lays claim to a superior objectivity in re-voicing the Victorians that ignores the politics of who has access to the agency of 'voice' at any given historical and cultural moment.

Catherine Bernard's work on the trope of ventriloquism in contemporary fiction suggests that it stems from aesthetic exhaustion, an anxiety about belatedness and the 'demise of originality' in literary production (Bernard, 2003, p. 11). Her use of *Possession* as an example of such ventriloquism does in part align Byatt's text with Jameson's definition of the uncritical intent of pastiche: it 'does not engage in a critical dialogue with the canon it elects as worthy of being appropriated' (Bernard, 2003, p. 19).[2] Byatt's own association between ventriloquism and 'love for the dead' would seem to preclude the accusation of parodically mocking her Victorian subjects in *Possession*, and yet I contend that Byatt's re-creation of Victorian voices in the form of her fictional poets Ash and LaMotte does not disclose an *anxiety* about her own authorial voice. The extensive passages of Ash's and LaMotte's poetry within the text serve to showcase Byatt's *talent* for Victorian ventriloquism, to self-consciously demonstrate the brilliant range of her own voice as opposed to deferring to the prior creative authority of nineteenth-century literature. Ann Hulbert's review of *Possession*, tellingly entitled 'The Great Ventriloquist', highlights the crucial issue in Byatt's 'Victorian' voice: 'There's a triumphant, sometimes slightly irritating exhibitionism at the core [...] for the many words we're meant to thrill to are, of course, all Byatt's own' (Hulbert, 1991, p. 49). As I will explore in more detail below, the 'voices' of Randolph Ash and Christabel LaMotte do have notable parallels with several 'real' Victorian poets yet we must recognize that they remain Byatt's original creations. Christian Gutleben's irritation with Byatt's ventriloquism is also palpable but he recognizes that such Victorian ventriloquism cannot be as easily removed from 'moral' or political concerns as Byatt would wish: 'Is it not possible that the quest for this self-satisfied pleasure obliterates the awareness of its ideological consequences?' (Gutleben, 2001, p. 27). Bearing Gutleben's question in mind, I want to turn now to *Possession* to tease out the ideological consequences of Byatt's enactment of Victorian ventriloquism.

Robert Browning is the poet most regularly cited as the model for Byatt's Randolph Ash and the work of Christabel LaMotte is frequently interpreted as a composite of Emily Dickinson, Christina Rossetti and Elizabeth Barrett Browning.[3] Robert Browning's influence on *Possession* has various facets. For example, the name of Byatt's contemporary protagonist Roland Michell alludes to Browning's poem 'Childe Roland to the Dark Tower Came' (the title of which is itself a reference to a line from Shakespeare's *King Lear*). Additionally, Browning's antipathy towards spiritualism, particularly the medium Daniel Home who inspired the damning 'Mr Sludge, the Medium', finds an echo in Ash's distaste for spiritualism and, indeed, Daniel Home (Byatt, 1991, pp. 170–1) and most explicitly in Ash's poem 'Mummy Possest'.[4] Perhaps the clearest indication of the connection between Browning and Ash comes in the latter's attachment to the dramatic monologue as a poetic form. Considering that the dramatic monologue relies upon the sustained projection of a poet's voice into an alternative persona – the poet must self-consciously speak in the voice of another – this form of writing does have a relationship with the concept of ventriloquism. Discussing her interest in Browning, Byatt notes that 'Browning [...] did refer to himself as a ventriloquist. Browning wrote a poem, just as an exercise, in almost every voice of almost every period, of almost every civilisation he'd ever begun to think about' (Noakes, 2004, p. 28). Byatt's reference to Browning's ventriloquial poems as 'exercises' implies that writing in historical voices is a demonstration of skill, a honing of ability as opposed to anxiety of influence, and her own impressive ventriloquization of Browning via Ash can presumably be classed as a comparable dexterity of authorial voice. In a letter to Priscilla Penn Cropper, the great-grandmother of the grasping academic Mortimer Cropper, Ash refers to how scientists, historians and authors such as him 'traffic with the dead', giving new voices to the past:

> *I myself, with the aid of the imagination, have worked a little in that line, have ventriloquised, have lent my voice to, and mixt my life with, those past voices and lives whose resuscitation in our own lives as warnings, as examples, as the life of the past* persisting in us, *is the business of every thinking man and woman. But there are ways and ways, as you must well know, and some are tried and tested, and others are fraught with danger and disappointment. What is read and understood and contemplated and intellectually* grasped *is our own, madam, to live and work with. A life-time's study will not make accessible to us more than a fragment of our own ancestral past [...] But that fragment we must thoroughly* possess *and hand on.* (Byatt, 1991, p. 104, emphasis in original)

Ash's acknowledgement of his status as an author-ventriloquist is justified by a universalizing impulse; re-creating the past through ventriloquism is instructive and relevant to 'every thinking man and woman'. Ventriloquism becomes a condition of all intellectual thought, not a process of active/passive domination and not confined to late twentieth-century anxieties about the lack of 'original' voice; Ash's reference to the desire to 'possess' the past obviously underscores a continuum between the Victorians and contemporary scholars of the novel. Ash's ventriloquism is couched in terms of giving voice to past history to make it 'our own', not exclusively, but as an inheritance for subsequent generations who will presumably re-voice it in turn. Ash's remarks lay the template for the 'possession' of historical knowledge that Roland and Maud will strive to achieve and metatextually affirm Byatt's ventriloquizing of Victorian forebears for her own literary creation. Whilst this understanding of ventriloquism appears to leave room for multiple voices to co-exist we must also be attuned to the value judgements within Ash's letter. He is writing to Cropper to discourage her interest in spiritualism and to disassociate his own dealings with 'dead' voices from such practices. His form of literary ventriloquism is a 'tried and tested' way of communing with the past, but the ventriloquism of mediumship is dangerous, fraudulent and not to be trusted. In other words, there is 'good' and 'bad' ventriloquism and thus the moral implications that Byatt so confidently tries to excise from her use of 'ventriloquism' are not so easily silenced.

Byatt's novel is clearly sympathetic to the role of the Victorian and neo-Victorian author-ventriloquist, but ventriloquial imagery also informs her representation of the academic critics of *Possession*. Ash is depicted as self conscious about his ventriloquial status; we are told that Mortimer Cropper's definitive biography of the poet takes its title – *The Great Ventriloquist* – from one of Ash's 'teasing monologues of self-revelation or self-parody' (Byatt, 1991, p. 107). His readiness to claim this role does not forestall condemnation from subsequent literary critics. James Blackadder, a prominent if gloomy scholar of Ash's work, has his academic fate to study Ash decided during a seminar whilst studying at Cambridge. Under the tutelage of F. R. Leavis the seminar group is confronted by a selection of texts from apparently different historical eras which Blackadder recognizes as all being penned by Ash, 'examples of his ventriloquism':

> He himself had two choices: to state his knowledge, or to allow the seminar to proceed, with Leavis enticing unfortunate undergraduates into making wrong identifications, and then proceeding to demonstrate his own analytic brilliance in distinguishing fake from authenticity, Victorian alienation from the voice of true feeling. Blackadder chose silence, and Ash was duly exposed and found wanting. Blackadder felt that he had somehow betrayed Randolph Henry Ash, though he might more justly have been thought to have betrayed himself, his grandfather, or possibly Dr Leavis. (Byatt, 1991, pp. 27–8)

Blackadder atones for his perceived 'betrayal' by proceeding to write his doctoral thesis on Ash and devote his academic career to the study of his work. The fictionalized version of Leavis dismissively relegates

Victorian ventriloquism to the realm of the fake, the inauthentic, the inferior copy, demonstrating the negative connotations of ventriloquism that are in currency but also subtly undermining such attitudes by pricking the domineering pomposity of 'Leavis'. Ironically, Leavis himself fulfils the archetype of a 'bad' Victorian ventriloquist who steals the independent critical voices of his students. There is a further ventriloquial facet to this scenario. In an interview with Philip Hensher Byatt mentions that she went to several of Leavis' seminars during her own time at Cambridge:

> Leavis was a very important figure for me in the sense that I perceived him as a kind of blockage to everybody who wanted to do what I wanted to do [...] I went to two of his seminars, which [...] is a story I have told in *Possession* – I decided that I wasn't going to go to any more because either I would get like the other people who worshipped him [...] but somehow didn't make anything, or I would get angrier and angrier with what I saw as his manipulation of his students into admiring him. (Hensher, 2001, n.p.)

Byatt's description of the real-life Leavis as a manipulator emphasizes the puppet-master role he fulfils in relation to his protégés and also reiterates his sinister ability to curtail the literary voices of would-be writers. The process of doubling which occurs between Byatt and Blackadder suggests that this is Byatt's 'personal' voice in the poly-vocal fabric of the novel but, crucially, Byatt succeeds where her fictional double fails; Byatt escapes from the oppressive ventriloquism of academic criticism and takes on the role of ventriloquist in her own right, whereas Blackadder is left struggling under the anxiety of critical influence. We learn that Blackadder, on seeing a television programme about a naturalist who dissects and reassembles owl droppings, is momentarily inspired to write a poem about the affinity he feels with this process in relation to his work as a literary critic. Sure enough, he then 'discovered that Ash had been beforehand with him [...] Blackadder could not think whether he had noticed the screen naturalist because his mind was primed with Ash's image, or whether it had worked independently' (Byatt, 1991, p. 29). Any creative thought that could enter Blackadder's mind is foreshadowed by Ash: the academic critic must follow the script of his Victorian authorial master.

The theme of the critic-dummy is made even more explicit when Blackadder meditates on his role as an academic editing the collected works of Ash: 'There were times when Blackadder allowed himself to see clearly that he would end his working life, that was to say his conscious thinking life, in this task, that all his thoughts would have been another man's thoughts, all his work another man's work' (Byatt, 1991, p. 29). Blackadder experiences his work as a form of ventriloquial possession; his mind and body are penetrated by the superior authorial voice of Ash and his very existence as a critic is parasitically dependent on this prior voice. Louise Yelin, Ann Marie Adams and Cora Kaplan have all written persuasively about the way in which *Possession* constructs a hierarchical relationship between creative and critical writing in which the former is privileged over the latter, and what I add to their voices is that criticism is repeatedly represented as 'bad' ventriloquism.[5] Byatt has remarked that 'ventriloquism became necessary' in *Possession* due to 'what I felt was the increasing gulf between current literary theory and the words of the literary text it in some sense discusses. Modern criticism is powerful and imposes its own narratives and priorities on the writings it uses as its raw materials' (Byatt, 2001, p. 45). Byatt is positioning her own ventriloquism as a defence strategy against the domination of academic voices, and the voice of literary theory is cast as an oppressive force. Her way of redressing this balance, however, is to relegate her academic critics to the role of dummy. The 'modern' characters of *Possession* are routinely characterized by the quality of their voices. For example, Maud's speaking voice is a 'deliberately blurred patrician; a kind of flattened Sloan' (Byatt, 1991, p. 39) whereas the voice of Beatrice Nest has 'a thick woollen quality' (Byatt, 1991, p. 111). Val, the unhappy girlfriend of Roland, 'had a rough voice gentled, between London and Liverpool, as the group voice was' (Byatt, 1991, p. 12). Both Maud and Beatrice are academics with disguised voices; Maud's is 'deliberately' contrived to present a certain image of her self and the equation of Beatrice's voice with 'wool' is a literal image of fabrication, a form of disguised utterance that is in keeping with Beatrice's anxiety about exposing her self and scholarship to hostile colleagues. Although Val is not an academic when we meet her in the novel, her altered voice is a result of coming to London to study at university. Lest it appears that Byatt recites the nineteenth-century script that associates artificial voices with women, it is important to recognize that Roland is also guilty of ventriloquial imitation. Eaun MacIntyre, the successful yuppy who will eventually woo Val away from her dysfunctional relationship with Roland, has a voice that is 'clear and ringing, not Scots, full of what Roland might inaccurately have called toffee-nosed sounds, or plummy sounds, sounds he had spent his childhood learning to imitate derisorily, hooting, curtailed, drawing, chipping sounds' (Byatt, 1991, p. 125). Roland's derisive mimicry of voices such as Eaun's is not shared by Byatt, for Eaun as an outsider from the poor ventriloquism of academia is granted the only 'clear' voice in this cacophony of imitations and deceptions. This propensity for imitation in the contemporary academia of *Possession* finds its most compelling manifestation in Roland's and Maud's re-tracing of Ash's and LaMotte's clandestine journey to Yorkshire. Although they initially determine to visit the locations mentioned in Ash's documents, the academics allow themselves a day off from pursuing the mystery of the poets' relationship. Roland suggests:

> 'There's a place on the map called the Boggle Hole. It's a nice word – I wondered – perhaps we could take a day off from *them*, get out of their story, go back and look at something for ourselves. There's no Boggle Hole in Cropper or the Ash letters – Just not to be caught up in anything?' (Byatt, 1991, p. 268, emphasis in original)

Roland's emphasis is on striving to achieve some independence from the weight of Ash's words, to literally free themselves from Ash's Victorian script which has dictated their movements so far and to have a 'new' experience. No such respite can be allowed for late twentieth-century academics, as their 'original' decision is exposed as a copy of Ash's and LaMotte's journey: 'He remembered most, when it was over, when time had run out, a day they spent in a place called the Boggle Hole, where they had gone because they liked the word' (Byatt, 1991, p. 286). The actions of both the Victorian and contemporary couple are motivated by words, hence the poststructuralist perspective that language use must condition and dictate our every experience is also made relevant to the nineteenth-century protagonists. More importantly, only the reader of *Possession* has access to this uncanny process of neo-Victorian doubling; the information about Ash's and LaMotte's visit to Boggle Hole is disclosed in one of the few sections of omniscient narration in the novel. Roland and Maud are condemned to repeat the script of their Victorian precursors, but they remain ignorant of their dummy status.

Roland and Maud are allowed some opportunities to reflect upon contemporary academia's predilection for repetition and it is significant that such moments in the novel are associated with meditations on late twentieth-century attitudes towards sexuality. During their trip to Yorkshire Roland remarks:

> 'Do you never have the sense that our metaphors *eat up* our world? I mean of course everything connects and connects – all

the time – and I suppose one studies – I study – literature because all these connections seem both endlessly exciting and then in some sense dangerously powerful – as though we held a clue to the true nature of things? [...] we were playing a professional game of hooks and eyes [...] and it all reduced like boiling jam to – human sexuality [...] And then, really, what is it, what is this arcane power we have, when we see that everything is human sexuality? It's really *powerlessness* [...] We are so knowing. And all we've found out, is primitive sympathetic magic. Infantile polymorphous perversity. Everything relates to *us* and so we're imprisoned in ourselves'. (Byatt, 1991, pp. 253–4, emphasis in original)

Roland voices Byatt's own views on the dangerous power of academic criticism to impose a script upon texts and it is the late twentieth-century fascination with sexuality which is figured as the oppressive force that foreshadows and manipulates the scholars into speaking in endless echoes. Maud's response is important in this respect: 'We live in the truth of what Freud discovered. Whether or not we like it [...] We aren't really free to suppose – to imagine – he could possibly have been wrong about human nature. In particulars, surely – but not in the large plan' (Byatt, 1991, p. 254). It is Freud that is offered as the master ventriloquist of twentieth-century scholarship; his theories make dummies of the academics who are compelled to repeat, with only limited transformation, his ideas. Roland and Maud are sympathetic characters in the novel as they are allowed to recognize the way in which such ventriloquism curtails their agency as thinkers, whereas the likes of Leonora Stern and Fergus Wolff are condemned to ignorantly regurgitate Lacanian theory without the benefit of self consciousness. As Roland and Maud draw closer to consummating their relationship they resort to silence: 'Speech, the kind of speech they knew, would have undone it' (Byatt, 1991, p. 424). To become literally dumb is preferable to the verbosity of academic ventriloquism and this self-imposed 'dummy' status offers safety from the manipulations of contemporary voices. Furthermore, at the end of the novel Roland comes to abjure academic ventriloquism and write poetry: 'He could hear, or feel, or even almost see the patterns made by a voice he didn't yet know, but which was his own [...] they came like rain and were real' (Byatt, 1991, p. 475). In a novel about ventriloquism such imagery is embarrassingly clear; Roland has found his 'real' voice through writing poetry as opposed to criticism and his potential for 'good' ventriloquism, like Ash's and Byatt's, becomes manifest.

There is another dimension to the currencies of ventriloquism which flow through *Possession*; the metatextual role of the critical reader of the novel itself. In Louisa Hadley's view, Byatt's text encourages the reader to actively engage with the process of bringing the past to life (Hadley, 2010, p. 118) but I question the optimism of this interpretation; perhaps it depends whether the assumed 'reader' also works in academia or not? Mark Hennelly reflects on the danger of the critical reader falling into the trap of the academics depicted in *Possession*, the 'anxiety of scholarly influence' which underpins Roland's and Maud's speculations about the originality of their work (Hennelly, 2003, p. 446). The experience of reading the novel with the intention of producing an academic commentary on it produces a strange sensation of losing one's 'critical' voice. For instance, in one of Ash's letters to Christabel he confesses that he feels 'at home' with her: '*I say "at home" – what extraordinary folly – when you take pleasure in making me feel most* unheimlich, *as the Germans have it, least of all* at home, *but always on edge, always apprehensive of failure*' (Byatt, 1991, p. 131). Of course, the reference to feeling 'unheimlich' reminds us of Freud's essay on 'The Uncanny' and can lead to a variety of speculations on how Ash's sense of discomfort with Christabel could stem from the sexual repression for which 'the Victorians' are so famous. I must confess that my initial interpretation of this passage was that Byatt was 'giving voice' to a stereotype of Victorian sexuality. Post-Freudian critical readers are primed for this response, make the sexual connection, and then must subsequently digest Maud's comments just over a hundred pages later on how Freudian theory has curtailed the freedom of academic criticism. Imposing a critical voice upon the Victorian poets not only makes the academics inside of *Possession* into dummies, but the critical reader 'outside' the text as well.

Another pertinent example of this sense of being 'spoken for' comes in the possible readings of Beatrice Nest's initial desire to study Ash as a postgraduate which is discouraged by her supervisor and re-directed to the more 'appropriate' feminine pursuit of studying the papers of Ash's wife, Ellen: 'What had she hoped for? Some intimacy with the author of the poems, with that fine mind and passionate nature' (Byatt, 1991, p. 114). Ellen is thus conceptualized as Beatrice's copy for Ash; women-focused criticism is an unsatisfactory substitute for the study of brilliant Victorian male poets. However, again this analysis is ventriloquized: on visiting Beatrice's home towards the end of the novel Maud sees her picture of Ash 'where those of a father or lover might have stood' on Beatrice's desk. Maud restrains herself from making a Freudian comment on the father/lover synthesis but 'automatically began to analyse it [...] The fact that the photograph was of the poet, not of his wife' (Byatt, 1991, p. 477). The 'academic' analysis has already been done for us and, as Jean-Louis Chevalier has noted of *Possession*, 'There is little need to comment on a text that does its own textual commentary so neatly' (Chevalier, 2001, p. 112).[6] The critical reader is either placed in the role of belatedly mouthing the work of Byatt's ventriloquial academics or is silenced altogether. Byatt is not only a Victorian ventriloquist, but a neo-Victorian ventriloquist in the sense that she speaks for the critical reader as well.

Nevertheless, this book has aimed to demonstrate that the fixed roles of ventriloquist and 'dummy' can be challenged in neo-Victorian literature and perhaps neo-Victorian criticism can also 'talk back' to Byatt's depiction of the critic-dummy. It is in *Possession*'s dealings with sexuality and gender that Byatt's attempts to distance herself from the politics of ventriloquism take on the most hollow tone. In an article on her official website, Byatt explains that the gendered connotations of the word 'possession' came from her teaching of Henry James' *The Bostonians*:

> to a generation of students involved in the politics of gender, who disliked Henry James' tragi-comic treatment of lesbian passion. It occurred to me that in the world of nineteenth-century spiritualism and feminism, *Possession* had both its meanings at once. So there was a need for the nineteenth-century woman to be a lesbian, or thought to be a lesbian, and the twentieth-century woman scholar to be a feminist. (Byatt, n.d.)

In an otherwise incisive article on the portrayal of lesbianism in *Possession*, Samantha J. Carroll interprets the above statement as Byatt's attempt to 'recuperate the representation of nineteenth-century homosexuality from James's reductive handling of it' (Carroll, 2008, p. 360). Carroll's reading of the text amply demonstrates that Byatt does not do this, but I contend that this was never the intention in the first instance. Elsewhere Byatt speaks of how *Possession*: 'wrote against the grain of what a feminist would have told. I made a feminist heroine, who since I'd invented her could be whatever I liked. So I made her a lesbian poet who turned out to have a heterosexual affair. I deliberately shifted the paradigm' (Walker, 2006, p. 332). Lesbian and/or feminist re-voicings of Victorian women have become a mould that apparently needs to be broken; Byatt's 'need' to include a nineteenth-century 'lesbian' and twentieth-century feminist is to expose how clichéd such representations have become, to demonstrate the oppressive force that same-sex desire can exercise upon women's voices. Various critics have highlighted the homophobic aspects of Byatt's novel: Blanche Glover, the assumed lover of Christabel, is depicted as neurotic and an inferior artist (Kaplan, 2007, p. 110); Christabel's relationship with Ash, though brief, is represented as defining her abilities as a writer and hence more fulfilling than her attachment to Blanche (Wallace, 2005, pp. 216–17); Leonora Stern, the bisexual academic, is figured as predatory and aggressive (Carroll, 2008, p. 372) but is finally neutralized by her unlikely heterosexual attachment to Blackadder. Carroll's reading is important for my purposes, as she recognizes connections between Blanche and Olive Chancellor in terms of their mutual spectrality and their position as thwarted lover in a hetero-homo love triangle (Carroll, 2008, p. 363). Byatt's acknowledgement of the sexualized implications of 'possession' via nineteenth-century spiritualism stops short of recognizing how this word, with its ambiguous fluctuations between objectification, agency and desire, is also a key term of ventriloquism.

Blanche remains a shadowy figure in the novel, but in the correspondence between Ash and LaMotte we can detect the return of the queer ventriloquist that haunts Victorian ventriloquism narratives. After receiving an anxious letter from Christabel suggesting that they should terminate their correspondence due to what people might think, Ash responds:

> *you write – do I go too far – as though your letter was in part dictated by the views of some other person or persons. I say this most tentatively – but it is very striking – some other voice speaks in your lines – do I divine truly? Now, this may be the voice of someone with much greater claims on your loyalty and attention than I may put forward – but you must be very sure that such a person sees truly and not with a vision distracted by other considerations.* (Byatt, 1991, p. 186)

Initially we might think that Ash is referring to the 'voice' of societal norms of gendered propriety, the script of Victorian femininity that Christabel must recite, but there is also the implication that she is being ventriloquized by Blanche. The link between Olive Chancellor and Blanche is most transparent when heard alongside the script of Victorian ventriloquism; I am reminded of Basil's speech to Verena where he makes her realize that she has become a 'preposterous puppet' under Olive's malign influence (James, 1998, pp. 325–6). Same-sex desire emerges as a manipulative, sinister force in *Possession* just as much as it does in *The Bostonians*. Does Byatt, in her skill at creating an 'authentic' Victorian voice for her poets, also need to replicate the perceived threat of queer ventriloquism?

It is also hinted that Christabel might have exercised a metaphorical silencing of her female partner. In a discussion between Maud and Leonora about the fate of Blanche's paintings – they have apparently been lost to history, unlike Christabel's covert heterosexual correspondence – Maud speculates: '"None of them have ever been found. I suppose Christabel may have kept them all. Or burned them in distress, we simply don't know"' (Byatt, 1991, p. 312). Although the loss of Blanche's work might be interpreted as a commentary on the ease with which lesbian history is lost, it, more disturbingly, also opines that lesbians themselves might collude with this silencing; Christabel might have destroyed her lover's legacy. Blanche's artistic 'voice' is triply silenced: broadly, as a nineteenth-century lesbian artist who, unlike Ash and LaMotte, has no 'real' traceable historical antecedents; personally, by her partner; and finally in the world of the novel, for if even James' queer ventriloquist might have been inspired to find a 'voice' as a result of her betrayal by Verena, Blanche remains mute. In a novel where artefacts from the past – often rather improbably – are being rediscovered, it is surely significant that Blanche's paintings stay missing. This is not to suggest that it is necessarily desirable to have a queer 'happy ending' for neo-Victorian novels to redress the Victorian script of ventriloquism. Chapter 5's commentary on *Affinity* underscored comparable themes of same-sex power struggles and queer self-silencing. However, the difference is that heteronormative power imbalances are revealed as irrevocably influencing the women's relationships in *Affinity*, whereas *Possession* seems content to proffer heteronormative attachments as a more fulfilling alternative.

This brings me to the last aspect of ventriloquism, gender and sexuality that I want to consider in *Possession*: the fate of Maud. Byatt's feminist critic is resistant to being defined by her beauty. When she looks in the mirror: 'The doll-mask she saw had nothing to do with her, nothing' (Byatt, 1991, p. 57). Maud is anxious about being objectified and also perceives her former relationship with Fergus as organized around a puppet/master dichotomy of power: Fergus is capable of 'giving little tugs at the carefully severed [...] puppet-strings which had once tied her to him' (Byatt, 1991, p. 140). Her self-awareness about the perils of objectification and her relative consciousness about the potential for academic critics to be manipulated by master discourses might seem to offer Maud a reprieve from becoming the dummy-woman of Victorian ventriloquism. On the other hand, the discovery of the lost letters of

Ash and LaMotte within a doll, stimulated by Maud's recitation of the poem 'Dolly Keeps a Secret', foreshadows the way in which Maud's 'doll-mask' *does* display her true identity. Maud is ultimately revealed to be the direct descendent of the progeny of Ash's and LaMotte's relationship and when Roland studies her face he recognizes that she looks like Christabel but also resembles Ash as well. Maud voices her concern about being 'possessed' by her forebears: '"I feel they have taken me over"' to which Roland reassures her that '"one always feels like that about ancestors"' (Byatt, 1991, p. 505). Indeed, the term 'possession' is imbued with multiple meanings in the novel: owning the literal artefacts of the past; desiring to own knowledge of the past; being inhabited by the past; simultaneously ventriloquizing and being ventriloquized.[7] 'Possession' only takes on a bodily manifestation for Maud, however, and the gendered discourse of the permeable female body which is particularly susceptible to ventriloquial 'possession' returns. This trope is reiterated when Maud and Roland finally have sex:

> And very slowly and with infinite gentle delays and delicate diversions and variations of indirect assault Roland finally, to use an outdated phrase, entered and took possession of all her white coolness [...] and he heard, towards dawn, from a long way off, her clear voice crying out, uninhibited, unashamed, in pleasure and triumph. (Byatt, 1991, p. 507)

Although the narrative voice articulates self-awareness about using 'an outdated phrase' to describe their coupling, the phrase is still invoked as preferable to a more frank expression of their sexual encounter. The late twentieth-century section of *Possession* ends with a neo-Victorian sex scene cloaked in euphemistic language, leaving us with the impression that such delicacy is preferable to post-Freudian explicitness but also reinstating the motif of the penetrable woman of the Victorian script of ventriloquism. If Roland is allowed to find his 'true' voice through his art, then Maud's disguised voice is restored to clarity and 'triumph' through heteronormative sexual fulfilment. In a novel which has already demonstrated that dolls must be penetrated to get to the 'true voice' of the Victorian poets, we are left with the alarming conclusion that the same logic is applicable to Roland's sexual possession of the doll-like Maud.

John J. Su has noted the conventional gendering of this sex scene (Su, 2004, p. 708), but I would like to offer a 'talking back' to Byatt's dismissal of same-sex attachments in her novel. Kate Mitchell's description of Maud's and Roland's union is thought-provoking: 'As [Roland] takes possession of Maud's body, and is possessed by hers, Roland joins himself to Ash's progeny and thus takes full possession of Ash himself' (Mitchell, 2010, p. 114). Mitchell's gloss on this exchange perceives it as the 'consummation' of Byatt's vision of the 'mutual possession of reader and text' (Mitchell, 2010, p. 114), but surely this is also a queer moment? Roland has 'possessed' Ash's letters, been 'possessed' by desire for knowledge about Ash, and now has the opportunity to sexually 'possess' an avatar for Ash. He has already informed Maud that now he has recognized her resemblance to Ash, 'I shall always see it' (Byatt, 1991, p. 505), and presumably this does not exclude his perception of Maud as they have sex. Ash is a ventriloquist whose influential voice has made dummies of his academic followers yet Roland has acquired Ash's poetic talent and made it his own 'voice'. In the sex scene, he is allowed the sexual privilege of the Victorian ventriloquist – penetrative power – and he exercises this upon a double of Ash. Byatt's novel might manipulate the critical reader as a demonstration of her ventriloquial mastery but queer ventriloquial currencies cannot be wholly silenced from *Possession*.

6.2   Talking back to pornography in *Fingersmith*

In contrast to Byatt's attempts to mute the connections between ventriloquism, gender and sexual politics, Sarah Waters' *Fingersmith* overtly engages with same-sex desire in relation to ventriloquial repetition. Our first introduction to Maud Lilly is in Sue's narrative; Sue is embroiled in a plot to assist Gentleman, alias Mr Rivers, to marry the wealthy Maud, inherit her fortune and then have her committed to a mental asylum. Sue is aware that Maud assists her uncle, Christopher Lilly, in compiling some sort of dictionary, and that she also regularly reads from his library to entertain his 'bookish gentlemen' friends, but it is not until we reach Maud's narrative that the nature of Lilly's book collection becomes clear; he is assembling a bibliography of pornography, and Waters' note at the end of the text explains that the character's project is inspired by the work of Henry Spencer Ashbee, who dedicated much of his life to the meticulous production of three such volumes.[8] Maud is tutored in bibliographical skills, but before she learns the content of her uncle's work she is instructed to read to Lilly's friends from his books: 'I read from foreign texts, not understanding the matter I am made to recite' (Waters, 2002, p. 198). Her unwitting recitation of the pornographic texts places her in the role of a 'dummy' in relation to the ventriloquist roles of both the anonymous pornographers and her uncle. She is not only condemned to act as an unthinking, unknowing vessel for the obscene repetitions, but is manipulated into this position by her guardian. After an initial erotic frisson on discovering the content of the texts, Maud becomes detached, disinterested from the subject of her readings: 'My hot cheek cools, my colour dies, the heat quite fades from my limbs. The restlessness turns all to scorn. I become what I was bred to be. I become a librarian' (Waters, 2002, p. 201). The vocabulary she uses to express this transformation is notable. Maud loses her bodily responses and thus becomes a sort of automaton who can calmly and coolly undertake her prescribed role. Sue's narrative repeatedly refers to Maud being 'as a puppet' (Waters, 2002, p. 131) or 'more like a clockwork doll' (Waters, 2002, p. 137). Such comparisons reveal Sue's guilt at the manipulations that Maud is receiving at the hands of their plot, but also inadvertently emphasize Maud's quasi-automaton role in relation to her uncle and his friends. Maud's narrative briefly reiterates the Trilby/Svengali relationship discussed in Chapter 2. Explaining Lilly's control over her voice and actions, she comments: 'He raises a brow, as a conductor of music might raise a baton [...] I am nothing if not obedient' (Waters, 2002, p. 234). Maud's latter remark has a double meaning, conveying her complete dedication to her prescribed role but also indicating her awareness that she has no option other than to conform to Lilly's instructions; her compliance to this Victorian ventriloquist defines her existence, and failure to recite his scripts would result in loss of identity, 'nothingness'.

In spite of the women being forced into competition for survival, Sue and Maud experience a growing attraction towards each other. Maud's explanation of this desire is related to her role as reader of and mouthpiece for a pornographic script:

> Even my uncle's books are changed to me; and this is worse, this is worst of all. I had supposed them dead. Now the words [...] start up, are filled with meaning. I grow muddled, stammer [...] I feel the stale words rouse me. I colour, and am ashamed. I am ashamed to think that what I have supposed the secret book of my heart may be stamped, after all, with no more miserable matter than this – have its place in my uncle's collection [...] When Sue comes to undress me I will suffer her touch, coolly, as I think a mannequin of wax might suffer the quick, indifferent touches of a tailor. And yet, even wax limbs must yield at last, to the heat of the hands that lift and place

them. There comes a night when, finally, I yield to hers. (Waters, 2002, pp. 280–1)

Whilst her repetition of the master voice of pornography disintegrates – Maud describes stumbling over her words, the breaking down of her utterances through stuttering – her personal desire becomes animated by the text. Maud's previous recitations of this script are transformed, and she expresses this awakening with an image of the 'mannequin' coming to life, a queer dummy who has the ability to garner an alternative meaning from the pornographic text, despite her not being the intended recipient of this stimulation. This is, however, an ambivalent experience for Maud; her 'shame' stems, not from her sexual arousal, but from a sense that she is still shackled to the script of male pornographic discourse. The text of her desire is written by another, and she fears that this is a mere extension of the thorough manipulation she has already experienced.

Both Sue's and Maud's narratives provide a perspective on their passionate love-making, a supposed 'preparation' for Maud's wedding night with Mr Rivers. Susan's account emphasizes Maud's innocence, and yet Maud's version of events is permeated with the 'script' of female desire she has learned from pornographic books. As she lies in bed:

> at first, it was easy. After all, this is how it is done, in my uncle's books: two girls, one wise and one unknowing... [...] It is easy. I say my part, and she – with a little prompting – says hers. The words sink back upon their pages. It is easy, it is easy... Then she rises above me and puts her mouth to mine. (Waters, 2002, p. 281)

Maud's account directly addresses the tropes of sex between women in pornography. As Emma Donoghue notes, this type of scenario is organized around a power imbalance of innocence and experience (Donoghue, 1993, p. 184), which would ostensibly appear to place Sue in a position of power to sexually manipulate Maud. Nevertheless, Maud underscores her self-conscious performance of this role as 'innocent'; her references to saying her 'part' and her 'prompting' of Sue stresses the 'scripted' aspect of this exchange, and the personae of 'experience' and 'innocence' become blurred. Potentially it is Sue who, though reciting the textual role of 'experience', is being naively manipulated by Maud. Maud's assessment of the pornographic script as 'easy' to follow is thwarted, however, by Susan's decisive and unexpected kiss. This moment has an important symbolism in terms of thinking about the women as passionate puppets in relation to pornographic representations of female desire. Maud's thoughts might be dominated by her uncle's books, yet the script fades away as their ownership of their desire becomes more intense. Pornography might have facilitated Maud's knowledge to construct a seduction scenario, and yet their mutual lust provides a deviation from this patriarchally-dictated exchange and renders the text inadequate to articulate their experiences.

At the end of the novel, Susan returns to Briar, Christopher Lilly's country residence, to find Maud among the remnants of his library. Maud confesses that she has taken to writing pornography to support herself financially, and explains to Susan:

> 'It is filled with all the words for how I want you... Look' [...] she had led me to the fire and made me sit, and sat beside me. Her silk skirts rose in a rush, then sank. She put the lamp upon the floor, spread the paper flat; and began to show me the words she had written, one by one. (Waters, 2002, pp. 547–8)

Paulina Palmer has interpreted Maud's 'showing' Sue her words as a form of lesbian reading practice, as Sue is illiterate and Maud's instruction enables her lover to access the written word (Palmer, 2008, pp. 77–8). I would add that the concept of Maud's demonstration of her text has a dual meaning. It implies reading but also an acting out of the script, as Maud has already deployed pornography as a way of shaping her sexual encounter with Sue. The implications of Maud teaching Sue to read are uncertain. On one level we might presume that this will imbue Sue with comparable agency as Maud to engage with texts rather than just repeating them. However, as Nadine Muller has argued, reading and writing are intrinsically connected by Maud's oppression at the hands of Lilly, and the images in Maud's narrative of ink as a form of poison 'raises the question whether or not Maud poisons rather than liberates Sue by teaching her how to read and write' (Muller, 2009/2010, p. 123). Maud's experiences of being 'given voice' by such texts have hardly been benign, and if Maud has necessarily been moulded by her experiences as 'dummy' to the master discourse of pornography mediated by her guardian-ventriloquist then to imagine that she can magically transcend such power dynamics when taking on the role of teacher to Sue is rather optimistic.

It is Maud's status as reader and writer of pornography that offers an avenue for considering the theme of metatextual neo-Victorian ventriloquism in *Fingersmith*. M. L. Kohlke interprets Maud's authorship as 'a lesbian profiteering from male desire by simulating fantastic sex on paper – presumably mainly heterosexual copulation' (M. L. Kohlke, 2008b, pp. 349–50). Why should we presume that the texts will be 'mainly' about hetero-sex, considering that the novel has already emphasized the theme of sex between women in pornography and that Maud explains to Sue that her writing is 'filled with all the words for how I want you'? This theme cuts to the heart of the metatextual debate that fuels the representation of pornography in Waters' novel: could women have authored pornographic texts in the nineteenth century? Could they have garnered pleasure from reading such texts? Paulina Palmer notes that *Fingersmith* addresses the issue of lesbian erotic representation in readings of the history of pornography and in contemporary debates about the role of pornography for lesbian communities (Palmer, 2008, pp. 78–9). Lillian Faderman acknowledges that sex between women has been a recurring trope of pornographic representation for several centuries, and yet suggests that this only occurs as a prelude to heterosexual copulation, and functions as titillation for men, authored by men: 'If any women wrote lesbian sex literature during the sixteenth to eighteenth centuries, it has been lost to posterity. Had such literature existed, the descriptions of lesbian lovemaking would have been different from the ones that are extant' (Faderman, 1985, p. 31). Faderman's analysis rests on the fundamental assumption that women not only write differently to men, but that there are certain aspects of lesbian sex that could never be imagined by a male heterosexual author and, indeed, that there are certain things that women *just don't do* in bed together.

Aside from the oddly prescriptive feeling of Faderman's remarks on how 'real' lesbian sex is conducted, her refusal to consider 'that there are myriad ways of discovering one's desire' is also problematic (Castle, 1993, p. 9). Terry Castle, Emma Donoghue and Martha Vicinus have all recognized the potential for lesbian-themed pornography to be accessed and enjoyed by women in the eighteenth and nineteenth centuries (Castle, 1993, p. 9; Donoghue, 1993, pp. 14–15; Vicinus, 1992, p. 476). Interestingly, critics such as Faderman who dismiss the erotic potential of historical lesbian pornography, and commentators such as Castle, Donoghue and Vicinus who are willing to consider pornographic representation as a potential outlet for female same-sex desire all do agree that these discourses would have been authored by men. Indeed, even Steven Marcus, whose study of Victorian pornography does not overtly address feminist or lesbian political perspectives, readily confirms that the vast majority of texts were male-authored (Marcus, 1969, p. 284).

In an interview with Abigail Dennis, Waters explains she is interested in 'how pornography might have worked for the women who read it or the women who wrote it' (Dennis, 2008, p. 44). Such information is lost to history, and yet Waters' depiction of Maud offers the possibility of hearing women's voices in pornographic narratives. It is a matter of the reader's interpretation as to whether the words will oppress and silence or stimulate and, as the dual narrative structure of *Fingersmith* indicates, there are multiple interpretations to be garnered from a narrative voice.

However, Waters must negotiate the subtle distinction between reinstalling the voice of silenced Victorian women and actually creating voice; as so little is known about nineteenth-century women's experiences of pornographic production and consumption it must necessarily be imagined. Waters' act of ventriloquism in giving Maud a 'voice' in *Fingersmith* might say more about a neo-Victorian desire to project contemporary interests in sexuality onto the Victorian period and yet *Fingersmith*'s sensitivity to the ways in which ventriloquial repetition inflects Maud's experience of pornography recognizes what might be at stake in speaking about sex. Steven Marcus delineates the genre of pornographic writing as an 'extremely conventionalized form of expression' in the sense that it depends upon the repetition of set tropes (Marcus, 1969, p. 60). Furthermore, I suggest that critical writing on pornography, often ironically, also depends upon repetition to an extent: even when subjected to the most searing condemnations, the content of a pornographic text needs to be described or cited.[9] If repetition always plays a role in pornography, then the potential for repetition with difference – Waters' neo-Victorian ventriloquism – allows some degree of agency to 'talk back' to patriarchal and heteronormative discourses of women's sexuality.

The liberatory potential of Maud's authorship is curtailed by neo-Victorian knowledge; the critical reader who is familiar with the controversies surrounding women and the history of pornography will know that there is no record of women such as Maud and so her attempt to produce a women-centred voice for sexuality has in fact been silenced. Additionally, if these texts were authored by women then they have had a dubious influence; debates surrounding the way in which pornography might objectify or empower women still rage.[10] Maud's authorship does not alter the script of history but may well have contributed to reiterating and strengthening the oppressive aspects of pornography on future generations of women. Even in the act of producing an authorial voice she cannot control the ways in which this voice will be manipulated in the future, and for what purposes. Andrew Davies' television adaptation of Waters' earlier novel *Tipping the Velvet* – a text which also engages with the erotic representation of queer desire between women – generates a pertinent parallel between Maud's and Waters' roles as authors of sexually explicit texts. There was a media furore surrounding the screening of Davies' 2002 adaptation on BBC 2, and his version of the dildo-wielding sex scenes between Nancy and Diana received particular attention. The interest of the mainstream tabloid newspaper the *Sun* was notable; although not generally known for queer-friendly cultural appraisals, the newspaper was keen that their readership should not miss some of the more salacious scenes of the adaptation. In a television guide for the evening of 16 October 2002, Gordon Smart identifies a programming quandary: the second episode of *Tipping the Velvet* clashes with the England team's football match against Macedonia, and in the words of Smart: 'It's the clash of the season and a dilemma for any self-respecting, hot blooded man' (Smart, 2002, n.p.). Smart provides the assumed readership of 'hot blooded men' a convenient time table for the 'juicy bits' of the Waters' adaptation, thus reassuring the viewer that he can 'send the missus out for the night and settle down for a game of two halves' (Smart, 2002, n.p.). Despite the absurdity of this example, it does encapsulate the ways in which an author's voice can be appropriated for multiple audiences and as Ann Heilmann and Mark Llewellyn have commented, 'the fact that Davies's adaptation [...] will be remembered as much for the golden phallus/dildo as anything about the narrative of women's rights presented in the novel is surely problematic' (Heilmann and Llewellyn, 2010, p. 243). Although Waters might deploy neo-Victorian ventriloquism to 'talk back' to the hetrocentric tropes of pornography, this re-voicing comes perilously close to being recited as an instrument of the very patriarchal script it attempts to re-articulate.

Voiceless Victorians in *Under the Poppy*

Several reviewers of Kathe Koja's *Under the Poppy* have mentioned the novel's similarities to *Fingersmith* and yet neither Jess Faraday or Devon Thomas elaborate on what this point of connection might be (Faraday, 2011, n.p.; Thomas, 2010, n.p.) It is tempting to speculate that Waters' name is invoked as a vague signifier for all things neo-Victorian, but presumably it is *Under the Poppy*'s focus on nineteenth-century sexuality which provokes these comparisons. 'The Poppy' of the title is a brothel which actually has more in common with Angela Carter's depiction of

Madame Schreck's establishment in *Nights at the Circus*, for the women of the Poppy offer sexual entertainment with a theatrical twist: one of the women employed in the brothel tells us that she dresses up for customers, pretending 'I'm an angel [...] wearing little white wings on my back' (Koja, 2010, p. 4). Although this costume is a faint echo of Fevvers' impressive wing span, there is a dumb pianist in the Poppy whose music accompanies the women's performances. Jonathan has had his tongue removed and, like the mouth-less Toussaint in Carter's novel, must bear silent witness to the degradation of his co-workers. He does have a narrative voice in the novel, however, and contemplates his fate: 'When you are silent, no one sees you, that is what I know. Onstage, the audience never looks to me' (Koja, 2010, p. 61). Jonathan's reflections remind us of the potent connection between 'voice' and power, and his silence represents his marginalization. But is not being looked at necessarily a bad thing, particularly in a world where the power of the gaze turns the actors into sexual objects that can be bought and sold? We should remember that Toussaint, though dumb, also refuses to participate in the sordid performances at Madame Schreck's brothel, and so even silent men are not as prone to manipulation as women in either text.

Here is where the similarities between Carter's and Koja's understandings of the gendered politics of ventriloquism end. It is telling that although Istvan the ventriloquist imparts some knowledge about the history of his craft – informing his protégé Lucy that the priestess of the Delphic oracle was a 'voice-thrower' (Koja, 2010, p. 54) – he appears to lack awareness of how ventriloquism becomes synonymous with masculine penetrative power as it develops from a supernatural event into a secular accomplishment. Istvan repeatedly ponders the difficulty in distinguishing 'how different, really, is a man from a mec?' (Koja, 2010, p. 29) and the role of puppet is not just reserved for women in *Under the Poppy*: when Istvan and his lover, Rupert, are boys living on the streets we learn that they are forced to be 'toys' for the men who will purchase their sexual favours. As they grow older, Rupert's desire for Istvan makes him 'shaking and helpless [...] as a puppet unstrung' (Koja, 2010, p. 83). However, Istvan as ventriloquist and puppet-master is never represented as in serious danger of losing his autonomy. Although he is a queer ventriloquist he is impermeable to the manipulations of others and takes advantage of his own penetrative privileges. The opening scene of the novel offers a shocking demonstration of his abilities. Rupert and the co-owner of the Poppy, Decca, are disturbed by cries of one of their employees, Pearl. They discover her being penetrated by two men, one wearing a 'white plague mask' and the other a 'dwarf': 'assaulting her simultaneously: the dwarf's arm is aiming up her back passage, the man is pounding at her front' (Koja, 2010, p. 2). Although the narrative voice recognizes that this is an 'assault', the problem for the brothel owners is that the 'dwarf' has not paid his fee. When the brothel's security man attempts to remove him the 'dwarf's' head is ripped off in the struggle, spurting blood across the bedroom. Unsurprisingly, 'Pearl goes mad, the hideous half-clothed body still attached to her by its arm, its hand still jammed inside' (Koja, 2010, p. 2). The denouement of this hideous scenario is that the 'dwarf' is a puppet manipulated and voiced by the other customer who is revealed to be Istvan, Decca's brother. Pearl is used as a mere prop for the ventriloquist's trick. Both ventriloquist and puppet penetrate the girl and the violence and horror of this opening scene is never really redressed in the novel. Pearl remains traumatized by the experience but elicits no sympathy from her fellow workers, as Lucy mocks her, imitating her cries of terror (Koja, 2010, p. 9).

What is the function of this neo-Victorian sex scene, inflected as it is by ventriloquial imagery? It renders explicit the sexual dynamics of the Victorian script of ventriloquism but makes no attempt to interrogate the gendered power division of the act. Pearl is represented as passive and easily manipulated by Istvan's deception; Istvan is depicted as a sexually potent, trickster character. Koja might allow her master ventriloquist to pontificate on the boundary between 'men' and 'mec', but not to recognize that *women* are more vulnerable to being cast as puppets in the world of the Poppy. Evacuated of critical impulse, Pearl's double penetration by ventriloquist and dummy is a lurid example of the exploitative ways in which neo-Victorian ventriloquism can operate when separated from sexual politics. Apart from its investment in Victorian ventriloquist narratives, the 'Victorian' element of *Under the Poppy* is actually rather obscure. It is significant that the action of the novel is very difficult to place in terms of location and date. The text is in two parts, and the publisher's blurb on the book's cover states that the second half of the story is in Brussels of the 1870s. The first half of the novel is set under the shadow of impending war, presumably in Europe, and yet names of towns are mentioned that could locate the plot in Britain, continental Europe or even North America. Indeed, the shadow cast by authorities intent on clamping down on the decadence of the Poppy might even be reminiscent of Berlin prior to World War Two.

There are various anachronistic references to fin-de-siècle British culture in the novel. Walter, a worker at the Gaiety Theatre local to the

Poppy, mentions actresses who call themselves 'the Jersey Lily' (Koja, 2010, p. 145) which is reminiscent of Lillie Langtry, the British society beauty. However, such a nickname would not be familiar to pre-1870s actresses, considering that Langtry was not performing onstage until the 1880s. Istvan refers to Benjamin, his rival for Rupert's affections, as 'The Happy Prince... dip him in whitewash, call him a statue' (Koja, 2010, p. 251). This appellation, referring as it does to same-sex desire, seems to invoke the name of Oscar Wilde's short story 'The Happy Prince', but this was first published in 1888, at least a decade after Istvan's use of the expression in 1870s Brussels. My intention in highlighting these details is not to denigrate Koja's research, but to probe the ways in which voices of 'the Victorian' era become strangely detached from a stable context in *Under the Poppy*. The novel gives the impression that is talking to a desire to present a certain image of the nineteenth century to a neo-Victorian readership, resplendent in sexual exploitation and tawdry glamour but bearing little relation to any specific historical moment or voice. *Under the Poppy* thus exemplifies the perils of neo-Victorian ventriloquism; the critical reader is not encouraged to scrutinize the dialogue between the Victorian and contemporary eras, as the historical allusions in the text buckle under interrogation. Instead, an uncritical reader is encouraged to digest neo-Victorian stereotypes of Victorian sexuality. Koja's novel functions as an example of neo-Victorianism talking to itself.

Conclusion

This chapter has broadened the concept of neo-Victorian ventriloquism to consider the role performed by the critical reading and interpretation of neo-Victorian texts. I have identified *Possession, Fingersmith,* and *Under the Poppy* as offering different perspectives on the ventriloquial process of reading. *Possession* offers a sustained justification and affirmation of the role of author-ventriloquist in engaging with Victorian literature; via her representation of Ash, Byatt casts ventriloquism as a necessary and desirable aspect of literary production for both Victorian and neo-Victorian authors. In this sense, she strives to distance ventriloquism from its negative connotations of artistic inadequacy, malign influence, oppressive manipulation or silencing. However, Byatt still reinstalls the power imbalances of Victorian ventriloquism in her depiction of contemporary academics as 'dummies' and in her metatextual manipulations of the critical reader of her novel. Ironically, she fulfils the role of the master Victorian ventriloquist by influencing the voice of the critic, casting critical ventriloquism as belated and repetitive for the critics inside and outside of *Possession*. Despite Byatt's confidence in her ability to control interpretations of her novel, she cannot mute the dubious sexual politics that surface in her textual depiction of ventriloquism.

Fingersmith is in various ways a novel about interpretation of narrative voice; though she has been forced into the position of dummy to the master discourse of pornography, Maud learns to read and write texts to produce a voice to articulate her own desire. Simultaneously, the critical reader of the novel is encouraged to listen again to the multiple voices and intentions that might be at work in patriarchal, heteronormative sexual scripts and to recognize that interpretation can be a way of 'talking back' to such scripts. Yet *Fingersmith* also teaches us that interpretations of an author's work cannot be wholly controlled, and that subversive repetitions run the risk of being absorbed back into the dominant discourse of heteronormative sex.

Close critical reading of *Under the Poppy* exposes the conservatism of its depiction of ventriloquism and sexuality, and also demonstrates that the echoes of the 'Victorian' era within the novel are an act of ventriloquial misdirection. The text is an echo-chamber of neo-Victorian voices dislocated from Victorian sources and the reader is left uncertain whether this is a self-conscious ventriloquial strategy on the part of Koja or an inadvertent indication of the problems of not 'listening' to the context of nineteenth-century voices. Understanding neo-Victorian literature as a process of ventriloquism can provide a way of conceptualizing the myriad voices and intentions that are involved in 'talking back' to the Victorians. In its most sophisticated incarnations, neo-Victorian ventriloquism both listens to and *generates* multiple voices for authors and critical readers. At its most problematic, neo-Victorian ventriloquism will recite the oppressive, manipulative impulses of Victorian ventriloquists such as Basil Ransom and Svengali. The promise and perils of neo-Victorianism reside in the slipperiness of ventriloquial power relations.

Afterword: Voices Beyond the Victorian Era? Wesley Stace and Ventriloquism

In the heyday of ventriloquism as a form of popular entertainment it was typically the dummy that had the last word and yet, as the discussion of the dummy stage performance in Chapter 1 explained, it is really never the 'dummy' speaking, but a knowing illusion on the part of the ventriloquist and a willing self-deception on the part of the audience. An attempt to have 'the last word' on any topic, particularly on such elusive matters as gender construction, sexuality, agency, authorial voice – let alone ventriloquism – is surely also self-deceptive and illusory. A central aim of this book has been to conceptualize neo-Victorian ventriloquism as a poly-vocal exchange. Lest I fulfil the role of dummy in trying to make an Afterword 'the last word', as if it ever could be, this final section of the book seeks to acknowledge the ways in which the representation of ventriloquism in contemporary literature with an investment in re-voicing the past cannot be confined wholly within the 'Victorian' era.

As a strategy to reflect upon the themes of gender and ventriloquism that have been explored throughout this study, my Afterword offers readings of two novels by Wesley Stace: *Misfortune* (2005) and *By George* (2007). Neither text actually finds a direct 'voice' from the Victorian era; the main plot of *Misfortune* is set in the late eighteenth/early nineteenth century and the narrative of *About George* is split between the 1930s–1940s and the 1970s onwards, but both develop the script of Victorian ventriloquism in various ways. *Misfortune* tells the story of a male child found by the melancholic Lord Geoffroy Loveall who, in his grief over the death of his beloved sister Dolores years earlier, ignores the baby's sex and raises the child as a girl, Rose, who is fashioned as a substitute for his lost 'Dolly'. The novel addresses the construction of Rose's cross-gendered subjectivity and her attempts to produce a 'voice' to narrate her life in the face of confused 'origins' and manipulative guardians. The concept of the author-ventriloquist and author-dummy is explicitly invoked by Stace's *By George*; part of the text is narrated by a ventriloquist's dummy, the property of Joe Fisher, son of the female ventriloquist Echo Endor. The novel also focuses on the childhood of George Fisher, grandson of Joe and heir to his dummy, and his relationship to his ventriloquial heritage. Both texts are concerned with the gendered dynamics of ventriloquism and the concept of displaced voice as a way of accessing the past, and I suggest that Stace's novels provide us with an opportunity to consider the powers and potential, perils and problems of Victorian and neo-Victorian ventriloquisms.

Geoffroy Loveall is the reclusive, eccentric heir to Love Hall, irrevocably marked by his childhood loss of Dolly. Of course, her name is reminiscent of the archetypal prop of ventriloquism and in the novel's description of the children's meeting with their governess, Anonyma, the woman who will subsequently become the wife of convenience to Geoffroy and adoptive mother to Rose, his ventriloquial designs upon Dolly become manifest. Under her brother's influence Dolores utters a greeting in French to Anonyma: 'Behind her, the elder boy mouthed every word with his sister, his pupil, and nodded, gratified by the finished result' (Stace, 2005, p. 58). Geoffroy's role as prompter of his sister is informed by sibling love, but also underscores the sense of superiority which comes from his puppet-master status: 'It was as though he felt above the world, invisible: the master pulling the puppet strings above the curtain' (Stace, 2005, p. 58). Geoffroy is confident in his manipulative abilities and perceives himself as immune to such voice-related influences. This is a motif of ventriloquial mastery which is now familiar to us; nineteenth-century ventriloquists from Valentine Vox to Svengali are defined by their ability to control the voices of others but to remain impenetrable. However, Anonyma responds to Dolly's address and furthermore 'talks back' to Geoffroy. The effect of this is to undermine his sense of detachment: 'there he sat, in plain view. He had concentrated all his efforts into providing Dolores with the most magnificent of entrances, and now he was trying not to blunder himself' (Stace, 2005, p. 58). Ventriloquists do not expect to be questioned or spoken to on an equal level and Geoffroy's machinations are exposed. This is the novel's first hint that voices are not always easy to control and that 'dollies' do not always behave as expected.

For years after Dolores' death Geoffroy persists in ventriloquizing his sister. His sanctuary is their former playroom which contains the Doll's House, a miniature replica of Love Hall and the supposed residence of

Dolly's spirit: 'Now, despite his thirty-three years, he still spoke to his sister in the doll's house. When he needed her help – *assisterance*, he called it – he sat in front of the doll's house and gently unclasped the front. He peered inside, worrying each time that she would no longer be there. Then she appeared' (Stace, 2005, p. 28). Indeed, it is 'Dolly' who whispers the advice to Geoffroy that he should 'build a new house' after finding the infant Rose and his mother's death, informing him that Anonyma will aid in this new era of Love Hall's history (Stace, 2005, p. 53). The novel never clarifies the source of Dolly's voice; is Geoffroy truly dictated to by voices from the past, or does he speak for and as Dolly to justify his actions? Either way, Rose becomes Geoffroy's way of revisiting history to inform his present, a double for the lost Dolly who will also be subjected to his misguided manipulations. What *Misfortune* teaches us is that the desire to replicate the past via ventriloquial dialogue has unpredictable results: Rose could never be Dolly, she is not even biologically female, but her adoptive father's insistence upon moulding her to a prior script produces a hybrid identity for his 'daughter'.

On a rare outing beyond the confines of his ancestral home, Geoffroy discovers a baby lying amongst the detritus of a rubbish site. Convincing himself that he can repossess his history, Geoffroy takes the child, names her 'Rose' and brings her up with Anonyma as the heir to Love Hall, but in his fixation on Dolly he either chooses or fails to acknowledge that Rose is a boy child. He uses the past to construct a script for the child's life and looking back at her infancy Rose acknowledges: 'I was just a baby, safe in my mother's arms, but he was drawing plans all around me' (Stace, 2005, p. 108). Geoffroy has always experienced gender trouble; as a child he cannot tell the difference between male and female dolls (Stace, 2005, p. 51) and his attire is described as 'fabulously effeminate' (Stace, 2005, p. 98). Anonyma colludes with his delusions, however, due to her own sense of duty to the memory of Dolly but also because of her faith in the work of the poet Mary Day. According to Day:

A baby's inner sense of itself was neither male nor female, until society taught it which role it was to assume. (Has this been entirely discredited yet? If not, it will be.) Boys and girls were therefore made and not born, and I would be made. I would without doubt be the most adorable and original child ever born, and an even more successful adult [...] My mother was giving me the greatest gift that she could offer. (Stace, 2005, p. 98)

Rose's cross-gendered upbringing is Anonyma's experiment, 'a chance to test her theories' (Stace, 2005, p. 98) and it dramatizes the dangers of trying to manipulate subjectivity to serve a personal agenda. Geoffroy and Anonyma both attempt to play puppet-master to their new 'Dolly' The apparent dismissal of a constructionist account of gender by the narrative voice in the above quotation is ambiguous; should we presume that Rose is 'originally' male and her compelled adherence to the script of femininity a mere 'copy'? I feel that this sense of scepticism towards Anonyma's project actually functions as a caution against fixing the complex interactions between sex, anatomy and gender to a master discourse that can 'speak for' all. As Rose reaches puberty her body rebels against her nominal gender role but later in life she reaches a 'true' identity that is a conspicuous blurring of both masculine and feminine signifiers: dresses, veils, and extravagant facial hair. When compared to a female impersonator, Rose is indignant: 'I am not doing an impersonation. You cannot imitate that which you really are' (Stace, 2005, p. 384). Rose's 'reality' is between boundaries; a combination of historical scripts dictated by her would-be ventriloquist father and mother and the performative dictations of masculinity and femininity. She both reiterates and subverts these scripts, revealing that gender identity is a multi-faceted construction which cannot be fixed to an origin but simultaneously acknowledging that she cannot transcend the historical scripts which have shaped her present identity. It is only on Geoffroy's deathbed that he can finally acknowledge Rose as his son. He sits up in bed 'as though a puppeteer has jerked suddenly on his invisible strings. The sheets fell down around him, revealing a pink nightdress' (Stace, 2005, p. 233). The puppet-master becomes puppet when he realizes that he cannot control his 'Dolly's' body. And what of Geoffroy's gender trouble? In a sense, the ventriloquist has become his own 'dolly', and Rose's response recognizes this alteration in their roles: 'A new script had been given me, though I didn't know where it was from, and the words came from deep inside me' (Stace, 2005, p. 234). She is still aware of reciting a pre-determined script yet also understands that the 'origin' of social scripts is perpetually obscure; the master ventriloquist is always already absent and gendered discourse will make puppets of both father and child.

The above quotation suggests that Rose does bring her own 'voice' to her performance but her claim that the voice comes from 'deep inside me' connects her utterance to the history of ventriloquism. The word 'ventriloquist' is the direct Latin translation of the older Greek term 'engastrimyth' meaning 'belly speaker', representing the belief in supernatural accounts of ventriloquism that this was where the speaking spirit was residing or the secular speculations that ventriloquists produced their voices from an anatomical location other than the normal organs of speech.[1] Rose's admission that her new voice might be an example of 'belly-speaking' takes on another dimension when considering Steven Connor's commentary on the early Christian rumours that Ancient Greek prophetesses spoke from their genitals (Connor, 2000, p. 69). Are Rose's new words dependent on her father's final acknowledgement that she is 'really' a boy, and hence the 'new script' is dictated by the anatomical fact of her penis? Rose does meditate on the gendering of voice in her narrative and her anxiety about the production of voice belies such an essentialist interpretation. The novel begins as a third-person, seemingly omniscient narration and yet the second section of the text introduces the first-person voice of Rose:

> I should apologize for not revealing myself in the first volume, which I chose not to tell in my own voice. "Why," you may ask, "when you are so very first person now?" The answer is simple [...] I didn't think my own voice would be persuasive enough, so I opted for the old-fashioned narrator, the All-Seeing One – or let's call him God. No one knows how God knows everything. He knows – after all, it's bound to be a man (and He blithely assumes that you are also male) – but He says He knows and we all believe Him. He speaks with knowledge and the force of history on His side [...] It was I who made up the first line of this confession, but when I read it to myself in His voice (deep, echoing) even I believed it. Print, too, is very persuasive – it has saved my life on more than one occasion. I have an entirely different style from God. I deal only in the truth, that is, the truth as I witnessed it. If I had written the foregoing part in my own voice, I would have been covering, waiting for what I knew and making up the rest: there would have been a few arias but also whole scenes of recitative and a good deal of rhubarb. (Stace, 2005, p. 77)

An act of authorial voice-throwing becomes necessary for Rose, as she understands her own marginalized position in relation to literary production and patriarchal discourse. Bearing in mind that as Rose is telling her story she is in full possession of the knowledge of her 'true' identity, she still clearly does not want to lay claim to the authority of 'male' voice. Although her self-conscious ventriloquism of the third-person narrative style might be perceived as a deferral of agency – an assumption of the 'dummy' role in relation to the master discourse of omniscient, quasi-divine authorial knowledge – she recognizes that this form of narration is also a ventriloquial act in the first instance; writing is always the assumption of another voice, it just depends which voice the author-ventriloquist has access to or utilizes to suit their purposes. Rose is also 'talking back' to the status of the quasi-divine, third-person narrative voice: 'I needed God, so I put Him to work for me. Of course, I also spoke in my own voice – for even God, however neutral He pretends to be, must commit a little of Himself' (Stace, 2005, p. 78). In other words, even a figure as marginalized as Rose can audaciously appropriate 'God's' voice for her own purposes. As an author, she is both ventriloquist and dummy but these roles can co-exist.

Like all of the neo-Victorian texts discussed in this study, *Misfortune* is a multi-voiced narrative and it engages with the way in which 'his-story' can be 'voiced', interpreted and manipulated for various purposes. But what can Stace's novel add to the neo-Victorian ventriloquisms that have already been explored? Although it has much in common with neo-Victorian literature, *Misfortune* is largely silent about the Victorian period; the revelation of Rose as the true heir to Love Hall comes in 1839 and her personal narrative ends with her death in 1918. There is an additional 'voice' in the form of the guide book to Love Hall as the novel's appendix, which is dated 2000, but the parable of Geoffroy Loveall whose obsession with the past leads him to ventriloquize – not wholly successfully – his daughter's present and future functions as a warning against fetishizing a bygone era. Like Rose, we might not be able, or even desire, to silence the prior discourses which shape us, but depending too heavily on the voices of specific historical moment as a fictive 'origin' or 'script' runs the risk of making dummies of us all.

The way in which historical scripts can become oppressive 'voices' for subsequent generations is a key concern of *By George*. The Fisher family contains several generations of ventriloquists: Vox Knight, who practices distant-voice ventriloquism in the nineteenth century; his daughter Echo Endor (otherwise known as Evie Fisher), who is part of the 'golden age' of ventriloquism and uses a dummy; Echo's son Joe Fisher, who is reluctantly coerced into following his mother's footsteps and performing with a dummy; George Fisher, Joe's grandson who inherits his father's dummy and his secret memoirs hidden inside the puppet. Ventriloquism is the inheritance – the familial 'script' – of the Fishers. There is also a tradition of naming the Fisher boys after ventriloquist's dummies. Joe is named after Coster Joe, the puppet used by the famous ventriloquist Fred Russell who popularized the performance centring on a single dummy (Stace, 2009, p. 31). George is named after his grandfather's dummy. Throughout this book I have concentrated on how the 'dummy' can be perceived as representing feminized traits prior to the dummy/vent performance act which dominates twentieth-century understandings of ventriloquism. However, the gendering of ventriloquism is overtly addressed in *By George* and the term 'dummy' is interrogated, ironically enough, by George the puppet: 'better call me *boy* rather than *doll* (a little girlish), *figure* (too formal), or *dummy* (for obvious reasons); *mannequin*, though preferable for its manliness, is archaic' (Stace, 2009, p. 11). George's preference for an appropriately gendered appellation emphasizes the way in which twentieth-century ventriloquism becomes about 'boys' and this connection between male children and the condition of the dummy offers a notable departure from the gendered currencies of manipulation in Victorian ventriloquism narratives which are the focus of the neo-Victorian ventriloquism texts examined in the main body of this book. Victorian and neo-Victorian narratives regularly address patriarchal ventriloquists – actual fathers such as Selah Tarrant in *The Bostonians* and Friedrich Wieck in *Clara*, but also symbolic patriarchs such as Svengali, Basil Ransom, Jeremiah/ Jerome, Simon Jordan and Jack Walser. The primary manipulative force of *By George* is Echo Endor and the Fisher family represents a matrilineage, characterized by forceful women and absent fathers. Evie/Echo remarks: '"The Fisher men are not to be relied upon, never were. Only the boys, only the boys"' (Stace, 2009, p. 75). The word 'boys' is imbued with a double meaning: Echo is adept at manipulating both dummies and sons. When asked whether Joe will follow her into the family profession she responds: '"He will [...] if I say so" (Stace, 2009 p. 14). She also demonstrates her ability to shape Joe's voice, onstage and off. Joe initially aspires to become a distant voice ventriloquist, but Echo refuses such relics of nineteenth-century ventriloquism: 'He had finally been ready to prove himself, to show off, to make her proud, but whatever confidence the speech had conjured vanished with her interruption' (Stace, 2009, p. 69). The matriarch-ventriloquist will not only silence her son, but furthermore will steal his voice: when Joe refuses to enter into a dialogue with her, Echo mimics his voice, explaining that '"if you won't speak for yourself, I'll speak for you"' (Stace, 2009, p. 69).

Evie's stage name engages with the history of displaced voice; 'Echo' refers to the mythical character who pines away to nothing more than a redundant voice for love of Narcissus, 'Endor' refers to the Witch of Endor, a biblical character famed for producing ventriloquial utterance.[2] At the same time, her rejection of past modes of ventriloquism belies her nominal debt to the gendered aspect of this history. Echo's success is, in part, due to her novelty as a female ventriloquist in the male-dominated era of the 1920s–1940s: 'No one had seen a boy partnered by a *woman*: only men had dared say such cheeky things' (Stace, 2009, p. 10). Echo's role as ventriloquist is a transgression of traditional gender roles but as we have also seen in relation to the female ventriloquists in neo-Victorian fiction – Fevvers, Grace Marks, Diana Lethaby, Margaret Prior, Selina Dawes, Ruth Vigers – this does not necessarily provide a permanent subversion of the oppressive relationship between ventriloquists and dummies. Echo cannot help but claim the domineering privileges of Victorian ventriloquists, even as she dismisses their art. The dummy might be a 'boy' but the power imbalance persists. Later in life Echo also recognizes her own role in relation to history. She is a benign presence in George's life but she will never allow her great-grandson to refer to her as 'Echo': '"Because now I am just an Echo, a memory, and I certainly don't want to be reminded of that fact"' (Stace, 2009, p. 130). As Evie was able to scorn the previous generation of ventriloquists, she is now subjected to the same fate. She in turn has become redundant, returned to the passive role of her namesake. Evie perceives herself as relic from a past age and although her presence in the Fisher family represents the persistence of historical voices it also indicates the ease with which past voices might be marginalized or misheard. Echo Endor's fate offers an avenue for reflecting upon the 'echoes' of past voices in neo-Victorian fiction. We must be attuned to the ways in which past voices will reverberate, resonate but also distort and even fade in contemporary contexts, but similarly how contemporary voices will 'echo' for subsequent generations. What 'voices' of the Victorians are we preserving as our inheritance, and what 'voices' of neo-Victorian ventriloquism will persist as a future inheritance? Like Evie, will our dismissal of certain voices come back to haunt us? Does neo-Victorian ventriloquism emulate the power imbalances of Victorian ventriloquism even as it 'talks back' to this prior script? This study has consistently addressed these questions, not to provide easy answers, but to stimulate further debate about the issues surrounding 'giving voice' to the past and to consider how ventriloquism can be situated as a key trope in such dialogues.

Passages of the book are narrated 'by George'; the dummy offers us an insight into Joe's life in the shadow of his mother, his unsuccessful relationship with his wife and his burgeoning friendship with the transvestite ventriloquist Bobbie Sheridan and his beautiful dummy Bella. Bobbie explains his cross-dressing act as a tribute to Echo Endor. George adores Bella, and tells us the story of their strange and passionate courtship. Initially, we are lead to believe that on some level George might have a voice and consciousness beyond his ventriloquist and yet when the real boy George finds his grandfather's dummy he discovers some manuscripts hidden within the puppet. In an echo of 'Dolly hides a Secret' in *Possession*, the dummy George harbours 'The Memoirs of George Fisher', a series of letters addressed to 'B' which reveals the author's sense of alienation from his family life and his love for his correspondent. But does 'B' stand for Bella the dummy, or Bobbie the ventriloquist? My study has identified a recurring trope of the queer ventriloquist, most clearly realized in a Victorian context by Oscar Wilde's work and featuring in Sarah Waters' neo-Victorian novels. This queerness is written into George's ventriloquial inheritance for it is his grandfather's dummy that can articulate 'the love that dare not speak its name' on behalf of his master. In *By George*, a ventriloquist's dummy reveals the 'truth' of the Fisher family history, but this is an occluded, unstable truth of multiple voices and perspectives.

After the discovery of the letters, George stops speaking and will only talk through his grandfather's dummy. His anxious family send him to a therapist who identifies the similarities between George and his grandfather: 'you had to disguise your voice in order to be heard' (Stace, 2009, p. 308). However, she also cautions George against emulating his grandfather's lack of interest in women and, implicitly, his queerness:

> If Joe did mistrust women, it's possible that men would have seemed safer and more nurturing in comparison. And yet where is Joe's father? Barely mentioned in the diary [...] With no male role model and an overbearing mother, Joe must have been ambivalent: perhaps he tried to love this man who claimed, however humorously, to have modelled himself on Joe's mother. (Stace, 2009, p. 309)

This assessment has dubious connotations; the female ventriloquist is blamed for producing a queer son and this idea that non-normative sexuality is due to familial relationships echoes Freudian understandings of sexual identity. Must we return to A. S. Byatt's image of Freud as a master ventriloquist, dictating the script of our sexual vocabulary? Not necessarily, as the therapist's version of Echo does not cohere with George's experience of his great-grandmother; ventriloquists are never all-powerful in *By George* and the therapist's attempts to fix the Fisher family within a stable narrative is undermined by the novel's conclusion.

Joe was supposedly killed whilst entertaining the troops out in Italy during the Second World War but his story does not end there. The teenage George meets an Italian collector of ventriloquists' dummies

who is desperate to acquire his grandfather's dummy and the manuscript he knows it contains. On visiting Italy to take the dummy to the
collector, George notices that an old man at the house bears an uncanny
resemblance to his grandfather. When George informs this man he has
discovered the memoirs, his suspicions are confirmed:

> He nodded, without turning to me, and said nothing. A smile crept
> across his lips, a remorseful smile not meant for me. Still there were
> no words. I filled the silence with his imagined thoughts: the life lost
> to him, the family he had fled, the lie in which he had taken refuge,
> the ghost he had become, the grandson he imagined and to whom
> he had spoken across decades. (Stace, 2009, p. 375)

Joe Fisher has retreated into silence and his grandson is left with the
task of 'voicing' his past. An act of narrative ventriloquism becomes
the only way in which George can access his family history. He must
form his own script for his ancestor, imagine his life, cast Joe as player
in a fiction. Joe's only communication is to write a note instructing
his grandson to 'tell them I'm sorry', to which George responds: 'How
could I when he was dead? I shook my head and walked away' (p. 376).
George refuses to speak for his grandfather, and also refuses to repeat
his words. He has recognized the limitations of a one-sided conversation with the past but makes the decision to keep the 'fictional' version
of Joe Fisher intact.

I began this study by rejecting the primacy of twentieth-century
understandings of ventriloquism which oscillate around an imbalance of
power between ventriloquist and dummy. Although *By George* is located
within the era of the dummy/ventriloquist performance it owes much to
the Victorian and neo-Victorian script of ventriloquism. It also encapsulates a collection of themes that have shaped this book: the gendered history of ventriloquism; the resistance of neo-Victorian ventriloquisms to
fixing voices to finite sources; the ways in which the roles of ventriloquist
and dummy might be negotiated to allow space for multiple voices to
emerge. The theme of ventriloquism in Stace's novel provides an opportunity for us to speculate on the ways in which authorship becomes a
process of ventriloquism, without clear distinctions between 'speaking
as', 'speaking through' or being 'spoken for'. Additionally, it offers a perspective on ventriloquism beyond the dominance of Victorian and neo-
Victorian voices, whilst simultaneously acknowledging that such voices
cannot be silenced. *By George* does feature a text that I have identified as
formative of the Victorian script of ventriloquism: *The Life and Adventures*

of Valentine Vox the Ventriloquist. Joe studies this book whilst learning how to throw his voice and it is sent to George whilst he is away at boarding school: 'He opened the front cover. In it was scratched: "For My Georgie, Impress your friends! See you at half-term. Love, Evie (Sep '73)". Above this, in the faded ink of a fountain pen: "For Joe, Practice makes perfect – I know! Echo (April '27)."' (Stace, 2009, p. 52). Significantly, this gift is from Evie. Two forms of 'script' come into focus: one of the foundational texts of Victorian ventriloquism and also the personal script of George's ventriloquial genealogy. Evie's changing relationship to her role as transmitter of ventriloquial heritage is underscored by the inclusion of her stage name and her real name. 'Echo' functions as signifier of matriarchal dictation – Joe is instructed to emulate his mother's success – and 'Evie' represents George's affectionate relationship with his great-grandmother.

However, George's engagement with the novel is ambivalent. Although Valentine's ventriloquial prowess inspires him to attempt to practice distant-voice ventriloquism, George is disconcerted by the 'mean-spirited' nature of Valentine's pranks and he begins to doubt the veracity of the novel's account of ventriloquism, as the explanation of Vox's powers is 'wilfully obscure': 'there was one thing that troubled George above all else: Valentine's skill, the very subject of this thick brick of a book – could it actually be done?' (Stace, 2009, pp. 82–3). George ponders the ethical implications of such ventriloquial demonstrations:

> If you could harness that 'power' – make people utterly believe that there was a voice coming from elsewhere – what could you use it for? How far would you go? Certainly the events in *Valentine Vox* were exaggerated, but would someone really have spent so long writing 512 pages, each filled with 700 words, if the whole thing could be dismissed just like that, as a kid's book? Were people so very stupid whenever the book was written or was their willingness to believe in Valentine a longing for magic that George could exploit even today? (p. 85)

Crucially, George comes to recognize that Valentine's purported powers are fictional; the 'origin' of his ventriloquial inheritance is a construct, albeit a compelling one. *By George* teaches us that Victorian ventriloquists were never as powerful as they pretended, their sinister power is a sham and the search for the 'true' ventriloquial voice is exposed as fruitless. This has thought-provoking implications for thinking about neo-Victorian ventriloquism, the fixation on 'talking back' to the Victorians and re-voicing the past. The 'Victorian' script that is being re-cited always already fictional, but nevertheless persists. In various ways, the texts on neo-Victorian ventriloquism that have been discussed in this book represent the 'longing for magic' that George identifies as characteristic of Victorian ventriloquism; the willingness to believe in the figure of the sinister, omnipotent masculine ventriloquist even as this trope is challenged. This is unsurprising for, as George muses, who wants to realize that the weighty tomes of Victorian ventriloquism might be a diversion, a trick of misdirection from 'real' Victorian voices? At the same time, we must acknowledge that these textual voices are our only access to the silent past; narrative reconstruction of Victorian voices is necessarily ventriloquial. But does George's impulse to 'exploit' this fictional power – with attendant connotations of abuse, manipulation and mastery – find a resonance in neo-Victorian exercises in ventriloquism? At times, perhaps. As George has identified, ventriloquial power is in the eye – or ear – of the reader. As ventriloquial voice might refuse location to a finite source, neo-Victorian ventriloquisms resist being fixed to a finite intention or agenda. *Gender and Ventriloquism in Victorian and Neo-Victorian Fiction* has sought to trace some of these voices, but actively encourages further dialogue.

Notes

Introduction: The Victorians for Dummies? Talking Back to the Nineteenth Century

1. See Louis Althusser's discussion in 'Ideology and Ideological State Apparatus (Notes towards an Investigation)' (1970) of how the discursive subject is brought into being through the process of interpellation (2001, p. 118). Judith Butler pursues this theory in her book *Excitable Speech: A Politics of the Performative* (1997) where she adapts Althusser's work to argue that the process of being interpellated into discourse also gives the subject the agency to 'talk back' to the prior call (Butler, 1997, p. 15).

2. To further complicate these series of definitions, it is worth noting that the concept of 'the Victorian' is in itself debateable. Andrea Kirchknopf writes of extending the boundaries of 'the Victorian era' to beyond Queen Victoria's reign, identifying 'the Victorian' as an aesthetic rather than historic designation (2008, p. 55). In an introductory article for the inaugural issue of the journal *Neo-Victorian Studies*, Marie-Luise Kohlke argues for 'the widest possible interpretation of 'neo-Victorian' and so [to] include the whole of the nineteenth century, its cultural discourses and products, and their abiding legacies, not just within British and British colonial contexts and not necessarily coinciding with Queen Victoria's realm' (Kohlke, 2008, p. 2). A comparably inclusive definition can be used in relation to the 'Victorian' era itself: although the nineteenth-century texts studied in this book were published within the reign of Queen Victoria, the North American setting of Henry James' *The Bostonians* extends the remit of 'the Victorian' to outside of an immediately English context.

3. See, for example, Rebecca Munford and Paul Young (2009, p. 4), Louisa Yates (2010, pp. 186–211), Rohan McWilliam (2009, p. 107) and Andrea Kirchknopf (2008, p. 54), amongst others.

4. See Susan Sniader Lanser (1992, p. 3) and Cora Kaplan (2001, p. 63) on the significance of the 'voice' and 'speech' metaphor in identity politics.

5. The phrase 'anxiety of influence' is taken from Harold Bloom's study of literary influence, *The Anxiety of Influence* (1973). Bloom's use of an oedipal model for conceptualizing generational conflict and rivalry is relevant to Louisa Hadley's recent discussion of the (grand)parent/child implications of neo-Victorianism's relation to the Victorians. Following the work of J. B. Bullen, Hadley remarks that if the Modernists perceived the Victorians as 'oppressive parent-figures', then for contemporary authors the Victorians are more like 'benign grandparents' (Hadley, 2010, p. 1). She posits: 'Removed by a generation, we escape the "anxiety of influence" that characterized the Modernists' reactions to the Victorians' (Hadley, 2010, p. 7). Whilst Hadley is right to recognize the differences between Modernist and postmodernist attitudes towards the Victorians, I contend that neo-Victorian 're-voicings'

of the nineteenth century are not as comfortable with their Victorian precursors as such an analogy might suggest. Indeed, Heilmann and Llewellyn's book emphasizes the 'anxiety of influence' as a process with which neo-Victorianism continues to struggle (Heilmann and Llewellyn, 2010, p. 3).

6. See Chapter 6 for a discussion of Jameson's distinction between 'parody' and 'pastiche', which I argue is reiterated by A. S. Byatt's justification of her use of the term 'ventriloquism' in her criticism and fiction.

7. Tatiana Kontou's and Louisa Hadley's usages of the ventriloquial metaphor are important exceptions to the otherwise very vague invocations of ventriloquism in academic commentaries on neo-Victorian literature. Kontou's brief discussion of the relationship between ventriloquism and mediumship acknowledges the ambiguity of the roles of 'ventriloquists and dummies' in neo-Victorian engagements with spiritualism (Kontou, 2009, p. 99). Hadley pauses to define ventriloquism as deployed in neo-Victorian fiction: 'Ventriloquism involves both "speaking like" and "speaking as" a Victorian, it can take the form of both impersonating a voice and "throwing" your voice so it appears to come from somewhere else [...] while "speaking like" a Victorian could result in a surface imitation of Victorian narrative forms, "speaking as" a Victorian requires an understanding of the historical conditions to which these forms are responding' (Hadley, 2010, p. 160). However, Kontou does not pursue the implications of challenging the roles of 'ventriloquist' and 'dummy' when considering the ventriloquial metaphor, and Hadley does not offer any comment on the ethical implications of either 'speaking like' or 'speaking as' a Victorian.

8. Mark Llewellyn's article, 'Neo-Victorianism: On the Ethics and Aesthetics of Appropriation' (2009) considers the ways in which these terms interact in the genre of the neo-Victorian, though this is not related to ventriloquism (Llewellyn, 2009, pp. 27–44).

9. Writing in the field of postcolonial studies, Gayatri Chakravorty Spivak has produced one of the most compelling commentaries on the perils of 'speaking for' the silenced. In 'Can the Subaltern Speak?' (1988), Spivak considers the politics of postcolonial and feminist critics providing the oppressed with 'a voice', arguing that even with the best intentions such strategies risk replicating the 'silencing' it intends to redress (Spivak, 1988, pp. 271–313). See also Heilmann and Llewellyn's discussion of how postcolonial neo-Victorianism poses a 'creative challenge' to the concept of the silent subaltern (Heilmann and Llewellyn, 2010, p. 69; pp. 66–105).

10. *De Profundis* has a complicated publication history. The letter was written circa 1896–1897 during Wilde's time at Reading Gaol. An expurgated version of the text was published by Robbie Ross in 1905 and a slightly extended version was published in Ross's 1908 volume of Wilde's 'Collected Works'. The manuscript of the letter was kept at the British Library but was not available for public access until 1960. The complete version was first published by Rupert Hart-Davis in *The Complete Letters of Oscar Wilde* (1962). As Chapter 4 discusses in further detail, *De Profundis* has a clear autobiographical context and hence to consider this letter as uncomplicatedly 'fictional' is not only erroneous but has serious ethical implications. Without losing sight of the circumstances under which the letter was produced, however, we can also view the letter as Wilde's self-conscious fictionalization of his own persona.

11. The blurb on the 1999 Virago paperback edition of *Tipping the Velvet* is taken from Mel Steel's review of *Tipping the Velvet* in the *Independent*, Sunday 22 March 1998, p. 33. See Diana Wallace (2005, pp. 209–10) and Mark Llewellyn (2007, p. 195) for discussions on the effects of the use of this quotation.

1 Voices from the Past: Rethinking the Ventriloquial Metaphor

1. I am, of course, making a generalization here about audience interpretation and I am specifically referring to an audience with a certain understanding about the conventions of ventriloquial performance. C. B. Davis' article, 'Reading the Ventriloquist's Lips: The Performance Genre behind the Metaphor' explicitly addresses children's reactions to ventriloquists and puppets/dummies (Davis, 1998, pp. 133–56). This is not to suggest that the ventriloquist/dummy illusion is not, in some circumstances, extremely compelling or convincing. Valentine Vox's book on the history of ventriloquism relates the anecdote of Eleanor Roosevelt's meeting with the then-renowned ventriloquist Edgar Bergen and his dummy Charlie. She automatically extended her hand to the doll, expecting him to shake it (Vox, 1981, p. 104).

2. There have been several works exploring the social and cultural history of ventriloquism which follow this trajectory. See, for example, Valentine Vox's *I Can See Your Lips Moving: The History and Art of Ventriloquism* (1981), Steven Connor's *Dumbstruck: A Cultural History of Ventriloquism* (2000), and Leigh Eric Schmidt's article 'From Demon Possession to Magic Show: Ventriloquism, Religion, and the Enlightenment' (1998).

3. She discusses *Paris is Burning* (1991), a film directed and produced by Jennie Livingstone that focuses on the drag balls of Harlem, New York, events that are mainly populated by black and Latino gay men. In a section of Livingstone's film we see that the balls have a category awarding 'realness' and the cross-dressing enacted in this section of the competition is concerned with how well the men can 'pass' as 'real' women. This is not drag as political subversion but as a performance that re-idealizes and perpetuates the normative construction of gender binaries (Butler, 1993, p. 131). In a comparable vein of interrogating the 'subversive' potential of drag, Butler also notes drag performances that are permitted as an established component of heteronormative entertainment. Butler provides examples such as Dustin Hoffman in *Tootsie* and Jack Lemmon in *Some Like it Hot*, whose cross-dressing functions as a negotiation of homophobic panic and as a form of 'ritualistic release', a carnivalesque inversion that will only serve to consolidate hegemonic gender boundaries when order is restored (Butler, 1993, p. 126).

4. Derrida's essay 'Signature Event Context' (1972) offers a sustained critique of Austin's assumptions about language use, particularly in relation to intention and context, and uses the concept of 'citationality' to destabilize the notions of 'originality' and 'intention'. Butler's work on the potential of transformation through re-citation is grounded in Derrida's ideas, and her own re-citation of the Derridean script of citationality introduces the new context of gendered repetitions, an issue that Derrida does not address in his 'original' text.

5. Butler's text is specifically referring to the potential to re-cite and therefore resignify *words* such as 'nigger' and 'queer'. Although theoretically her concept is applicable to longer examples of hate speech – the racist and homophobic speeches of the current British National Party leader Nick Griffin, for instance – she does not elaborate on the differences in resignificatory potential between an individual word and a sustained racist/homophobic monologue. I am indebted to Mary Eagleton for identifying this issue in the course of our discussions of Butler's ideas in *Excitable Speech*.

2   Victorian Ventriloquists: Henry James and George Du Maurier

1. See Valentine Vox for a detailed account of Russell's influence on twentieth-century ventriloquism (Vox, 1981, pp. 79–97). The author Valentine Vox is a practising ventriloquist and published his history of ventriloquism – *I Can See Your Lips Moving: The History and Art of Ventriloquism* – under his stage name. His own indebtedness to the history of ventriloquism is emphasized by this name for, as Chapter 2 explains, 'Valentine Vox' was the name of Henry Cockton's ventriloquizing protagonist in *The Life and Adventures of Valentine Vox the Ventriloquist.*
2. It is important to note, of course, that the life and work of Henry James has played an important role in neo-Victorian fiction such as Cólm Toíbin's *The Master* (2004) and David Lodge's *Author, Author* (2004). For a discussion of the cultural afterlife of James' *The Turn of the Screw* (1898), see Ann Heilmann (2010, pp. 111–30).
3. See Larzer Ziff (1962, p. 51), Charles C. Bradshaw (2003, p. 376) and William A. Manly (1963, pp. 319–20) for examples of brief discussions of the ventriloquism theme in *Wieland*. Eric A. Wolfe's article, 'Ventriloquizing Nation: Voice, Identity and Radical Democracy' (2003, pp. 431–57) offers a sustained discussion of the ventriloquial plot of Brown's novel, but this is placed in the context of eighteenth-century American politics.
4. Robert Halliday cites a review of *Valentine Vox* in *The Age*, published 10 November 1839, saying of Cockton 'we shall be much mistaken if he does not achieve a fame surpassed not even by C. Dickens' (Halliday, 1994, p. 349). Sadly the reviewer was mistaken, as Cockton's subsequent novels did not live up to his early promise and he died in poverty and obscurity (Halliday, 1994, p. 351). *Valentine* Vox's place in the *Daily Telegraph's* top 100 books of the nineteenth century is mentioned in Allan Massie's article for the same publication written 100 years later, 'The problem of predicting what will last' (4 January 2000).
5. See Susan Sniader Lanser (1992, p. 3) and Elizabeth Wilson (1982, p. 153) for a discussion of the significance of the 'voice' metaphor in second-wave feminism.
6. The sexuality of Olive Chancellor has emerged as a contentious issue in commentaries on James' novel. See Terry Castle for a summary of critics who either disregard the lesbian themes of *The Bostonians* or who argue that James' depiction of Olive is wholly condemnatory (Castle, 1993, pp. 150–1). Castle herself argues – via her metaphor of the 'apparitional lesbian' – that James' text 'insinuate[s] the *idea* of lesbianism into *The Bostonians* without [...] actually representing it' (Castle, 1993, p. 159). In Castle's terms, Olive is

a haunting presence in the novel and in Chapter 5 we shall see how Sarah Waters' *Affinity* talks back to the plot of *The Bostonians* via her depiction of ventriloquism in the séance room. Lillian Faderman also explores the theme of lesbianism in *The Bostonians*, discussing the connection between Olive and Verena in the context of 'Boston marriages' between women in nineteenth-century New England (Faderman, 1985, pp. 190–203).

7. Daniel Pick's *Svengali's Web* (2000) offers a sustained consideration of the theme of mesmerism/hypnotism in *Trilby* and this theme is also significant in the analyses of the text by Pamela Thurschwell (2001, pp. 50–4) and Hilary Grimes (2008, pp. 67–83), amongst many others.

8. Nina Auerbach has remarked upon the ambiguous gendering of Du Maurier's illustrations for *Trilby* (1981, p. 289) and Dennis Denisoff has discussed the relationship between cross-gendering and queer sexualities in the novel (Denisoff, 1998, pp. 153–62).

9. See Pick (2000) for an extended discussion of the significance of Svengali's 'Jewishness' in the novel.

3   Sirens and Svengalis: *Nights at the Circus, Alias Grace* and *Clara*

1. 'Dora' (whose real name was Ida Bauer, 1882–1945) featured as a case study in Freud's work on hysteria and through the analysis of his patient's dreams Freud was to reveal Dora's repressed desires for her father and a male family friend. From a ventriloquial perspective, the physical manifestation of Dora's hysteria is noteworthy; she suffered from aphonia (loss of voice). See Claire Kahane's consideration of the Freud/Dora relationship which focuses on the concept of 'voice' and narration in their sessions (Kahane, 1995, pp. 14–33).

2. Of course, Fevvers' status as a winged woman engenders a further comparison between the trapeze artist and the Sirens.

3. The conclusion of *Nights at the Circus* leaves the reader uncertain about the 'truth' of Fevvers' wings and her purported virginity. As the supine Jack Walser asks why she went to such lengths to convince him she was the 'only fully-feathered intacta in the history of the world', Fevvers begins to laugh: 'Gawd, I fooled you!' (Carter, 1985, p. 294). It is unclear whether the confidence trick has been in relation to her wings, her intact hymen, or both.

4. For an extended discussion of the trope of the double in twentieth-century horror films featuring ventriloquists, see Leonard G. Heldreth (1991, pp. 81–94).

5. I use the term 'proto-psychoanalytic' because although Jordan's strategies seem to echo those of Freudian psychoanalysis, the time frame of Jordan's sessions with Grace (1859) pre-dates Freud's research in the field of psychology.

6. Various critics have also noted this connection between Grace and Jordan. See Jeannette King (2005, pp. 76–7) and also Sandra Stanley (2003, p. 381). Coral Ann Howells considers Simon as becoming 'one of Grace's doubles' via his amnesia (Howells, 2003, p. 36).

7. The bond between the men in the novel emulates Eve Kosofsky Sedgwick's queered reading of the 'erotic triangle' in literature, in which 'the bond that links the two rivals is as intense and potent as the bond that links either of the rivals to the beloved' (Sedgwick, 1985, p. 21).

4 Queering the Dummy/Ventriloquist Dichotomy: Oscar Wilde and Ventriloquial Influence

1. There is very little published criticism on Wilde's 'The Harlot's House'. For a reading of the poem which assumes all puppet references in the poem to be in relation to female prostitutes, see Rhianna Shaw, 2010, www.victorianweb.org/authors/wilde/shaw.html. I am indebted to Ruth Robbins for her thoughtful comments on the poem in our conversations about Wilde and gender ambiguity.
2. The second edition of *The Oxford English Dictionary* (1989) notes that the word 'harlot' was first used in the context of masculine gender from the thirteenth century onwards, and to refer to feminine gender from the fifteenth century onwards.
3. In her article on the various ways of defining 'neo-Victorianism', Andrea Kirchknopf considers the multiple definitions of the signifier 'Victorian' (Kirchknopf, 2008, pp. 55–9). Mark Llewellyn has also acknowledged the 'anxiety of identification and periodisation' surrounding the term 'Victorian' (Llewellyn, 2008, p. 166).
4. Jonathan H. Grossman, implicitly recognizing the etymological history of the word 'influence' discussed in Chapter 2, also remarks on the significance of 'influence' in the novel: 'Appropriately fluid, "influence" seems to run all over this novel' (Grossman, 1996, p. 535). Pamela Thurschwell also engages with the theme of influence in Wilde's novel (Thurschwell, 2001, pp. 60–3).
5. See Grossman (1996, p. 536), Pick (2000, pp. 28–9) and Thurschwell (2001, pp. 37–64) for commentaries on the intertextual connections between *Dorian Gray* and *Trilby* in relation to hypnotism/mesmerism.
6. It is worth noting that Dorian's influence over Henry, and Basil, is linked to another sense: vision, or the power of the gaze. A discourse that unites both facets of this sense-related influence – the oral/aural and visual – and is also relevant to ventriloquism is the nineteenth-century interest in hypnotism or mesmerism. As Daniel Pick has remarked, the figure of the hypnotist is frequently associated with the power of the gaze; the trope of 'piercing eyes' recurs in narrative accounts of mesmeric influence (Pick, 2000, p. 51; 169). The process of hypnotic/mesmeric influence is also dependent on aural suggestibility hence the dual senses of gazing and listening/speaking are necessary to exercise such powers (Pick, 2000, p. 60). Deborah McCollister emphasizes the significance of both visual and aural influence in *Dorian Gray*, specifically in relation to mesmerism and 'charming' (1995, p. 18) and Pamela Thurschwell offers a fascinating analysis of *Dorian Gray* in relation to fin-de-siècle concerns about the morality of hypnotic influence (Thurschwell, 2001, pp. 37–64). My interest in the theme of aural/oral influence in *Dorian Gray* is not intended to reject the significance of the concept of 'the gaze' or to suggest that the senses of hearing/seeing can be wholly separated. Steven Connor, for example, addresses this issue: 'One of the problems of building an aesthetic around the principles of sound and hearing is the fact that they are hard to consider as autonomous [...] We ask of a sound "What was that?", meaning "Who was that?", or "Where did that come from?" We do not naturally ask of an image "What sound does

that make?"' (Connor, 1997, p. 213). The relationship between sound/sight is also an important aspect of the ventriloquial illusion: 'The fascination and the menace of ventriloquism derived from a belief that it represented the power of sound to countermand the evidence of sight [...] In so far as the eye may be associated with the government of space [...] the disturbing effect of ventriloquism may derive from its transcendence or disruption of seen space' (Connor, 2000, pp. 14–15). Having registered the difficulty in separating the concepts of sound/sight, however, the significance of 'the voice' and influence in Wilde's work has remained largely unaddressed in previous critical accounts of his novel, whereas 'the gaze' in *Dorian Gray* has been discussed by Cohen (1987, pp. 805–11) and Craft (2005, pp. 109–36), amongst others. My decision to focus specifically on the oral/aural dynamics of ventriloquial influence seeks to redress a relative dearth of scholarship.

7. Despite the ways in which the ways in which parrots' abilities to mimic the human voice have ensured their use as a signifier of repetition or copying, Paul Carter's study of parrots in the Western cultural imagination consistently challenges the assumption that parrots 'merely' repeat the human voice. Anyone who has spent time in the company of parrots that are able to talk will know that their 'recitations' are rarely exact and parrots have the ability to transform human speech through repetition, 'talking back' to their human interlocutor in a comparable way to the 'unruly dummy' of the ventriloquial exchanges considered in this chapter. On a personal note, my own interest in the connection between ventriloquism and parroting stems from my loquacious pet parrot named, aptly enough, Oscar.

8. Wilde's original title for the letter was *Epistola: In Carcere et Vinculis* (Wilde, 2000, p. 781). As Ruth Robbins has suggested, Wilde's decision to give the seemingly private document both a title and a genre ('Letter: in Prison and in Chains') supports the argument that the letter was written with view to being published (Robbins, 2011, p. 168). It was Robbie Ross, Wilde's friend and literary executor, who received the original copy of the letter for safekeeping and made the decision to publish an expurgated version of the text under the title of *De Profundis* ('Out of the depths') in 1905. See Merlin Holland for a detailed history of the afterlife of the manuscript (Holland, 2003, pp. 251–67).

9. In a comparable way to many details of Wilde's biography, the actual location of this incident is disputed. As this quotation suggests, Wilde claims that the exchange took place at Wandsworth, whereas Ellmann, following Gide, states that this happened during the first six weeks of Wilde's time at Reading Gaol (1988, p. 466).

10. The story of Wilde's conversation with the prisoner is first told by André Gide in *Oscar Wilde* (Gide, 1951, p. 37), and is subsequently retold by H. Montgomery Hyde (Hyde, 1990, p. 385) and Richard Ellmann (Ellmann, 1988, p. 466).

11. David Goldblatt explains that one of the conventional signifiers of skill in a ventriloquist/dummy performance is the ventriloquist's apparently motionless lips (Goldblatt, 2006, p. 40).

12. See Merlin Holland (2003, pp. 251–67) and Ian Small and Josephine Guy (2006, pp. 47–76) for discussions of the text's production. The letter was written during Wilde's time at Reading gaol. Merlin Holland provides

a summary of how Wilde came to be allowed to write whilst in prison: '[Wilde] had begun to fear for his sanity. On 2 July 1896 he petitioned the Home Secretary in cringing terms for some relaxation of the harsh prison regime [...] The petition did not fall on deaf ears. It reached the desk of the recently appointed, young and enlightened chairman of the Prison Commissioners, Evelyn Ruggles-Brise, who, after having Wilde medically examined, gave instructions on 27 July that the prisoner "should be provided with foolscap paper, ink and pen, for his use in his leisure moments in his cell" as well as a more liberal supply of books. The order coincided fortuitously with the appointment of a new governor at Reading, Major James Nelson, who additionally suggested "a strongly but coarsely bound notebook which would afford less facilities for improper use than sheets of foolscap"' (Holland, 2003, pp. 254–5). By the end of the year, however, Wilde was allowed to use the potentially 'improper' sheets of foolscap paper and he began working on the letter to Douglas.

13. See Merlin Holland (1997, pp. 3–17) and Joseph Bristow (2004, pp. 6–35) for commentaries on the blurring of 'fact' and 'fiction' in biographies of Wilde, and also Angela Kingston's *Oscar Wilde as a Character in Victorian Fiction* (2007) for a book-length study of fictional incarnations of Wilde in late nineteenth-century literature.

14. See Helen Davies, 'Original Copy: Neo-Victorian Versions of Oscar Wilde's "Voice"' for a discussion of the significance of Wilde's voice in his lifetime and cultural afterlife (2011, pp. 1–21).

15. Douglas, also known as Bosie, was not Wilde's first same-sex lover and therefore cannot be held responsible for Wilde's 'criminal' activities that led to his conviction. It was, however, Wilde's relationship with this young man that inflamed the wrath of Douglas' volatile and irrational father, the Marquis of Queensberry, to such an extent that Queensberry instigated a campaign of all-too-public defamation of Wilde. This vendetta culminated in an infamous card left at Wilde's club, accusing him of 'posing as a Somdomite [sic]'. (There is some debate as to how the scribbled handwriting should be deciphered. Ellmann, for example, argues that the card reads 'Ponce and Somdomite' (1988, p. 412). In either interpretation the intended insult – and misspelling – is clear). Bosie actively encouraged Wilde to sue Queensberry for libel, despite there being ample evidence that could, and would, be brought to trial to suggest that Wilde could himself be prosecuted under the Labouchere Amendment. Critics such as Julia Wood argue that Wilde's unabashed flouting of the laws of the era would have led to his prosecution at some point anyway and claim that Douglas has been unfairly cast as a villain in the drama of Wilde's fall from grace (Wood, 2007, pp. 65–6). Quibbling over how blame should be allocated is not particularly illuminating but it is impossible to deny that Wilde's relationship with Douglas and the strength of his devotion to the younger man were instrumental in his conviction.

16. There is evidence to suggest that Douglas was protected from prosecution by his father and also that Wilde was made a scapegoat for the indiscretions of the English upper classes and prominent Parliamentary figures of the time. Ellmann explains: 'the case was conducted by the Treasury with considerable hypocrisy. Not only was homosexuality common in the English public schools which most of the legal personages present had attended. Also there

had evidently been an agreement between Gill [the prosecutor at Wilde's first trial] and Charles Russell, Queensberry's solicitor, that Douglas' name would be kept out of the case as far as possible in return for Queensberry's detailed evidence against Wilde [...] There was also the old difficulty that Rosebery's name had been mentioned in one of Queensberry's letters' (Ellmann, 1988, p. 434). Lord Rosebery, the Foreign Secretary who was to become Gladstone's successor as Prime Minister in 1894 was also persecuted by Queensberry, in part because of his suspicions with regards to Rosebery's relationship with Lord Francis Douglas Drumlanrig, Queensberry's eldest son. Drumlanrig was to die in a 'shooting accident' in October 1894, widely thought to be a suicide and rumours circulated at the time suggesting that Drumlanrig was anxious that he would be blackmailed on account of his alleged relationship with Rosebery (Ellmann, 1988, p. 402). Queensberry held Rosebery responsible for his son's death and referred to Rosebery as a 'Snob Queer' (Ellmann, 1988, p. 402). It is obvious why such incriminating rumours would need to be quashed and one can speculate that Wilde's trials provided the government with an avenue for detracting attention from the condemnation of their party members.

17. See Ellmann for a summary of the press responses to Wilde's conviction (1988, pp. 450–1) and Ed Cohen (1993) for a nuanced reading of the media reactions to Wilde's trial and conviction. See, for example, the sympathetic coverage of Wilde's conviction provided by *Reynolds's News*. The paper pertinently noted that Wilde had not 'corrupted' any innocent men and that it was unfair that the young men appearing at the trials should go unpunished for their activities (Ellmann, 1988, p. 450).

5   Sexual Re-scripting: Ventriloquial Repetitions and Transformations in Sarah Waters' *Tipping the Velvet* and *Affinity*

1. Charles Dickens and Wilkie Collins have been cited in numerous book reviews and in academic criticism as important influences on Waters' neo-Victorian novels. Cora Kaplan also includes Charlotte Brontë, Oscar Wilde and Robert Louis Stevenson as authors to which Waters 'owe[s] a great deal in tone, structure, story and language' (Kaplan, 2007, p. 110). Mariaconcetta Constantini mentions Wilde in her list of Waters' Victorian forebears, in addition to Christina Rossetti, Elizabeth Barrett Browning, Alfred Tennyson, Mrs Henry (Ellen) Wood, Joseph Sheridan Le Fanu and Thomas Hardy (Costantini, 2006, p. 18). Paulina Palmer is notable for considering the lesbian-centred literary genealogy to which Waters' work belongs, citing the 1920s Parisian salon of Natalie Barney and the Greenwich Village literary scene of New York in the 1950s, including Ann Bannon, Valerie Taylor and Claire Morgan (Palmer, 2008, p. 71).

2. In a book chapter co-authored with Laura Doan, 'Making up for lost time: Contemporary lesbian writing and the invention of history', Waters offers a sustained commentary of the drawbacks – and benefits – of the relative absence of lesbian history for contemporary lesbian novelists, and again addresses the contrast between the histories of gay men and lesbian women (Doan and Waters, 2000, pp. 12–28).

3. Alison Oram's work on male impersonation acts in the Victorian and Edwardian music hall provides a very useful historical context for Waters' fictional representation of these performances as signalling same-sex desire to a knowing audience. Oram suggests that male impersonation was not necessarily an active critique of conventional gender roles but often a form of emulation that upholds and pays tribute to the traditions of masculine signification. She also notes that the convention of male impersonation in the theatre could operate as a licensed space for carnivalesque gender inversion as opposed to offering a subversive challenge to patriarchal and heteronormative gender (Oram, 2007, pp. 5–13). She acknowledges, however, that 'there is plenty of evidence of women's homoerotic response to male impersonators' and cites some fascinating examples of postcards of famous male impersonators that were collected and exchanged between women (Oram, 2007, pp. 51–2). This historical evidence surely informs Waters' depiction of the young women who visit and write to Nancy, and the later scene in the novel where Nancy and Florence visit a local women's pub and discover a queer cult following of Nancy's former music hall act (Waters, 1999, pp. 420–1).

4. To my knowledge, there is no historical evidence to suggest that queer women who were contemporaries of Wilde put his work to any such erotic usages and this is possibly because, as Waters' comments have suggested, there are very limited historical records about same-sex desire between women. However, the figure of Salomé does become an erotic signifier for women in the early twentieth century via a sensational trial that would interrogate notions of male and female sexual 'decency'. In February 1918 the Independent MP Noel Pemberton-Billing published an article in his paper the *Vigilante*, entitled 'The Cult of the Clitoris'. The subject of his commentary was the well-known dancer Maud Allan, a young woman who became famous for her interpretation of Salomé's 'dance of the seven veils'. The piece stated: 'To be a member of Maud Allen's [sic] private performance in Oscar Wilde's *Salome* one has to apply to Miss Valetta of 9 Duke St., Adelphi. If Scotland Yard were to seize the list of these members I have no doubt they would secure the names of several thousand of the first 47,000' (cited in Bland, 1998, p. 183). As Lucy Bland explains, a reference to the 'first 47,000' had appeared in an article in a sister-publication to the *Vigilante*, the *Imperialist*, suggesting that the German government was in possession of a 'black book' naming 47,000 English women and men who were vulnerable to blackmail by German intelligence due to their 'sexual perversions'. The article commented: 'The names of Privy Councillors [...] wives of Cabinet ministers, dancing girls, even Cabinet Ministers themselves [...] In lesbian ecstasy the most sacred secrets of the state were betrayed' (Bland, 1998, p. 184). This combination of lesbian sexuality, decadence and potential threat to the nation's security was a provocative accusation. Allan herself was provoked enough to bring a libel case against Pemberton-Billing, claiming that he was implying that she was a lesbian. The sensational case spanned six days, from late May to early June of 1918 and summaries of the complexities and implications of the case can be found in Philip Hoare's book (1997) which provides a detailed examination of the events surrounding the trial. Lucy Bland's article 'Trial by Sexology?: Maud Allan, *Salome* and the "Cult of the Clitoris" Case' also offers an excellent summary of the key facts of the trial and the role it played drawing attention

to and pathologizing lesbianism in the first decades of the twentieth century (Bland, 1998, pp. 183–98). Through a strange turn of events, the name 'Oscar Wilde' was not only considered to be synonymous with male same-sex desire but could also be used to suggest sexual activities between women. Pemberton-Billing's article constructed a titillating vision of a secret circle of women, united by their interest in clitoral sexuality, mediated through the seductive spectacle of a woman performing as Salomé. We can see that Nancy's description of how she dances as Salomé and strips 'down to her drawers' for the erotic stimulation of Diana's Sapphic coterie emphasizes this association (Waters, 1999, p. 281).

5. Sarah Gamble also remarks on the novel's 'self-consciously utopian ending' which she perceives as 'authenticity replacing performativity'. She clarifies this statement by acknowledging that Nancy's identity remains 'queer', 'unrecognized and unauthenticated by Victorian society' (Gamble, 2009, pp. 135–6). The concept of an 'authentic' queerness is surely paradoxical, and the problems with Gamble's conflation of the terms 'performance' and 'performativity' are discussed in Chapter 1.

6. Aside from *Affinity*, other neo-Victorian texts which focus on the figure of the female medium include Michèle Roberts, *In the Red Kitchen* (1990), A. S. Byatt, *Angels and Insects* (1992) and Victoria Glendinning, *Electricity* (1995).

7. Steven Connor briefly comments upon the connection between mediumship and ventriloquism in *Dumbstruck: A Cultural History of Ventriloquism* (2000, p. 390) and offers a more sustained consideration of the issue of 'voice' and the ventriloquial dynamics of spiritualism in 'The Machine in the Ghost: Spiritualism, Technology and the "Direct Voice"' (Connor, 1999b, pp. 203–25).

8. Terry Castle's theory of the 'apparitional lesbian' is an important intertext for Waters' use of spiritualism as a forum for same-sex desire. Castle argues that there is a recurring literary association between lesbianism and spectrality (Castle, 1993). Several other critics have noted the connection between *Affinity* and Castle's work. See, for example, Jeannette King (2005, p. 189), Lucie Armitt and Sarah Gamble (2006, p. 155) and Mark Llewellyn (2004, p. 211), amongst others.

6 Talking to Ourselves? Ventriloquial Criticism and Readership in Neo-Victorian Fiction

1. I use the term 'critical reader' as a way of encompassing literary critics who read neo-Victorian literature for work and pleasure (often simultaneously) and readers of neo-Victorian texts who might not be reading from an 'professional' perspective but who still bring some degree of knowledge of Victorian intertexts to the reading experience. For a discussion of the 'divided' readership of neo-Victorian fiction, see Ann Heilmann and Mark Llewellyn (2010, pp. 17–18).

2. Bernard subsequently argues that in some ways Byatt's novel refutes Jameson's comments on postmodernity's loss of historicity, 'the random cannibalization of all the styles of the past' (Jameson, 1991, p. 18) and that although nostalgia – another aspect of postmodernism criticized by Jameson – plays

a role in *Possession* it is represented as 'far from playful, far from soothing' but articulating a conscious sense of mourning and loss (Bernard, 2003, p. 20). The ways in which neo-Victorianism might both adhere to and challenge Jameson's designation of postmodernism as 'an attempt to think the present historically in an age that has forgotten how to think historically in the first place' (Jameson, 1991, p. iv) and as uncritically nostalgic has been debated by Dana Shiller and Sally Shuttleworth, amongst numerous other critics (Shiller, 1997, pp. 538–60 ; Shuttleworth, 1998, pp. 253–68). It is questionable whether Byatt's *Possession* can be understood as a 'postmodern' novel. Jackie Buxton has offered a convincing argument against the 'postmodernity' of *Possession* by emphasizing the ways in which the novel is suspicious and even condemnatory of postmodern challenges to authorship (Buxton, 2001, pp. 89–104).

3. Ann Marie Adams has also suggested that the representation of Ash's poetry in the novel bears the influence of Milton, Wordsworth and Coleridge (Adams, 2003, p. 121), Jennifer M. Jeffers figures Ash as being like Alfred Tennyson as well as Browning (Jeffers, 2002, p. 136). Louise Yelin adds George Meredith as an additional source for Ash's voice (Yelin, 1992, p. 38). It is thus worth noting that Byatt's ventriloquization of Victorian poets defy reduction to a finite location.

4. Peter Lamont's 2005 biography of Daniel Dunglas Home offers a detailed account of the animosity which Browning felt towards the medium.

5. Louise Yelin perceives that Byatt locates critics of Victorian literature, both inside and outside of the novel, as in 'a critical wilderness from which we cannot escape' (Yelin, 1992, p. 40). Ann Marie Adams suggests that Byatt's 'privileging of aesthetics and devaluation of politicized criticism' is influenced by Matthew Arnold (Adams, 2008, p. 339). Cora Kaplan explains that in *Possession*, 'the cards are subtly stacked against even the most sympathetic academic characters from the start: their own preoccupations pale against Byatt's own rich and above all literary authorial voice' (Kaplan, 2007, p. 95). Kaplan recognizes that the superiority of creative writing over critical is overtly linked to the concept of 'voice' but does not relate this to the theme of ventriloquism in *Possession*.

6. Indeed, on attempting to write about *Possession* it often feels as if everything has already been said; a sense of repeating the words of other critics which adds a further metatextual dimension to the theme of ventriloquism.

7. See Thelma J. Shinn's detailed article on the numerous connotations of the word 'possession' (Shinn, 1995, pp. 164–83).

8. Henry Spencer Ashbee (1834–1900) published his texts under the pseudonym Pisanus Fraxi. The titles of the three volumes are as follows: *Index Librorum Prohibitorum: being Notes Bio- Biblio – Icono-graphical and Critical, on Curious and Uncommon Books* (1877); *Centuria Librorium Absconditorum: being Notes Bio – Biblio – Icono-graphical and Critical, on Curious and Uncommon Books* (1879); *Catena Librorum Tacendorum: being Notes Bio – Biblio – Icono-graphical and critical, on Curious and Uncommon Books* (1885). A short biography, and a lengthy assessment of Ashbee's considerable contribution to the world of Victorian pornography, can be found in Steven Marcus's *The Other Victorians: A Study of Sexuality and Pornography in Mid-Nineteenth Century England* (1969, pp. 34–77).

9. For example, Andrea Dworkin's *Pornography: Men Possessing Women* (1981) is notable for its unequivocal condemnation of pornography and detailed descriptions of pornographic pictures and texts.
10. The body of work on feminism and pornography is extensive. Andrea Dworkin's book *Pornography: Men Possessing Women* (1981) is a landmark study in the field, and she has regularly contributed to the debates. Catharine Mackinnon is another prominent anti-pornography feminist, and her book *Only Words* (1993) is another exemplary feminist discussion of pornographic representation. A comprehensive collection of anti-pornography feminist thought is featured in a collection edited by Diana E. H. Russell, *Making Violence Sexy: Feminist Views on Pornography* (1993). Pat(rick) Califia has been a frequent and audacious defender of both S/M practices and pornography and his text *Public Sex: The Culture of Radical Sex* (2000) collects twenty years of his writing on the feminist and lesbian sexuality debates. An excellent overview of the field of feminist writing on pornography, the controversies and the implications that this might have for thinking about censorship, race and a multitude of sexual identities is provided in a collection edited by Drucilla Cornell, *Feminism and Pornography* (2000). The volume contains contributions from both pro- and anti-pornography feminist commentators and is an invaluable resource for surveying the debates surrounding this highly sensitive feminist concern. Emma Healey's *Lesbian Sex Wars* (1996) focuses specifically on the lesbian feminist engagements with pornographic representation, and also provides a useful summary of the issues.

Afterword: Voices Beyond the Victorian Era? Wesley Stace and Ventriloquism

1. Valentine Vox describes the belief that ventriloquial voice 'came from the diviner's stomach where the departed spirit was thought to dwell' (Vox, 1981, p. 17). He also comments on the book about ventriloquism written by the Abbé de la Chappelle, published in 1772, which was one of the first documents to identify that 'the ventriloquist does not speak from the stomach, as the name implies, but makes the ventriloquial sounds in the same way as sounds are normally produced, except that he diffuses the sound in such a way as make it appear distant' (Vox, 1981, p. 44).
2. The story of the Witch of Endor is found in the First Book of Samuel, Chapter 28, verses 3–25. After the death of Samuel, Saul has forbidden the practice of divination or mediumship in Israel. However, having prayed to God about the outcome of an impending battle and having received no answer, Saul resorts to going in disguise to a witch at Endor. The spirit of Samuel supposedly speaks through this woman, but the question of the source of this voice has been the topic of intense theological debate. See Steven Connor for a detailed analysis of the ventriloquial issues surrounding the story of the Witch of Endor (Connor, 2000, pp. 75–101).

Bibliography

Primary texts

Atwood, Margaret. *Alias Grace*. 1996; London: Virago, 1997.
Brown, Charles Brockden. *Wieland; or The Transformation*. 1798; Oxford: Oxford University Press, 1998.
Byatt, A. S. *Possession: A Romance*. 1990; London: Vintage, 1991.
Byatt, A. S. *Angels and Insects*. London: Chatto & Windus, 1992.
Carter, Angela. *Nights at the Circus*. 1984; London: Picador, 1985.
Cockton, Henry. *The Life and Adventures of Valentine Vox the Ventriloquist*. 1840; London: George Routledge and Sons, 1889.
Du Maurier, George. *Trilby*. 1894; Peterborough, Ontario: Broadview Press, 2003.
Faber, Michel. *The Crimson Petal and the White*. Edinburgh: Canongate Books Ltd, 2002.
Galloway, Janice. *Clara*. 2002; London: Vintage, 2003.
Glendinning, Victoria. *Electricity*. 1995; London: Simon & Schuster UK Ltd, 1997.
James, Henry. *The Bostonians*. 1886; Oxford: Oxford University Press, 1998.
Koja, Kathe. *Under the Poppy*. Easthampton, Massachusetts: Small Beer Press, 2010.
Lodge, David. *Author, Author*. London: Random House, 2004.
Rhys, Jean. *Wide Sargasso Sea*. 1966. London: Penguin, 1997.
Roberts, Michèle. *In the Red Kitchen*. 1990; London: Vintage, 1999.
Self, Will. *Dorian: An Imitation*. 2002; London: Penguin, 2003.
Stace, Wesley. *Misfortune*. London: Jonathan Cape, 2005.
Stace, Wesley. *By George*. 2007; London: Vintage, 2009.
Toíbin, Cólm. *The Master*. London: Picador, 2004.
Waters, Sarah. *Tipping the Velvet*. 1998; London: Virago, 1999.
Waters, Sarah. *Affinity*. 1999; London: Virago, 2000.
Waters, Sarah. *Fingersmith*. London: Virago, 2002.
Wilde, Oscar. 'The Harlot's House' (1885). In *The Complete Works of Oscar Wilde*. Glasgow: Harper Collins, 2003, p. 867.
Wilde, Oscar. *The Picture of Dorian Gray* (1891). In *The Complete Works of Oscar Wilde*. Glasgow: Harper Collins, 2003, pp. 17–159.
Wilde, Oscar. *De Profundis* (1962). In *The Complete Works of Oscar Wilde*. Glasgow: Harper Collins, 2003, pp. 980–1059.

Secondary criticism

Adams, Ann Marie. 'Dead Authors, Born Readers, and Defunct Critics: Investigating Ambiguous Critical Identities in A. S. Byatt's *Possession*'. *The Journal of the Midwest Modern Language Association*, 36:1 (Spring 2003), pp. 107–24.
Adams, Ann Marie. 'Defending "Identity and the Writer": A. S. Byatt's Delineation of the Proper "Function of Criticism at the Present Time"'. *Critique*, 49:4 (Summer 2008), pp. 339–55.

Althusser, Louis. 'Ideology and Ideological State Apparatus' (1970). In *Lenin and Philosophy and other essays*. Trans. by Ben Brewster. New York: Monthly Review Press, 2001, pp. 85–126.

Armitt, Lucie, and Gamble, Sarah. 'The Haunted Geometries of Sarah Waters' *Affinity'*. *Textual Practice*, 20:1 (2006), pp. 141–59.

Atwood, Margaret. *Negotiating with the Dead: A Writer on Writing*. Cambridge: Cambridge University Press, 2002.

Auerbach, Nina. *Communities of Women: An Idea in Fiction*. Cambridge: Harvard University Press, 1978.

Auerbach, Nina. 'Magi and Maidens: The Romance of the Victorian Freud'. *Critical Inquiry*, 8:2 (Winter 1981), pp. 281–300.

Austin, J. L. *How to Do Things with Words*. Oxford: Clarendon Press, 1962.

Ayto, John. *Word Origins*. 2nd edn. London: A & C Black Publishers Ltd, 2006.

Beizer, Janet. *Ventriloquized Bodies: Narratives of Hysteria in Nineteenth-Century France*. Ithaca and London: Cornell University Press, 1994.

Benhabib, Seyla. 'Feminism and Postmodernism: An Uneasy Alliance'. In Seyla Benhabib, Judith Butler, Drucilla Cornell and Nancy Fraser. *Feminist Contentions: A Philosophical Exchange*. New York and London: Routledge, 1995, pp. 17–34.

Bernard, Catherine. 'Forgery, Dis/possession, Ventriloquism in the works of A. S. Byatt and Peter Ackroyd'. *Miscelánea: a Journal of English and American Studies*, 28 (2003), pp. 11–24.

Blackford, Holly. 'Haunted Housekeeping: Fatal Attractions of Servant and Mistress in Twentieth-Century Female Gothic Literature'. *LIT: Literature Interpretation Theory*, 16 (2005), pp. 233–61.

Bland, Lucy. 'Trial by Sexology?: Maud Allan, *Salome* and "The Cult of the Clitoris"'. In Lucy Bland and Laura Doan (eds), *Sexology in Culture: Labelling Bodies and Desires*. Oxford: Polity Press, 1998, pp. 183–98.

Bloom, Harold. *The Anxiety of Influence: A Theory of Poetry*. New York: Oxford University Press, 1973.

Bradshaw, Charles C. 'The New England Illuminati: Conspiracy and Causality in Charles Brockden Brown's "Wieland"'. *The New England Quartley*, 76:3 (September 2003), pp. 356–77.

Brindle, Kym. 'Diary as Queer Malady: Deflecting the Gaze in Sarah Waters's *Affinity'*. *Neo-Victorian Studies*, 2:2 (Winter 2009/2010), pp. 65–85.

Bristow, Joseph. 'Biographies: Oscar Wilde – the Man, the Life, the Legend'. In Frederick S. Roden (ed.), *Palgrave Advances: Oscar Wilde Studies*. Basingstoke: Palgrave Macmillan, 2004, pp. 6–35.

Burgass, Catherine. *A. S. Byatt's Possession: A Reader's Guide*. London and New York: Continuum, 2002.

Butler, Judith. 'Performative Acts and Gender Constitution: An Essay in Phenomenology and Feminist Theory'. *Theatre Journal*, 40:4 (December 1988), pp. 519–31.

Butler, Judith. *Gender Trouble: Feminism and the Subversion of Identity* (1990). New York and London: Routledge, 1999.

Butler, Judith. *Bodies That Matter: On the Discursive Limits of 'Sex'*. New York and London: Routledge, 1993.

Butler, Judith. 'For a Careful Reading'. In Seyla Benhabib, Judith Butler, Drucilla Cornell and Nancy Fraser. *Feminist Contentions: A Philosophical Exchange*. New York and London: Routledge, 1995, pp. 127–43.

Butler, Judith. *Excitable Speech: A Politics of the Performative*. New York: Routledge, 1997.

Butler, Judith. *The Psychic Life of Power: Theories in Subjection*. Stanford, California: Stanford University Press, 1997.

Butler, Judith. *Undoing Gender*. London and New York: Routledge, 2004.

Buxton, Jackie. '"What's love got to do with it?" Postmodernism and *Possession'*. In Alexa Alfer and Michael J. Noble (eds), *Essays on the Fiction of A. S. Byatt: Imagining the Real*. West Port, Connecticut: Greenwood Press, 2001, pp. 89–104.

Byatt, A. S. 'Choices: On the Writing of *Possession'*. (n.d.) <www.asbyatt.com/ Onherself.aspx> (accessed 11 September 2011).

Byatt, A. S. 'Forefathers'. In A. S. Byatt. *On Histories and Stories: Selected Essays* (2000). London: Vintage, 2001, pp. 36–64.

Califia, Pat(rick). *Public Sex: The Culture of Radical Sex* (1994). San Francisco, California: Cleis Press, 2000.

Carroll, Rachel. 'Rethinking Generational History: Queer Histories of Sexuality in Neo-Victorian Feminist Fiction'. *Studies in the Literary Imagination*, 39:2 (Fall 2006), pp. 135–47.

Carroll, Samantha J. 'Lesbian dis*Possession*: The Apparitionalization and Sensationalization of Female Homosexuality in A. S. Byatt's *Possession: A Romance'*. *Critique*, 49: 4 (Summer 2008), pp. 357–78.

Carter, Paul. *Parrot*. London: Reaktion Books Ltd, 2006.

Castle, Terry. *The Apparitional Lesbian: Female Homosexuality and Modern Culture*. New York: Columbia University Press, 1993.

Chevalier, Jean-Louis. 'Conclusion in *Possession'*. In Alexa Alfer and Michael J. Noble (eds), *Essays on the Fiction of A. S. Byatt: Imagining the Real*. West Port, Connecticut: Greenwood Press, 2001, pp. 105–21.

Cohen, Ed. 'Writing Gone Wilde: Homoerotic Desire in the Closet of Representation'. *PLMA*, 102: 5 (October 1987), pp. 801–13.

Cohen, Ed. *Talk on the Wilde Side: Towards a Genealogy of Discourse on Male Sexuality*. New York: Routledge, 1993.

Cohu, Will. 'The BBC make it sound quite filthy'. *Daily Telegraph*, 8 October 2002, p. 23.

Coll, Fiona. '"Just a Singing-machine": The Making of an Automaton in George Du Maurier's *Trilby'*. *University of Toronto Quarterly*, 79: 2 (Spring 2010), pp. 742–63.

Connor, Steven. 'The Modern Auditory I'. In Roy Porter (ed.), *Rewriting the Self: Histories from the Renaissance to the Present*. London and New York: Routledge, 1997, pp. 203–23.

Connor, Steven. 'The Ethics of the Voice'. In Dominic Rainsford and Tim Woods (eds), *Critical Ethics: Text, Theory and Responsibility*. Basingstoke: Macmillan Press Ltd, 1999a, pp. 220–37.

Connor, Steven. 'The Machine in the Ghost: Spiritualism, Technology and the "Direct Voice"'. In Peter Buse and Andrew Stott (eds), *Ghosts: Deconstruction, Psychoanalysis, History*. Basingstoke: Macmillan Press Ltd., 1999b, pp. 203–25.

Connor, Steven. *Dumbstruck: A Cultural History of Ventriloquism*. Oxford: Oxford University Press, 2000.

Cornell, Drucilla (ed.) *Feminism and Pornography*. Oxford: Oxford University Press, 2000.

Costantini, Mariaconcetta. 'Faux-Victorian Melodrama in the New Millennium: The Case of Sarah Waters'. *Textual Practice*, 18:1 (2006), pp. 17–39.

Craft, Christopher. 'Come See About Me: Enchantment of the Double in *The Picture of Dorian Gray'*. *Representations*, 91 (Summer 2005), pp. 109–36.

D'Alessandro, Jean M. Ellis. 'Intellectual Wordplay in Wilde's Characterization of Henry Wotton'. In George C. Sandulescu (ed.), *Rediscovering Oscar Wilde*. Gerrards Cross: Colin Smythe Limited, 1994, pp. 61–75.

Davies, Helen. '"They whisper into my ears the tale of their perilous joy": The Powers of the Feminine Voice in Oscar Wilde's "The Fisherman and his Soul"'. In Naomi Wood (ed.) *A Giant's Garden: Special 'Fairy Tale' Issue*, special issue of *The Oscholars*, (Spring 2009) <http://www.oscholars.com/TO/Specials/Tales/Fisherman_Davies.htm> (accessed 6 October 2011).

Davies, Helen. 'Passive Puppets and Unruly Dummies: Gender and Ventriloquism in Sarah Waters' *Affinity'*. *Autopsia*, 1:1 (November 2010), pp. 41–64.

Davies, Helen. 'The Trouble with Gender in *Salomé'*. In Michael Y. Bennett (ed.), *Oscar Wilde's Salomé*. Amsterdam: Rodopi, 2011, pp. 55–69.

Davies, Helen. 'Original Copy: Neo-Victorian Versions of Oscar Wilde's "Voice"'. *Neo-Victorian Studies*, 4:1 (Winter 2011), pp. 1–21.

Davis, C.B. 'Reading the Ventriloquist's Lips: The Performance Genre Behind the Metaphor'. *The Drama Review*, 42:4 (Winter 1998), pp. 133–56.

Denisoff, Dennis. '"Men of My Own Sex": Genius, Sexuality, and George Du Mauriecor's Artists'. In Richard Dellamora (ed.), *Victorian Sexual Dissidence*. Chicago and London: University of Chicago Press, 1999, pp. 147–69.

Dennis, Abigail. '"Ladies in Peril": Sarah Waters on neo-Victorian celebrations and why she stopped writing about the Victorian era'. *Neo-Victorian Studies*, 1:1 (Autumn 2008), pp. 41–52.

Dentith, Simon. *Parody*. London: Routledge, 2000.

Derrida, Jacques. 'Signature Event Context' (1972). In *Limited Inc*. Trans. Samuel Weber and Jeffrey Mehlman. Evanston, Illinois: Northwestern University Press, 1988, pp. 1–23.

Doan, Laura and Waters, Sarah. 'Making up for lost time: Contemporary lesbian writing and the invention of history'. In David Alderson and Linda Anderson (eds), *Territories of Desire in Queer Culture*. Manchester: Manchester University Press, 2000, pp. 12–28.

Dolar, Mladen. *A Voice and Nothing More*. Cambridge, Massachusetts, and London: The MIT Press, 2006.

Dollimore, Jonathan. *Sexual Dissidence: Augustine to Wilde, Freud to Foucault*. Oxford: Oxford University Press, 1991.

Donoghue, Emma. *Passions Between Women: British Lesbian Culture 1668–1801*. London: Scarlet Press, 1993.

Dryden, Linda. *The Modern Gothic and Literary Doubles: Stevenson, Wilde and Wells*. Basingstoke: Palgrave Macmillan, 2003.

Dunn, Leslie C. and Jones, Nancy A. 'Introduction'. In Leslie C. Dunn and Nancy A. Jones (eds), *Representing Female Vocality in Western Culture* (1994). Cambridge: Cambridge University Press, 1996, pp. 1–13.

Dworkin, Andrea. *Pornography: Men Possessing Women*. London: The Women's Press Ltd, 1981.

Ellmann, Richard. *Oscar Wilde* (1987). London: Penguin, 1988.

Faderman, Lillian. *Surpassing the Love of Men: Romantic Friendship and Love between Women from the Renaissance to the Present* (1981). London: The Women's Press Ltd, 1985.

Faraday, Jess. 'Review: *Under the Poppy* by Kathe Koja'. *Speak its Name*, 12 February 2011. <www.speakitsname.com/2011/02/12/review-under-the-poppy-by-kathe-koja/> (accessed 11September 2011).

Ferguson, Christine. 'Footnotes on *Trilby*: The Human Foot as Evolutionary Icon in Late Victorian Culture'. *Nineteenth-Century Contexts*, 28: 2 (June 2006), pp. 127–44.

Ferguson, Christine. 'Victoria-Arcana and the Misogynistic Poetics of Resistance in Iain Sinclair's *White Chappell Scarlet Tracings* and Alan Moore's *From Hell*'. In Rebecca Munford and Paul Young (eds), *Engaging the Victorians*, special issue of *LIT: Literature Interpretation Theory*, 20:1–2 (2009), pp. 45–64.

Fraser, Nancy. 'False Antithesis: A Response to Seyla Benhabib and Judith Butler'. In Seyla Benhabib, Judith Butler, Drucilla Cornell and Nancy Fraser. *Feminist Contentions: A Philosophical Exchange*. New York and London: Routledge, 1995, pp. 59–74.

Gagnier, Regenia. *Idylls of the Marketplace: Oscar Wilde and the Victorian Public*. Aldershot: Scholar Press, 1986.

Galloway, Janice. 'Silent Partner'. *Guardian*, 20 June 2002, p. 16.

Gamble, Sarah. '"You cannot impersonate what you are": Questions of Authenticity in the Neo-Victorian Novel'. In Rebecca Munford and Paul Young (eds), *Engaging the Victorians*, special issue of *LIT: Literature Interpretation Theory*, 20:1–2 (2009), pp. 126–40.

Gide, André. *Oscar Wilde*. Trans. by Bernard Frechtman. London: William Kimber & Co. Ltd, 1951.

Goldblatt, David. *Art and Ventriloquism*. London and New York: Routledge, 2006.

Goring, Rosemary. 'Remarkable Voice for Silent Woman'. *Herald* [Glasgow], 30 November 2002, p. 4.

Grimes, Hilary. 'Power in Flux: Mesmerism, Mesmeric Manuals and Du Maurier's *Trilby*'. *Gothic Studies*, 10:2 (November 2008), pp. 67–83.

Grossman, Jonathan H. 'The Mythic Svengali: Anti-Aestheticism in *Trilby*'. *Studies in the Novel*, 28: 4 (Winter 1996), pp. 525–42.

Gustar, Jennifer. 'Re-Membering Cassandra, or Oedipus Gets Hysterical: Contestatory Madness and Illuminating Magic in Angela Carter's *Nights at the Circus*'. *Tulsa Studies in Women's Literature*, 23: 2 (Fall 2004), pp. 339–69.

Gutleben Christian. *Nostalgic Postmodernism: The Victorian Tradition and the Contemporary British Novel*. Amsterdam: Rodopi, 2001.

Hadley, Louisa. *Neo-Victorian Fiction and Historical Narrative: The Victorians and Us*. Basingstoke: Palgrave Macmillan, 2010.

Halliday, Robert. 'New Light on Henry Cockton'. *Notes and Queries*, 41:3 (September 1994), pp. 349–51.

Harvey, Elizabeth D. *Ventriloquized Voices: Feminist Theory and English Renaissance Texts*. London and New York: Routledge, 1992.

Healey, Emma. *Lesbian Sex Wars*. London: Virago, 1996.

Heilmann, Ann. 'The Haunting of Henry James: Jealous Ghosts, Affinities, and *The Others*'. In Rosario Arias and Patricia Pulham (eds), *Haunting and Spectrality in Neo-Victorian Fiction*. Basingstoke: Palgrave Macmillan, 2010, pp. 111–30.

Heilmann, Ann and Llewellyn, Mark. *Neo-Victorianism: The Victorians in the Twenty-First Century, 1999–2009*. Basingstoke: Palgrave Macmillan, 2010.

Heldreth, Leonard G. 'Variations on the Double Motif in Ventriloquist Films: *The Great Gabbo*, *Dead of Night* and *Magic*'. *Journal of the Fantastic in the Arts*, 3: 2 (1991), pp. 81–94.

Hennelly, Mark M. '"Repeating Patterns" and Textual Pleasures: Reading (In) A. S. Byatt's *Possession: A Romance'*. *Contemporary Literature*, 44:3 (Autumn 2003), pp. 442–71.

Hensher, Philip. 'A. S. Byatt, The Art of Fiction No. 168'. *The Paris Review*, 159 (2001) <www.theparisreview.org/interview/481/the-art-of-fiction-no-168-a-s-byatt> (accessed 11 September 2011).

Hoare, Philip. *Oscar Wilde's Last Stand: Decadence, Conspiracy and the Most Outrageous Trial of the Century*. New York: Arcade Publishing, 1997.

Holland, Merlin. 'Biography and the Art of Lying'. In Peter Raby (ed.), *The Cambridge Companion to Oscar Wilde*. Cambridge: Cambridge University Press, 1997, pp. 3–17.

Holland, Merlin. 'De Profundis: The Afterlife of a Manuscript'. In Robert Keane (ed.), *Oscar Wilde: The Man, his Writings, and his World*. New York: AMS Press, Inc., 2003, pp. 251–67.

Howells, Coral Ann. *Contemporary Canadian Women's Fiction*. New York and Basingstoke: Palgrave Macmillan, 2003.

Hulbert, Ann. 'The Great Ventriloquist'. *The New Republic*, 7 and 14 January 1991, pp. 47–49.

Hutcheon, Linda. *A Poetics of Postmodernism: History, Theory, Fiction*. London: Routledge, 1988.

Hyde, H. Montgomery. *Oscar Wilde* (1976). London: Mandarin, 1990.

Jameson, Fredric. *Postmodernism, or The Cultural Logic of Late Capitalism*. London: Verso, 1991.

Jeffers, Jennifer M. 'The White Bed of Desire in A. S. Byatt's *Possession'*. *Critique*, 43:2 (Winter 2002), pp. 135–47.

Jeremiah, Emily. 'The "I" inside "her": Queer Narration in Sarah Waters's *Tipping The Velvet* and Wesley Stace's *Misfortune'*. *Women: A Cultural Review*, 18:2 (Summer 2007), pp. 131–44.

Kahane, Claire. *Passions of the Voice: Hysteria, Narrative, and the Figure of the Speaking Woman, 1850–1915*. Baltimore and London: The John Hopkins Press, 1995.

Kaplan, Cora. '"Talk to me": Talk Ethics and Erotics'. In S. I. Salamensky (ed.), *Talk Talk Talk: The Cultural Life of Everyday Conversation*. New York and London: Routledge, 2001, pp. 63–75.

Kaplan, Cora. *Victoriana: Histories, Fictions, Criticism*. Edinburgh: Edinburgh University Press, 2007.

King, Jeannette. *The Victorian Woman Question in Contemporary Feminist Fiction*. Basingstoke: Palgrave Macmillan, 2005.

Kingston, Angela. *Oscar Wilde as a Character in Victorian Fiction*. Basingstoke: Palgrave Macmillan, 2007.

Kirchknopf, Andrea. '(Re-)workings of Nineteenth-Century Fiction: Definitions, Terminology, Contexts'. *Neo-Victorian Studies*, 1:1 (2008), pp. 53–80.

Knox, Melissa. *Oscar Wilde: A Long and Lovely Suicide*. New Haven and London: Yale University Press, 1994.

Koestenbaum, Wayne. 'Wilde's Hard Labor and the Birth of Gay Reading' (1990). In Jonathan Freedman (ed.), *Oscar Wilde: A Collection of Critical Essays*. Upper Saddle River: Prentice Hall, Inc., 1998, pp. 234–47.

Kohlke, M. L. 'Into History through the Back Door: The "Past Historic" in *Nights at the Circus* and *Affinity'*. *Women: A Cultural Review*, 15:2 (2004), pp. 153–66.

Kohlke, M. L. 'Introduction: Speculations in and on the Neo-Victorian encounter'. *Neo-Victorian Studies*, 1:1 (2008a), pp. 1–18.
Kohlke, M. L. 'The Neo-Victorian Sexsation: Literary Excursions into the Nineteenth Century Erotic'. In M. L. Kohlke and Luisa Orza (eds), *Probing the Problematics: Sex and Sexuality*. Oxford: Inter-Disciplinary Press, 2008b, pp. 345–56. <www.inter-disciplinary.net/publishing-files/idp/eBooks/ptp% 202.2.pdf> (accessed 11 September 2011).
Kontou, Tatiana. *Spiritualism and Women's Writing From the Fin de Siècle to the Neo-Victorian*. Basingstoke: Palgrave Macmillan, 2009.
Kucich, John and Sadoff, Dianne F. (eds), *Victorian Afterlife: Postmodern Culture Rewrites the Nineteenth Century*. Minneapolis and London: University of Minnesota Press, 2000.
Lamont, Peter. *The First Psychic: The Peculiar Mystery of a Notorious Victorian Wizard*. London: Little, Brown Book Group, 2005.
Lanser, Susan Sniader. *Fictions of Authority: Women Writers and Narrative Voice*. Ithaca and London: Cornell University Press, 1992.
Lefkovitz, Lori Hope. 'Inherited Holocaust Memory and the Ethics of Ventriloquism'. *The Kenyan Review*, 3:2 (1991), pp. 34–43.
Llewellyn, Mark. '"Queer? I should say it is criminal!" Sarah Waters' *Affinity*'. *Journal of Gender Studies*, 13:3 (2004), pp. 203–14.
Llewellyn, Mark. 'Breaking the Mould? Sarah Waters and the Politics of Genre'. In Ann Heilmann and Mark Llewellyn (eds), *Metafiction and Metahistory in Contemporary Women's Writing*. Basingstoke: Palgrave Macmillan, 2007, pp. 195–210.
Llewellyn, Mark. 'What is Neo-Victorian Studies?' *Neo-Victorian Studies*, 1:1 (2008), pp. 164–85.
Llewellyn, Mark. 'Neo-Victorianism: On the Ethics and Aesthetics of Appropriation'. In Rebecca Munford and Paul Young (eds), *Engaging the Victorians*, special issue of *LIT: Literature Interpretation Theory*, 20:1–2 (2009), pp. 27–44.
Lloyd, Moya. 'Performativity, Parody, Politics'. In Vikki Bell (ed.), *Performativity and Belonging*. London: SAGE Publications Ltd, 1999, pp. 195–213.
Lovelady, Stephanie. 'I Am Telling This to No One But You: Private Voice, Passing, and the Private Sphere in Margaret Atwood's *Alias Grace*'. *Studies in Canadian Literature*, 24 (1999), pp. 35–63.
Mackinnon, Catharine A. *Only Words* (1993). London: Harpercollins Publishers, 1994.
Manly, William A. 'The Importance of View in Brockden Brown's *Wieland*'. *American Literature*, 35:3 (November 1963), pp. 311–21.
Marcus, Steven. *The Other Victorians: A Study of Sexuality and Pornography in Mid-Nineteenth-Century England* (1964). London: Corgi Books, 1969.
Massie, Allan. 'The problems of predicting what will last'. *Daily Telegraph*, 4 January 2000. <http://www.telegraph.co.uk/culture/4719492/The-problems-of-predicting-what-will-last.html> (accessed 4 February 2011).
McCollister, Deborah. 'Wilde's *The Picture of Dorian Gray*'. *The Explicator*, 54 (1995), pp. 17–20.
McCormack, Jerusha. 'Wilde's Fiction(s)'. In Peter Raby (ed.), *The Cambridge Companion to Oscar Wilde*. Cambridge: Cambridge University Press, 1997, pp. 96–117.

McWilliam, Rohan. 'Victorian Sensations, Victorian Romances'. *Victorian Studies*, 52:1 (Autumn 2009), pp. 106–13.

Michael, Magali Cornier. 'Angela Carter's *Nights at the Circus*: An Engaged Feminism via Subversive Postmodern Strategies'. *Contemporary Literature*, 35: 3 (1994), pp. 492–521.

Millard, Rosie. 'I'm going to give the lesbians a little rest'. *The Sunday Times*, 28 December 2008, p. 5.

Miller, Karl. *Doubles: Studies in Literary History*. Oxford: Oxford University Press, 1985.

Mitchell, Kate. *History and Cultural Memory in Neo-Victorian Fiction: Victorian Afterimages*. Basingstoke: Palgrave Macmillan, 2010.

Muller, Nadine. 'Not My Mother's Daughter: Matrilinealism, Third-wave Feminism and Neo-Victorian Fiction'. *Neo-Victorian Studies*, 2:2 (Winter 2009/2010), pp. 109–36.

Munford, Rebecca and Young, Paul. 'Introduction: Engaging the Victorians'. In Becky Munford and Paul Young (eds), *Engaging the Victorians*, special issue of *LIT: Literature Interpretation Theory*, 20:1-2 (2009), pp. 1–11.

Noakes, Jonathan. 'Interview with A. S. Byatt'. In Margaret Reynolds and Jonathan Noakes (eds), *A. S. Byatt: The Essential Guide*. London: Vintage, 2004, pp. 11–32.

O'Connell, John. 'The Tipping Point'. *Time Out*, 8 February 2006, p. 18.

O'Neill, John. 'Adam's Novel? The *Omphalos* and the Ending of *Possession*'. *Critique*, 47:4 (Summer 2006), pp. 331–44.

Oram, Alison. *Her Husband Was a Woman! Women's Gender-Crossing in Modern British Popular Culture*. London and New York: Routledge, 2007.

Owen, Alex. *The Darkened Room: Women, Power and Spiritualism in late Victorian England*. London: Virago, 1989.

The Oxford English Dictionary 2 edition. Oxford: Oxford University Press, 1989, <http://www.oed.com> (accessed 13 July 2011).

Page, Philip. 'The Curious Narration of *The Bostonians*'. *American Literature*, 46:3 (November 1974), pp. 374–83.

Paglia, Camille. *Sexual Persona: Art and Decadence from Nefertiti to Emily Dickinson*. New Haven and London: Yale Nota Bene, 1990.

Palmer, Paulina. '"She began to show me the words she had written, one by one": Lesbian Reading and Writing Practices in the Fiction of Sarah Waters'. *Women: A Cultural Review*, 19:1 (2008), pp. 68–86.

Pick, Daniel. *Svengali's Web: The Alien Enchanter in Modern Culture*. New Haven and London: Yale University Press, 2000.

Powell, Kerry. 'A verdict of death: Oscar Wilde, actresses and Victorian women'. In Peter Raby (ed.), *The Cambridge Companion to Oscar Wilde*. Cambridge: Cambridge University Press, 1997, pp. 181–94.

Rée, Jonathan. *I See a Voice: A Philosophical History*. London: Flamingo, 1999.

Robbins, Ruth. *Subjectivity*. Basingstoke: Palgrave Macmillan, 2005.

Robbins, Ruth. *Oscar Wilde*. London and New York: Continuum, 2011.

Russell, Diana E. H. (ed.) *Making Violence Sexy: Feminist Views on Pornography*. Buckingham: Open University Press, 1993.

Saxey, Esther. 'The Maid, the Master, her Ghost and his Monster: *Alias Grace* and *Mary Reilly*'. In Rosario Arias and Patricia Pulham (eds), *Haunting and Spectrality in Neo-Victorian Fiction*. Basingstoke: Palgrave Macmillan, 2010, pp. 58–82.

Schmidt, Leigh Eric. 'From Demon Possession to Magic Show: Ventriloquism, Religion, and the Enlightenment'. *Church History*, 67:2 (June 1998), pp. 274–304.

Schwartz, Hillel. *The Culture of the Copy: Striking Likenesses, Unreasonable Facsimiles*. New York: Zone Books, 1996.

Scott, Anthony. 'Basil, Olive and Verena: *The Bostonians* and the Problems of Politics'. *Arizona Quartley*, 49 (Spring 1993), pp. 49–72.

Sedgwick, Eve Kosofsky. *Between Men: English Literature and Male Homosocial Desire*. New York: Columbia University Press, 1985.

Sedgwick, Eve Kosofsky. *Tendencies*. London: Routledge, 1993.

Segal, Charles, 'The Gorgon and the Nightingale: The Voice of Female Lament and Pindar's Twelfth *Pythian Ode*'. In Leslie C. Dunn and Nancy A. Jones (eds), *Embodied Voices: Representing Female Vocality in Western Culture* (1994). Cambridge: Cambridge University Press, 1996, pp. 17–34.

Shaw, Rhianna. 'The Great Social Evil "The Harlot's House" and Prostitutes in Victorian London'. *Victorian Web*, 2010. <www.victorianweb.org/authors/wilde/shaw.html> (accessed 13 July 2011).

Shiller, Dana. 'The Redemptive Past in the Neo-Victorian Novel'. *Studies in the Novel*, 29:4 (1997), pp. 538–60.

Shinn, Thelma J. '"What's in a Word?" Possessing A. S. Byatt's Meronymic Novel'. *Papers on Literature and Language*, 31 (1995), pp. 164–83.

Shuttleworth, Sally. 'Natural History: The Retro-Victorian Novel'. In Elinor S. Shaffer (ed.), *The Third Culture: Literature and Science*. Berlin: de Gruyter, 1998, pp. 253–68.

Small, Ian and Guy, Josephine. *Studying Oscar Wilde: History, Criticism, and Myth*. Greensboro: ELT Press, 2006.

Smart, Gordon. 'Guide to Match of the Gay', *Sun*, 16 October 2002. <http://www.thesun.co.uk/sol/homepage/showbiz/bizarre/180567/guide-to-match-of-the-gay.html> (accessed 11 September 2011).

Sokoloff, Naomi B. 'Narrative Ventriloquism and Muted Feminine Voice: Agnon's *In the Prime of Her Life*'. *Prooftexts*, 9 (1988), pp. 113–37.

Spivak, Gayatri. 'Can the Subaltern Speak?' In Cary Nelson and Lawrence Grossberg (eds), *Marxism and the Interpretation of Culture*. Urbana, Illinois: University of Illinois Press, 1988, pp. 217–313.

Stanley, Sandra Kumamoto. 'The Eroticism of Class and the Enigma of Margaret Atwood's *Alias Grace*'. *Tulsa Studies in Women's Literature*, 22: 2 (Autumn 2003), pp. 371–86.

Steel, Mel. 'Books: Fiction in Brief'. *The Independent*, 22 March 1998, p. 33.

Su, John J. 'Fantasies of (Re)Collection: Collecting and Imagination in A. S. Byatt's *Possession: A Romance*'. *Contemporary Literature*, 45:4 (Winter 2004), pp. 684–712.

Summers, Claude J. *Gay Fictions: Wilde to Stonewall: Studies in a Male Homosexual Literary Tradition*. New York: The Continuum Publishing Company, 1990.

Thomas, Devon. 'Fiction Reviews'. *Library Journal*, 15 September 2010. <www.libraryjournal.com/lj/ljinprint/currentissue/886443-403/story.csp.> (accessed 11 September 2011).

Thurschwell, Pamela. *Literature, Technology and Magical Thinking, 1880–1920*. Cambridge: Cambridge University Press, 2001.

Tolan, Fiona. *Margaret Atwood: Feminism and Fiction*. Amsterdam and New York: Rodopi, 2007.

Tromp, Marlene. *Altered States: Sex, Nation, Drugs, and Self-Transformation in Victorian Spiritualism*. Albany: State University of New York Press, 2006.

Tyler, Carole-Anne. 'Boys Will Be Girls: The Politics of Gay Drag'. In Diana Fuss (ed.), *Inside/Out: Lesbian Theories, Gay Theories*. New York and London: Routledge, 1991, pp. 32–70.

Vicinus, Martha. '"They wonder to which sex I belong"; The historical roots of the modern lesbian identity'. *Feminist Studies*, 18:3 (Fall 1992), pp. 467–97.

Voights-Virchow, Eckart. 'In-yer-Victorian-face: A Subcultural Hermeneutics of Neo-Victorianism'. In Rebecca Munford and Paul Young (eds), *Engaging the Victorians*, special issue of *LIT: Literature Interpretation Theory*, 20:1–2 (2009), pp. 108–25.

Vox, Valentine. *I Can See Your Lips Moving: The History and Art of Ventriloquism*. Tadworth: Kaye & Ward Ltd, 1981.

Walker, Jonathan. 'An Interview with A. S. Byatt and Lawrence Norfolk'. *Contemporary Literature*, 42:3 (August 2006), pp. 319–42.

Wallace, Diana. *The Woman's Historical Novel: British Women Writers, 1900–2000*. Basingstoke: Palgrave Macmillan, 2005.

Wardley, Lynn. 'Women's Voice, Democracy's Body, and *The Bostonians*'. *ELH*, 56: 3 (Autumn 1989), pp. 639–65.

Warner, Marina. *No Go the Bogeyman: Scaring, Lulling and Making Mock* (1998). London: Vintage, 2000.

Weliver, Phyllis. 'Music, Crowd Control and the Female Performer in *Trilby*'. In Sophie Fuller and Nicky Losseff (eds), *The Idea of Music in Victorian Fiction*. Aldershot: Ashgate, 2004, pp. 5780.

Widdowson, Peter. '"Writing Back": Contemporary Re-visionary Fiction'. *Textual Practice*, 20:3 (2006), pp. 491–507.

Wilson, Cheryl A. '"From the Drawing Room to the Stage": Performing Sexuality in Sarah Waters's *Tipping the Velvet*'. *Women's Studies*, 35 (2006), pp. 285–305.

Wilson, Elizabeth. *Mirror Writing: An Autobiography*. Virago: London, 1982.

Wolfe, Eric A. 'Ventriloquizing Nation: Voice, Identity and Radical Democracy in Charles Brockden Brown's *Wieland*'. *American Literature*, 78:3 (September 2006), pp. 431–57.

Wolstenholme, Susan. 'Possession and Personality: Spiritualism in *The Bostonians*'. *American Literature*, 49:4 (January 1978), pp. 580–91.

Wood, Julia. *The Resurrection of Oscar Wilde: A Cultural Afterlife*. Cambridge: The Lutterworth Press, 2007.

Wormald, Mark. 'Prior Knowledge: Sarah Waters and the Victorians'. In Rod Mengham and Philip Tew (eds), *British Fiction Today*. London and New York: Continuum International Publishing Group, 2006, pp. 186–97.

Yates, Louisa. '"But it's only a novel, Dorian": Neo-Victorian Fiction and the Process of Revision'. *Neo-Victorian Studies*, 2:2 (Winter 2009/2010), pp. 186–211.

Yelin, Louise. 'Cultural Cartography: A. S. Byatt's *Possession* and the Politics of Victorian Studies'. *Victorian Newsletter*, 81 (Spring 1992), pp. 38–41.

Ziff, Larser. 'A reading of *Wieland*'. *PMLA*, 77:1 (March 1962), pp. 51–7.

Index

204 *Index*